EST. 1898

The BERGHOFF Family COOKBOOK

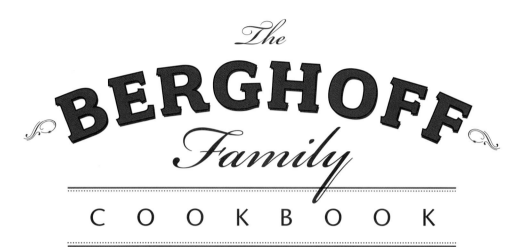

The BERGHOFF Family COOKBOOK

From Our Table to Yours,
Celebrating a Century of Entertaining

CARLYN BERGHOFF and JAN BERGHOFF

with NANCY ROSS RYAN

Andrews McMeel
Publishing, LLC
Kansas City

08 09 10 11 SDB 10 9 8 7 6 5

Library of Congress Cataloging-in-Publication Data

Berghoff, Carlyn.
   The Berghoff family cookbook : from our table to yours, celebrating a century of entertaining / Carlyn and Jan Berghoff with Nancy Ross Ryan.
         p. cm.
      ISBN-13: 978-0-7407-6362-5
      ISBN-10: 0-7407-6362-8
         1. Entertaining. 2. Cookery. I. Berghoff, Jan. II. Ryan, Nancy Ross. III. Title.
   TX731.B4185 2007
   641.509773'11—dc22

                              2006043037

Photo credits
The Berghoff Restaurant: v, ix, 2, 3, 4, 5, 6, 7 (bottom), 8, 9, 10, 11 (top), 13, 14,15, 25, 26, 29, 55, 71, 75, 116, 135, 155, 175, 193, 195, 196, 213, 219, 229
Eric Craig: vi, xii, 11 (bottom), 17, 19, 20–21, 27, 28, 33, 35, 37, 41, 42, 47, 48, 51, 57, 63, 69, 77, 83, 85, 87, 97, 98, 101, 103, 107, 109, 111, 113, 115, 119, 129, 131, 133, 141, 145, 149, 151, 159, 162, 165, 169, 171, 173, 177, 181, 183, 199, 201, 203, 205, 211, 216, 221, 223, 225, 231, 233, 241, 245, 249, 258, 261, 266, 267, 272
Susan Berghoff Prowant: 117
Gary Sigman: 16
Oil painting by Mark Melnick: ii, 7

Design by Catherine Jacobes

www.andrewsmcmeel.com

ATTENTION: SCHOOLS AND BUSINESSES
Andrews McMeel books are available at quantity discounts with bulk purchase for educational, business, or sales promotional use. For information, please write to: Special Sales Department, Andrews McMeel Publishing, LLC, 4520 Main Street, Kansas City, Missouri 64111.

We dedicate this book first to our founder, Herman Berghoff (1852–1934), whose vision, optimism, and hard work made our family and our restaurant possible. Second, we dedicate this book to our family, past and present, who made the restaurant's growth and prosperity possible: third-generation Herman Berghoff, Peter, Tim, and Julie Berghoff; Jim McClure, Lindsey, Sarah, and Todd McClure. Above all, we dedicate this book to our customers, who have supported us for the past 107 years and made it all possible.

Contents

Foreword / viii

Preface / x

Acknowledgments / xi

OUR STORY	**1**
APPETIZERS: Libations and Nibbles	**22**
SOUPS: Bowls for All Seasons	**52**
SALADS: Main Dish and Side Salads	**72**
SANDWICHES: A Sandwich with Your Dime Stein of Beer	**94**
MAIN DISHES: Our Crown Jewels	**126**
SIDES: Vegetables and Grains That Matter	**166**
GRILLING: From Barbecue to Oktoberfest	**190**
DESSERTS: Happy Endings	**206**
BREAKFAST & BRUNCH: Bright Beginnings	**234**
THE FAMILY PARTY: Yours and Ours	**254**

Letter from the Honorable J. Dennis Hastert / 268

State of Illinois House of Representatives Resolution / 269

City of Chicago City Council Resolution / 270

Index / 272

Foreword

by Herman J. Berghoff

I never met my grandfather, Herman Joseph Berghoff, who passed away on December 31, 1934, a few months before I was born. But he left me his name and a gift beyond my wildest dreams: his legacy.

His legacy includes founding the Berghoff Restaurant, to which my wife, Jan, and my sons, Peter and Timothy, and I dedicated ourselves heart and soul to continue running. His legacy also includes bringing three of his brothers to America. At this writing, the living descendants of those four Berghoff brothers—Herman, Henry, Hubert, and Gustav—account for more than one thousand U.S. citizens. Without my grandfather Herman, the restaurant and the family would not exist.

Every generation faces its own set of challenges. My grandfather's was to move to a new land with no money worth counting, to put down roots, to establish a family, and to create a family business using his wits, character, and honor. The second Berghoff generation—my father, Lewis, and my uncle Clement—were challenged to expand their father's café into a full-fledged restaurant that became an institution in their lifetime. These two were responsible for enlarging the menu and the business, and for creating the oak-paneled west dining room, with its stained-glass windows, murals, and chandeliers. They gave our customers a piece of Old World Europe in the heart of Chicago's Loop.

The challenge of my third generation was keeping pace with the public's changing tastes, and balancing the old with the new. During my time food trends changed rapidly, not just from decade to decade, but often from year to year. It was a fine line to walk between introducing new menu items and keeping customers interested in the old classic dishes on which the restaurant was founded. I was aided by the fourth Berghoff generation, Peter and Timothy, to manage this balancing act. And it was the fourth generation—Peter and Carlyn—who joined with Jan and me to open the Berghoff Café at O'Hare International Airport, one hundred years after Grandfather Herman opened the first Berghoff Café.

On a very basic level, running Berghoff's meant maintaining every inch of the 45,000-square-foot building that dates from 1872, built right after the Chicago Fire.

But Berghoff's was much greater than a building or a business, and it created a deep kinship among our staff, many of whom stayed with us for multiple decades. They became our second family, and over the years we responded to them with the kind of involvement that family creates.

Even though Berghoff's was a big complex restaurant with a menu of sixty-plus items, we were able to uncomplicate it. We took each new day as it came, adjusted to the changing times, and remained flexible. In the end, our basic instincts were correct—and after one hundred years we were still successful.

If my grandfather were here today I would say, "Thank you from the bottom of my heart. I hope I have fulfilled your wishes, and I am happy to have carried on your tradition all these years."

Herman J. Berghoff

Happy days! The Berghoff Café after repeal of Prohibition, April 1933.

Preface

The Berghoff Restaurant in Chicago was a rarity. It stood among a mere handful of American restaurants not only more than a century old, but also family-owned and -operated from day one. Ours remained in continuous operation on the same city block under our family's ownership for a record-breaking 107 years.

Our founder, Herman Berghoff, sailed at age seventeen from his native Germany in 1870, and landed in Brooklyn. Before bringing his three brothers to America to work with him in the Indiana brewery he founded, he worked variously on cotton and sugar cane plantations, on a freighter, on the railroad, and in the Buffalo Bill Wild West Show.

The Berghoff Restaurant began with the Berghoff Café (really a saloon), opened by Herman to serve his own beer when he was denied a license to sell it in Chicago. But you may read all about that in "Our Story," which follows.

Herman's sons Lewis and Clement joined their father in the business. During Prohibition, they expanded the saloon and its menu to serve food, and his brewery began producing soft drinks, including the still-famous Berghoff Root Beer.

Until his death, Herman was at Berghoff's daily. He died at the age of eighty-two, at home, on December 31, 1934. His grandson and namesake Herman was born a few months later.

Until February 28, 2006, the Berghoff Restaurant was run by our third and fourth generations.

The last hundred years of entertaining people have been marked by memorable parties and wonderful food. Some of our signature dishes—such as creamed spinach, apple strudel, and Wiener schnitzel—are famous. Fourth-generation Peter Berghoff called our enterprise the "Scratch House" because all the food (with one notable exception) was made from scratch. The 45,000-square-foot restaurant had its own bakery, butchered its own meat and fish, and had its own laundry and carpentry shop.

All the while we ran the business, we were also living as a family, one that entertained at home and celebrated holidays, graduations, anniversaries, and other milestones together . . . with great food ever an important part of our festivities.

Longevity is one sure measure of success, so our family must know something about good food. We have a few secrets, and we're willing to share.

The Berghoff clan can think of no better way to begin our second century of entertaining than by sharing our recipes, the secrets of our hospitality, and the tremendous pleasure that it gives us all. Our fondest hope is that you will receive the same pleasure from preparing these recipes and entertaining in your own home. Let the party begin!

Carlyn A Berghoff
Jan Berghoff

Acknowledgments

We wish to thank the following, without whom this book would never have come to life. First, we thank each other for mutual collaboration, shared memories, and hours of work.

We thank our families for their unselfish support during this long project.

We are humbly grateful to all Berghoff's staff who, for the past 107 years, made the restaurant what it was and whose names and life stories would fill a much bigger book. Among these is Michael Santiago, an employee for fifty years, who began as a busboy and became our indispensable floor manager. And Neemis Ortiz, our buyer for thirty years. We save a special place in our hearts for our thirty-one-year former executive chef, Mohammed Hussein. And we salute his successor, executive chef Matt Reichel, and pastry chef Enrique Sta. Marie (our "Bong"), and executive chef of artistic events Paul Larson and pastry chef Chon Reynozo.

For the past thirty-four years Dean Coronato, our chief engineer, held our enormous facility together and made it hum.

We are grateful to Susan Berghoff Prowant, our first family historian, who supplied several one-of-a-kind photos for the book, and to Lisa Berghoff, who compiled our official family history.

Blake Swihart and Kathleen Sanderson performed miracles, scaling down our recipes—written for huge restaurant and catering volume—and testing them for the home kitchen and making them work.

BBj Linen, Halls Rental, and the Flower Firm provided snazzy linens, great china, and gorgeous flowers for photography.

A special thanks to our literary agent, Lisa Ekus, our advocate and our friend, who had faith in us; our editor and publisher at Andrews McMeel, Jean Lucas and Kirsty Melville, who patiently guided us and shaped the book; Andrews McMeel's executive art director, Tim Lynch, whose vision illuminates every page; our graphics wizard Agnes Policarpio, who brought the past alive by translating historic photos into images for today; Catherine Jacobes, who brought our family history alive with her design; and our food stylist Carol Smoler and our photographer Eric Craig, who made our food look good enough to eat!

We thank Esther Herschenhorn for putting one (Nancy Ryan) and two (Carlyn and Jan) together as a great threesome. Lastly we thank Nancy Ross Ryan, the writer who turned our creative thoughts, memories, and dreams into words.

Our Story

OUR STORY BEGINS WITH HERMAN JOSEPH BERGHOFF, who was born November 13, 1852, in Dortmund, Westphalia, Germany (then Prussia). He was the third child—and the third son—of Franz Anton Berghoff, a carpenter, and Lizette Boelhauve Berghoff, the daughter of a miller (Franz and Lizette had seven children; in order, they were Anton Jr., Theodor, Herman, Henry, Hubert, Gustav, and Elizabeth). Herman received a basic education in the common schools of Dortmund. But when he turned seventeen, he decided to leave home and sail for the United States. He arrived in June 1870, six months before his eighteenth birthday.

Herman Joseph Berghoff, the restaurant's founder, at age seventeen.

This was a bold move, assuming he spoke only German, and our family has speculated for generations: Why? We settled on three possible reasons. The law in Prussia at that time declared the eldest son (which would have been Anton Jr.) the only legal inheritor of his father's estate; Herman was the third son. Also, military service was compulsory for every male, and Prussia was pursuing a policy of expansion. And lastly, family stories say that young Herman was captivated by tales of the American "Wild West" and fancied that he might share those adventures and strike it rich in the process. The closest he got to the Wild West was working for a year in Buffalo Bill Cody's Wild West Show. And as for getting rich quick, one of his first experiences when he landed in Brooklyn was being fleeced of everything he owned, by a con artist.

Sugar Cane, Ships, Rodeos, and Railroads

As described in later years by his brothers, the young Herman was friendly and outgoing and—remarkable for men of his era—six feet tall. The first four years after he immigrated, he held a variety of jobs. He worked for a season on a sugar plantation where, as another family anecdote describes it, the plantation owner cheated Herman and his fellow workers out of their end-of-the-season pay. In retribution, the workers burned down the man's barn—and Herman left town fast.

Thereafter he went to work as a pastry chef on a small freighter that sailed the southern and eastern U.S. coasts. But the captain soon discovered that Herman could not bake—not even a biscuit. Herman's ability to talk fast kept him from a very long swim, and he wound up as a deckhand. Following the freighter job, he worked for a year with Buffalo Bill. Then he spent time working on the railroads out west. Herman brought his younger sibling Henry to America in 1872. By 1874, the brothers found themselves in Fort Wayne, Indiana, where Herman became the "& Co." at J. E. Capps & Co., a jewelry and watch business.

Citizenship and Marriage

On November 20, 1876, Herman was naturalized in Allen County, Indiana, becoming an American citizen. In 1877, Henry married Theresa Mayer, and Herman moved in with the young couple. For the next year he worked briefly as a clerk with Root & Co. Dry Goods, and then became a salesman for B. Trentman & Son, a large wholesale grocery house. Talk about a small world. Trentman & Son also employed Theresa's father, Lorenz Mayer, as a teamster, who turned out to be the father of two other daughters: the youngest, Johanna, who was destined to marry a third Berghoff brother, Hubert; and Walburga, whom Herman married in 1878. Before Walburga's untimely death in 1896, she and Herman had eight children, six of whom survived.

And Baby Makes Seven

In 1879, Herman and his new wife, Walburga, had their first child, Alfred Charles. They were all living with Henry and Theresa, making five in the household. That year, Herman was working as a traveling salesman for Carnahan & Hanna Boots & Shoes. He had arranged for Hubert, another younger brother, to work in trade for his passage and to apprentice as a clerk and bookkeeper to Trentman Company. Hubert arrived in 1880, and moved in with Henry, Theresa, Herman, Walburga, and baby Alfred, making six. In 1881, Herman's second child, Leo Henry, was born. But if six was company, seven was a crowd. When Hubert married Johanna Mayer in 1882, this couple moved out and established their own home.

And Gustav Came Last

The youngest Berghoff brother, Gustav, was just seven years old when Herman, the third eldest, left Prussia for America. Gustav was still in

Walburga Mayer Berghoff and Herman Berghoff, shortly after their 1878 marriage.

Berghoff brothers who came to America. *Clockwise from left:* Henry, Herman, Hubert, and Gustav.

The Herman Berghoff Brewing Company and staff, Fort Wayne, Indiana, 1888.

school when both fourth-born Henry and fifth-born Hubert left for America. After Gustav completed his basic education in 1880, he received three years' training at the Union Brauerei, in Dortmund. When, in 1883, Gustav decided to come to America, the same arrangement as Hubert's was made for passage and apprenticeship with the Trentman Company. By that time, Herman and Henry were operating the Berghoff Brothers East End Bottling Works in Fort Wayne, Indiana. And, of course, Gustav moved in with Henry's family. Gustav worked at Trentman until Herman and Henry established the Herman Berghoff Brewing Co.; soon after that, he went on the road selling Berghoff Dortmunder-style beer for his brothers.

His three brothers were already married to three Mayer daughters, and the only remaining Mayer daughter, Mary Sophia, was fourteen years older than Gustav. But their mother, Maria Mayer, had a niece, Julia, around Gustav's age, living in nearby Dayton, Ohio. They visited back and forth and, in October 1890, Gustav and Julia were married. They moved to their own house, and their first child arrived in 1891.

A Dream Come True

For years Herman dreamed not only of being his own boss, but also of opening a brewery modeled after those in his hometown of Dortmund. He apparently inspired confidence because, in 1882, he got financial backing from

Henry, his brother's employer A. C. Trentman, and others, and purchased the East End Bottling Works in Fort Wayne, Indiana. Their advertising that year read, "Berghoff Brothers, Wholesale Dealers and Bottlers of Beer." Herman was president of the company. And he moved his wife and two children to their own home in Fort Wayne.

Some Bad Dreams, Too

Herman and Walburga had a third son in February 1883. The baby died that August. But Hannah, their first daughter, was born a year later, in 1884.

Back at the brewery, Henry had been appointed city treasurer of Fort Wayne and became less active in the business. So the Herman Berghoff Brewing Company was incorporated in April 1887 with $100,000 capital, and construction began on a new brewery. On its completion Dortmunder beer, named for the Berghoffs' town of origin, was introduced on June 1, 1888. It was characterized by a lighter color and flavor, and brewed solely from hops imported from Germany, and barley malt. The first brew master, William Breuer, had held the same job in one of Dortmund's leading establishments. The new Berghoff beer was an instant success and a keen competitor to Centlivre, the "other" Fort Wayne beer.

Early in 1888, Herman and Walburga lost a second child, a ten-month-old son.

On August 22, 1888, barely two months after the new brewery was completed, fire destroyed $50,000 worth of brewery property. According to newspaper accounts, Herman was

Herman Berghoff, *center,* and his six children, *clockwise from bottom left:* Leo Henry, Lewis Windthorst, Alfred Charles, Johanna, Clement Anthony, and Robert Sixtus.

in his office while the fire raged overhead, writing telegrams to manufacturers about the damaged equipment, reordering new equipment, and asking for skilled workers to be sent post haste to install the new equipment. A newspaper quoted him on the night of the fire: "Every dollar I have in the world is represented in that burning building, but you can tell your readers that we will rebuild, and we will be brewing beer again in a month at the latest." By September 22, he had the damage repaired, most of the equipment replaced, and resumed brewing. At that time he announced a new beer, Salvator, "a select beer for the table and for family use." The formula was that of a Munich beer, light brown with a stronger flavor than the Dortmunder beer.

Herman and Walburga had three more sons: Robert Sixtus, June 1889; Lewis Windthorst, March 1891; and Clement Anthony, March

Top: From Fort Wayne, Indiana, to Chicago go barrels of Berghoff beer.
Bottom: The first Berghoff location at West Adams and State streets.

1894. But shortly after her last child, Clement, was born, Walburga was diagnosed with cancer. She underwent surgery, fought bravely, but died on March 3, 1896. Her death left Herman with six children ranging in age from two to sixteen. Walburga's oldest sister, Mary Sophia, who had never married, became the children's caretaker—their beloved "Tante Mayme."

Marketing Meister

After the death of his wife, although he was still the brewery president, Herman also became a traveling salesman. Production had increased and the firm was ready to expand into new markets.

Herman had a remarkable gift for presenting himself and his product favorably to the press, the public, and his business colleagues. He believed in advertising, and placed eye-catching ads on the cover of the city directory and in the newspapers. He knew the effect that a good cigar and a foamy stein of his quality beer had on business associates and friends. And he understood the value of well-placed humor, an interesting story, and a personal, handwritten note. He was known for his resourcefulness and his ability to find ways around obstacles. For example, in 1893, during the World's Columbian Exposition in Chicago, Herman couldn't get a license to sell his beer on the fairgrounds, so he set up a stand outside the grounds and sold his beer to fairgoers as long as the fair lasted.

Two years after the death of his wife, Herman met Mary Jansen, the daughter of one of his business associates, Henry Jansen, a wine merchant and a fellow countryman. In 1898, Herman and Mary were married and Herman moved his family to Chicago.

The Berghoff Café

But none of his charm or business acumen could get him a wholesale license to sell his beer in Chicago to hotels, restaurants, and saloons.

Mural of the 1893 World Exposition in the Berghoff's west dining room, painted by Mark Melnick.

The city officials felt that the last thing they needed was an out-of-town beer to compete with the thirty local brewing companies. So the resourceful Herman inquired about a retail license, which would entitle him to sell food and drink retail—in a restaurant. This, he was granted. In 1898, he furnished a Chicago storefront bar in rich wooden panels, put in some plain tables and armless rattan-seated stools, and polished up the mahogany bar. He opened the Berghoff Café, advertising Berghoff Dortmunder Beer, light and dark, at five cents a glass and ten cents a stein, and a free sandwich. Also available was his own label of blended whiskey. It was a very masculine bar, situated on West Adams Street among predominantly women's stores. His detractors remarked, "We'll give the

Prohibition-era sign advertising Bergo soft drinks.

Mobile advertising after Prohibition.

Herman with the first liquor license issued by the City of Chicago, in 1933.

Dutchman [sic] six months." The bar is still open today, but it moved from its original location on West Adams and State when the building was razed in 1913 to a location one door down at 17 West Adams, where it now stands.

Early in Herman's second marriage he and Mary became parents of a son, who did not survive. In October 1907, their daughter, Mary Elizabeth, was born, who would live to the age of eighty-two.

The Berghoff Café prospered and provided for the education of all seven of his children. Three went to Harvard: Alfred Charles, Lewis Windthorst, and Clement Anthony. Robert Sixtus became a prominent cardiologist. Leo Henry moved to France and opened a hotel in Monte Carlo. Hannah attended Josephinum Academy in Chicago, Mary Elizabeth attended St. Mary of the Woods College in Terre Haute, Indiana, and (the accepted destiny for women of their generation) both married. Two of Herman's sons would join him in the business. But before Lewis Windthorst and Clement Anthony joined Herman, Prohibition became law in January 1920.

Prohibition, Near Beer, and New Directions

The 18th Amendment (the Volstead Act) banned the sale, transportation, and manufacture of alcohol in America. But this "Noble Experiment" that the American temperance movement had fought so long for resulted in a level of lawlessness the country had never seen. Organized crime recognized the huge market for a now-illegal commodity, and stepped in to supply it. Major U.S. cities all had gangsters, but Chicago became the capital of organized crime. Legitimate breweries and distilleries were closed, and illegal operations sprang up to supply bootleggers with unregulated spirits that were often toxic. Saloons were driven out of business as thousands of speakeasies took their place. In 1927, Chicago mayor William Hale Thompson ("Big Bill") said, "We'll not only reopen places these people have closed, but we'll open ten thousand new ones." The "people" he was referring to were reformers, and the "places" were speakeasies.

Herman's options seemed to be either close the brewery and the bar, or engage in illegal business. He was forced to make his choice early because Prohibition began in Indiana, where his brewery was located, in April 1918—two years earlier than in Chicago. But rather than accept Prohibition as the grim reaper of his growing business, Herman made it the midwife for a new one. He began brewing the legal near beer (containing less than one-half of one percent—0.5 percent—alcohol), and his own line of Bergo soda pops. Berghoff Root Beer is still popular today. When Prohibition began Herman had three bars or cafés in Chicago. He closed two of them and concentrated his efforts on the original café on West Adams. In addition to serving near beer and Bergo soft drinks, he expanded the service and began turning it into a full-service restaurant.

During the next fourteen years the sandwich menu expanded to include Wiener schnitzel, sauerbraten, German pot roast, apple strudel, potato pancakes, and dozens of other classics that made the restaurant one of the best-known eateries in Chicago.

When Prohibition ended in 1933, Herman managed to get retail liquor licenses Number 1 (for the bar) and Number 2 (for

Second-generation Lewis Windthorst Berghoff.

Second-generation Clement Anthony Berghoff.

OUR CEILING PRICES

All prices a la carte unless specified

#	Item	Price	#	Item	Price
1	TOMATO JUICE	.10	21	LAKE TROUT	.65
2	SOUP DU JOUR	.15 - .20 - .25	22	HAM SANDWICH	.25
3	BACON OR HAM & EGGS	.50	23	AMERICAN CHEESE SANDWICH	.20
4	TWO EGGS, ANY STYLE	.40	24	CREAM " "	.20
5	OMELETTE, PLAIN	.40	25	LETTUCE & TOMATO "	.20
6	FILET OF SOLE — PLATE LUNCH	.40	26	HAM & CHEESE "	.35
7	LIVER & BACON	.60	27	APPLE PIE	.10
8	PORK CHOPS	.70	28	VEGETABLE PLATE	.45
9	ROAST HAM	.60	29	COFFEE (CUP)	.10
10	CORNED BEEF HASH	.50	30	TEA (POT)	.10
11	VEAL GOULASH	.55	31	MILK (HALF PINT)	.10
12	COMBINATION SALAD - SMALL .15 - LARGE	.30	32	LIVER DUMPLINGS	.45
13	LIMBURGER CHEESE SANDWICH	.20	33	VEAL CHOP, BREADED	.65
14	THUERINGER (FRESH)	.50	34	FRIED JUMBO FROG LEGS	.80
15	FRESH PORK SHANK	.55	35	WHOLE BABY PIKE	.60
16	BRISKET OF CORNED BEEF	.60	36	FRIED JUMBO SCALLOPS	.55
17	BREADED VEAL CUTLET	.65	37	POT ROAST	.55
18	BROILED WHITEFISH	.85	38	SMOKED THUERINGER	.55
19	FRANKFURTERS	.45	39	BRAISED OX JOINTS	.55
20	PORK TENDERLOIN	.70	40	STEAMED FINNAN HADDIE	.65

Name BERGHOFF RESTAURANT CO.
Address 17 W. ADAMS ST. - CHICAGO, ILL.
Form OPA 4167-1836

Signed by *Lewis W. Berghoff*
(OWNER OR MANAGER)

ERASURES OR CHANGES OF PRICES ON THIS POSTER ARE UNLAWFUL

Ceiling prices menu, 1945.

the restaurant)—framed and on permanent display at the restaurant. And that year on December 31, the restaurant was wall-to-wall with revelers celebrating the first New Year's Eve after the repeal of Prohibition.

The Second Generation

In 1929, Clement Anthony joined his father in the restaurant business; Lewis Windthorst joined them in 1935. Working every day for the next thirty years, they made Berghoff's into not only a full-service restaurant but a Chicago institution. Clement worked in the front of the house—managing, meeting guests, and supervising staff. Lewis worked in the back—on the food, the menu and innovations, and managing the bottom line.

Until his death, even though Lewis and Clement were actively running the restaurant, Herman was at Berghoff's daily. He died unexpectedly at home on December 31, 1934.

During the three decades that the second generation, Lewis and Clement, was at the helm, Berghoff's was a major destination for not only the food but for the restaurant's location, central to shopping, entertainment, and transportation.

Berghoff's grew into three restaurants under one roof. The original bar (an all-male bar until 1968) retained its 1913 location. It was connected by a large open pass-through to a large two-room restaurant with dark paneling, brass light fixtures, leaded glass windows, and large murals of scenes from the 1890s and the 1893 World Columbian Exposition. In 1939, a more casual downstairs café, called the Annex, was opened.

Rationing and Price Controls

Few restaurant-goers today remember World War II rationing. From 1943 until 1946, food was rationed not only to citizens but to restaurants. Rationing regulated the amount of several basic commodities that consumers could obtain: sugar, meat, butter, oils and other fat, and most cheeses. Restaurants were subject to a menu price freeze. During the war, Lewis signed an official government document that ensured Berghoff's would not raise prices. In the family archives is its 1944 menu, called "Our Ceiling Prices," which had been filed with the War Price and Rationing Board. Those ceiling prices included Bacon or Ham and Eggs, 40 cents; Filet of Sole Plate Lunch, 40 cents; Corned Beef Hash, 50 cents; Veal Goulash, 55 cents; American Cheese Sandwich, 20 cents; Coffee (cup), 10 cents; Fried Jumbo Frog Legs, 80 cents; Braised Ox Joints, 55 cents; and Steamed Finnan Haddie, 65 cents.

The Third Generation

Herman Berghoff—Lewis's son and founder Herman's grandson—with his wife, Jan

Top: Third-generation Herman Berghoff with cases of bottled beer. *Bottom:* Herman and Jan Berghoff.

Berghoff, owned and ran the restaurant until February 2006. Herman was the business and management arm, and Jan was involved in the food and menu development, adding contemporary entrées and salads to the hearty German favorites.

But before they took over, there was a period of musical family chairs. In third-generation Herman's words: "Making generational changes is not easy, and passing on ownership is not easy." Lewis and Clement were active in the restaurant until about 1960 (Lewis passed away in 1969, Clement in 1980). To succeed themselves, they brought in siblings from each family, one being third-generation Herman Berghoff (Lewis's son). Management styles differed and, in 1973, Herman withdrew and moved with his wife and four children to Stevensville, Michigan. There, he and Jan owned and ran the highly successful Tosi's restaurant from 1973 to 1983, when they sold it. That year, the remaining Berghoff partners asked Herman to return and work with them. Herman offered to buy them out. They agreed, and from 1986 until its official closing in February 2006, Herman and Jan owned and ran the Berghoff Restaurant. "We put our hearts and souls into it," says Herman.

It was Herman in 1980 who had the Joseph Huber Brewery in Monroe, Wisconsin, put Berghoff beer into bottles. (Huber had been brewing the beer since 1960 to exacting Berghoff standards.)

Three Out of the Fourth Generation

In 1959, third-generation Herman, who grau-

ated from Michigan State University School of Business and Hospitality, met Janice Edith Clapp. They were both guests at a wedding in Chicago's South Side neighborhood where Janice grew up. She graduated from Purdue University with a degree in special education. Her chosen vocation, as a teacher to hearing-impaired children, was deferred when she and Herman were married in June 1960. The following year their first child, Carlyn, was born. Although Peter, Julie, and Timothy followed, Jan soon had another career—as Herman's partner in Tosi's and, starting in 1986, in the Berghoff Restaurant in Chicago.

The only one of Jan and Herman's four children who didn't go into the restaurant business in some form was their third child, Julie Marie. She has a master's degree in art and works as a film studio set designer in California.

In 1989, their older son, Peter, who has a degree in business administration, joined them at the Berghoff and became its CEO. In 1997, their younger son, Timothy, who had worked there part time when he was in college studying photography, entered the family business full time and became the beverage manager. He ran Berghoff's bar, by this time a Chicago institution.

In 1986, their older daughter, Carlyn, named for her paternal grandmother, went into business for herself. She graduated from the Culinary Institute of America, Hyde Park, New York, and has a degree in hospitality management from Florida International University, Miami. With a loan from her dad, she opened her own catering firm in Chicago—Artistic

Events by Carlyn Berghoff Catering. In 2006 her company served more than 100,000 meals in venues ranging from private homes to museums and earned more than $6 million in revenues. Her clients include U.S. presidents, international heads of state, national and local government officials, and celebrities in sports and entertainment. In 1998, she partnered with the Berghoff Restaurant to open the Berghoff Café at O'Hare International Airport. Says Jan, "We're proud that our daughter has achieved success outside of the family business, and we know that she will continue to succeed." Adds Herman, "She's a great Berghoff!"

"With my culinary and entertaining enthusiasm," says Carlyn, "I saw the opportunity to create a cookbook that would preserve the best of the old and the new."

Memories

Peter Berghoff remembers the huge quantities of raw ingredients—tons of potatoes, massive amounts of halibut, hundreds of pounds of flour—that were transformed daily into mashed potatoes, fish sandwiches, bouillabaisse, rye bread, and Black Forest cake. It was Peter who dubbed the restaurant the "Scratch House," a name that stuck.

As long as Peter can remember, there were lines of people waiting to get into Berghoff's every day for lunch and dinner. One line was for the street-level main dining rooms; one line was for the popular downstairs café (the former Annex, which was renamed and revamped in 2003). One day there came a sudden heavy shower, and there was still a long line of cus-

Jan and Herman Berghoff with the Oktoberfest float, 1990s.

tomers waiting outside. Peter raced to the lost-and-found department, grabbed twenty-plus umbrellas, ran outside, and gave them to the customers. As the customers came into the restaurant, they returned the umbrellas.

His favorite memory is of a waiter who worked at the Berghoff until he was ninety or older (the man was very cagey about his exact age). This waiter invested heavily in the stock market and became very rich. His stockbroker used to call Berghoff's to discuss his client's portfolio, and Peter says that the broker thought the waiter owned the restaurant. But although the employee lived in a luxury lakefront high-rise, he walked to and from work every day, twelve city blocks each way. In his early nineties, he retired and moved to Las Vegas. When he died, he left friends and colleagues unexpected large sums of money.

Timothy knew by heart the names—and personalities—of the fifty or so regulars who

Centennial poster redesigned from original early 1900s poster, provided by Susan Berghoff Prowant.

patronized Berghoff's bar every week. In 1994, when he was in college and working at the bar part-time, he was on duty one night during the World Cup soccer match. "The bar was ablaze with about one hundred fans and players—all wearing soccer jerseys—quite a sight."

The bar began as a men-only bar, and, even though it was opened to women in 1969, it remained a de facto men's bar because, says Timothy, "we didn't put in stools until 2001." (The original bar in founder Herman's day had some stools with brass spittoons on the floor between then. But somewhere after the end of Prohibition, the stools and the spittoons disap-

peared.) Until then, men would put one foot on the long brass rail that snaked around the bottom of the big mahogany bar, and drink their beer and eat their sandwiches standing up.

Tim recounts the story of Tim Phelan, a bartender for fifteen years, who was asked by a woman if it was okay for her husband to smoke a cigar at the bar. Phelan replied, "It's a saloon, darlin', not a tearoom."

His eeriest memory was in the late '90s, when "Two guys in town for a hardware convention came to the bar. They had a flight scheduled back to Pittsburgh that night, but they were having such a good time—nothing rowdy, mind you—that they decided to cancel their tickets and stay one more night in Chicago. The flight they were originally scheduled on crashed in Pittsburgh, and everyone on board was lost."

Says Carlyn, "I decided to go into the restaurant business because from the time I was six I can remember being in a kitchen. Then, I was in the kitchen with my mom at dinnertime, helping her cook dinner and learning how to tie a bow using the back of her apron. When we kids were really little, Dad used to take us with him to town on Saturdays and Sundays, to the Berghoff Restaurant. He would check all the incredible mechanics—temperatures, water flow, sewage. One of my favorite things to do was play in the bar behind the cigar counter, where there was a stash of chewing gum and penny candies. As we got older, I'd hang out more in the kitchen. Berghoff's kitchens were overwhelming. The pots were as big as I was. And then when I was thirteen, and my mom and dad bought Tosi's restaurant in Michigan, I started cooking in the kitchens there. Everything about our family lives focused on the restaurant. It kind of consumes you, so I figured if you can't beat it, join it."

The 100th Anniversary

In April 1998, the Berghoff Restaurant celebrated its hundredth anniversary with a series of parties. During one, the menu and prices from the original café were revived. The original Berghoff beer, light and dark, was sold for a nickel, and sandwiches, just as in the good old days in founder Herman Berghoff's time, were free.

Former chef Karl Hertenstein, *center left,* and Mrs. Hertenstein, and former chef Mohammed Hussein, *center right,* and Mrs. Hussein.

On the Fourth of July that year, the Berghoff family held a reunion: 875 descendants of the four Berghoff brothers attended, and more than 500 of them got up early enough that morning to have their family portrait taken under Berghoff's sign.

That year the annual Oktoberfest (always held in September) was the biggest Herman and Jan ever hosted. It lasted for four days, during which 45,000 sandwiches and 100,000 beverages (Berghoff Beer and Root Beer) were consumed by hungry, thirsty, happy Chicagoans.

Berghoff's Chefs

Chefs have always been the backbone of the Berghoff, but before 1948 their names are lost to memory. That year, the first chef of record was the Swiss-born executive chef Karl Hertenstein, who manned the kitchens from 1948 until 1964. He was a classically trained European chef adept at organizing and teaching, and Berghoff's

The entire Berghoff staff in the 1990s.

benefited from his expertise. It was Chef Hertenstein who created our famous creamed spinach, made then—as it is today—from frozen spinach. (Our creamed spinach is the one not-made-from-scratch dish on the menu.)

Working with him was floor chef Augustine Diezinger, who came on board in 1955 and worked at Berghoff's until 1970, with one year off for military service. Also working until the late 1970s was sous-chef James Cannon.

But our most famous—we consider him legendary—chef was Mohammed Hussein, who was with us for forty-one years. We hired him in 1954 as a food runner. This tall, hard-working, observant, and earnest young man

originally from Palestine systematically learned from the European chefs everything there was to learn about Berghoff's kitchen and food. By 1958, he was our executive chef. He retired in 1995.

One of Berghoff's greatest treasures is pastry chef Enrique Sta Maria, affectionately known as "Bong." When Jan and Herman bought out the partners in 1986, the commissary—for butchering meats and making pastry—was located in a building on Wabash Avenue, several blocks north of the restaurant. Herman immediately moved that facility to the main restaurant on West Adams. However, the pastry chef at that commissary, a man whose name has been forgotten, lives on in the memory of all who worked with him because of his ferocious temper. One of his apprentices was Bong. Bong learned all that the very talented rage-aholic chef had to teach about pastry, and then brought it with him to Berghoff's on West Adams. Bong was there every day, baking breads and turning out amazing desserts and pastries, all in the best of spirits.

The last Berghoff executive chef, Matt Reichel, was hired in 1993 and became executive chef in 1995. Until Berghoff's closed in 2006, Chef Matt ran the entire huge multi-restaurant operation, from recipes to food production to supervising the kitchen staff. It was Matt who oversaw the opening of the lower-level Berghoff Café in 2003 when we created a new concept for it, and it was Chef Matt who developed all the recipes for the café.

Auf Wiedersehen!

After Herman celebrated his seventieth birthday in 2005, he and Jan announced to the press that they would be closing the Berghoff Restaurant in the spring of 2006 after 107 years of serving Chicago's residents and visitors.

"We share the sadness that many feel about the closing," he said. "It's been an honor to be part of the fabric of Chicago, but after being in the business for more than half a century, Jan and I feel that now is the right time to start a new chapter in our lives.

"We thank our tremendous staff, the people of Chicago, and our customers from around

Johnny Wagner's German band.

the world who have contributed to more than one hundred years of success."

"I had the fun side of the business," says Jan. "I worked with the food and the menu and I knew the life stories of all of our people—the soul of this family business. Carlyn and I always talked about writing a cookbook together—and what better time than now to share recipes with the thousands of people who have eaten at and written to the restaurant."

Shortly after the announcement of the closing was made, letters and e-mails by the hundreds came from customers past and present. All were filled with regret, most were sad, a few were angry.

However, in true Berghoff fashion, Jan, Herman, Peter, and Timothy closed with a celebration that will remain a cherished memory for everyone who dined at Berghoff's during the final two months and especially the final day, February 28, 2006. Special memorial menus were printed. The lines of customers waiting to get in stretched around the block. Many had come from all over America to dine one last time at Berghoff's. Every weekend for those last two months, Johnny Wagner's German band played as they strolled around the huge dining room. The restaurant served more meals in the last two months than it had at any time in its history, including the four thousand meals per day it traditionally produced during the Christmas season. And on the very last night, the family who had made the restaurant run was there: Herman, Jan, Peter, and Timothy. The waiters worked harder than they had ever worked before (and, in the process, amassed bigger tips). The line of customers around the block waiting to get in was the longest it had ever been. At eleven P.M., closing time, the manager told Jan that there were still fifty-five people waiting outside. "Let them in," she said. And nobody went home until the last guest was fed.

The Next Chapter

Peter Berghoff retired, but only from Berghoff's on West Adams. For years he wore two hats: He owns and operates two related firms in Michigan that supply and transport limestone and aggregates to industrial, governmental, commercial, and residential customers. Today Peter continues to operate his transport business, and he has switched his former Berghoff's CEO hat for another as the COO (chief operating officer) of the Berghoff Café at O'Hare airport.

At this writing, Timothy Berghoff is going to open his own bar and grill, and is scouting locations. He is pursuing photography on the side.

Carlyn Berghoff, after twenty years of off-premise catering in one location, learned that her landlord was going to buy out her lease. So, to find a home for her rapidly growing business, she purchased the assets of the family business at 17 West Adams and moved her company there. She will continue to operate her catering business with her team at this address, where she has converted half of the former dining room into an event space called the Century Room, used for large catered parties. She has expanded her business by opening a café on the lower level that serves carved sandwiches, healthy salads, and freshly baked pizzas. She has also opened 17 West at the Berghoff, a cocktail bar where she is serving the best of the Berghoff's classics with a new look. "I call it tradition with a twist," she says. At 17 West customers can also sample some of the dishes that made her company famous. So the fourth generation continues the Berghoff's tradition of entertaining in a new and creative way.

Jan and Herman pop in to 17 West and walk down to the café every now and then—but only to dine. Jan says, "We not only raised a family together, but together we shared in the great experience of the historical icon that was Berghoff's. We did not move from the twentieth to the twenty-first century alone, but with our staff—many of whom shared our founder's experience of coming to America

Above: During the final days in February 2006, lines of customers stretched down the block. *Next page:* Customers savor their final meal before the Berghoff Restaurant closed, February 2006.

from another land. They were part of our lives, both as friends and second family, and we made music together." Finally, Jan and Herman are able to realize some long deferred dreams. One, they say, is "to enjoy the city we live in and have taken for granted for so many years. We want to walk along the shoreline of Lake Michigan and through the park and just enjoy the culture and architectural aspects of this beautiful Chicago." Another is to spend more time at their home in Michigan, where

Herman, who always wanted to be a builder, has a wood-working shop. A third is to spend more time with their three grandchildren (who are growing up fast), including a Disney cruise to celebrate Jan's upcoming seventieth birthday. And at last they can travel. "First I want to see this wonderful country we live in," says Herman. Next he wants to see Argentina. After that, they have a European vacation planned, with a stop in Dortmund, Germany— where it all began.

APPETIZERS

Libations and Nibbles

Berghoff Classics

CHEF MATT'S SPINACH DIP 30

GRILLED PORTOBELLO MUSHROOMS MARINATED
in BALSAMIC VINAIGRETTE 31

BEER-BATTERED VEGETABLES with TERIYAKI SAUCE 32

GERMAN CHEESE, MEAT, and FRUIT BOARD 34

MUSHROOM STRUDEL 36

Carlyn's Favorites

SWEET POTATO CHIPS with GREEN ONION DIP 38

SALTIMBOCCA SKEWERS with PESTO CREAM DIP 39

BRIE CHICKEN SKEWERS with CANDIED PECANS
and APPLE CHUTNEY 40

CREAMED SPINACH STUFFED MUSHROOMS 42

DILLED SHRIMP CUCUMBER CUP with BOURSIN CHEESE 43

HAZELNUT QUESADILLAS with CHIHUAHUA CHEESE
and RED PEPPER SAUCE 44

BRUSCHETTA with PEARS, GORGONZOLA, and WALNUTS ... 45

PESTO CHEESECAKE 46

GRAPES ROLLED in GOAT CHEESE 48

CURRIED CHICKEN CRÊPE BITES with PEANUT SAUCE 49

SHRIMP MARTINI 50

AS A FAMILY, THE BERGHOFFS have been tending bar for more than a century, ever since our founder Herman Joseph Berghoff opened the Berghoff Café (really a saloon) in 1898, mainly to sell his own Dortmunder beer, named after Dortmund, Germany's biggest beer-brewing city. This unique beer is golden-colored but darker and smoother than pilsner, and paler but with more body than Münchener beer. But he was smart enough to know that man does not live by beer (even Dortmunder) alone—so he threw in a free sandwich.

For our family and, we believe, for anyone with a superbusy life, drinks and hors d'oeuvres top the list of stress-free ways to entertain. There's only one secret: knowing how to set up a bar. Granted we had a head start on the bar know-how. But it was an easy step to take all the lessons we learned from serving customers in the Berghoff Café and bring them home for entertaining guests. We think it will be just as easy for you.

When planning any party, we always consider the season. For winter and spring we think

cocktail parties; for summer and fall we think a beer party. We have suggested menus for both, based on the slightly different spirit of each. A cocktail party is festive, fancy, and sophisticated (see page 259). A beer party is informal, relaxed, and lots of fun (see page 259).

With a cocktail party, you can stick to serving just beer, wine, and soft drinks. Or you can set up a full bar, and offer cocktails and mixed drinks. Or you can do a bourbon tasting, which third-generation Herman Berghoff held at Berghoff's all the time.

At a beer party, you can even add root beer floats (see page 213). What's more, you can present a beer tasting, a welcome change of pace from the ubiquitous wine tastings.

Depending on the size of the party, you can hire a bartender for the party so that you can be hands-free, or just let guests serve themselves.

Instead of spending the time and effort to prepare food for any of these parties, there's no reason not to create your own antipasto platter or simple buffet from the excellent cheeses, meats, breads, and condiments offered by gourmet food shops. Where is it written that you can't have a good time at your own party?

Setting Up the Bar

- Plan on a four-hour party.

- Make the bar/beverage station as simple or as complex as you wish, taking your guests' preferences into account. Decide on a beer and wine bar, or else a full bar with spirits. But don't confuse guests by sticking in a lone bottle of vodka with the wine.

- Set beverages and glassware on a six-foot-long table with a protected surface.

- Consider spills. You might think they won't happen, but they will. If you care about protecting your carpeting or furniture, then avoid serving anything red: red wine, tomato juice, cranberry juice, grenadine, or cherries.

- Remember nonalcoholic beverages: bottled water, both still and sparkling; juices; and soft drinks. Stock about half of your soft drinks sugar free, and don't forget some decaffeinated options.

Liquor License No. 1

When founder Herman Berghoff opened the Berghoff Café in 1898 to showcase his celebrated Dortmunder-style beer, he didn't count on Prohibition (1920–33). Always resourceful, Herman made sure his saloon thrived even during Prohibition because he expanded the bar into a full-service restaurant and began serving the great food for which the Berghoff Restaurant became famous. The day after Prohibition ended, Berghoff's was issued Liquor License #1 (for the bar) and Liquor License #2 (for the restaurant). Berghoff's has been awarded the first liquor license issued by the city every year since then.

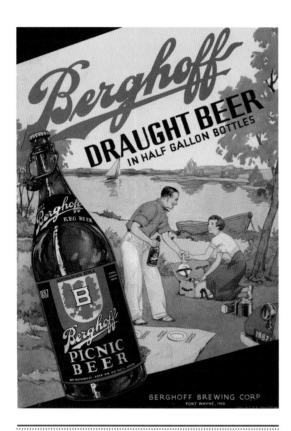

Berghoff's Beverages

During the thirteen years of Prohibition, when making and selling beverages with any alcohol content was illegal, Herman took the dry spell as an opportunity and started making soft drinks and near beer at the Berghoff brewery. (Mass-marketed during Prohibition, near beer was a malt beverage containing half of 1 percent or less, by volume, of alcohol; its official classification was a "cereal beverage.") At Prohibition's end, Berghoff's once again served its regular and seasonal beers and private label bourbon.

- How much is enough? For a beer and wine bar, figure on three-quarters of, to one full 750 ml bottle of wine per guest, and three to four 12-ounce bottles of beer per guest. Guesstimate how many red- vs. white-wine drinkers you may have, and purchase accordingly: two red to one white, or vice versa. Buy 750 ml bottles, not large sizes, so you can uncork as needed and eliminate waste.

- Raising the bar: For a full bar, in addition to red and white wines, beer, or nonalcoholic beverages—and perhaps champagne—you need a fifth each of vodka, gin, bourbon, scotch, rum, blended whiskey, sweet and dry vermouth, plus mixers. Mixers include tonic and club soda; orange, lemon, cranberry, and tomato juice; and Bloody Mary mix. Drink garnishes include lemon and lime wedges, olives, maraschino cherries, and pickled onions. Remember accoutrements: stirrers and bar picks, a cocktail shaker, an ice bucket and scoop, and glasses of real glass or plastic—five per person—plus ten cocktail napkins per person. (If you don't want to wash glassware, rent it. If you don't want to rent or wash glassware, use plastic.)

- How much ice? For serving with drinks in the summer for a full bar, the ratio is two pounds of ice per guest. In nonsummer months, you can manage with one pound per guest. Whichever the season, you will need additional ice for chilling beer and wine.

Beers through the ages: A lineup of some of Berghoff's famous beers.

A Beer Tasting

A beer tasting is not a blind tasting or a guessing game. The beers are labeled and poured to view, taste, and enjoy.

For each guest, supply:

- One plain paper placemat or an $8^1/_2$ by 11-inch piece of white paper, on which you have drawn five glass-base-size circles, with the name of the beer to be tasted beneath each circle. (You can create one mat and then photocopy the rest to save time.)

- Five plastic glasses, each with a 6-ounce capacity.

- Pencil and paper for making notes

We suggest tasting the following beers, all offered on Berghoff's menu in the summer:

Berghoff Summer Solstice Wit Beer

Berghoff Hefe Weizen Beer

Berghoff Original Lager

Berghoff Red Ale

Berghoff Genuine Dark

For the fall-winter, we suggest:

Berghoff Oktoberfest

Berghoff Winter Ale

And the original lager, red ale, and genuine dark

- For each tasting, pour 3 ounces of beer into a glass and place it on its labeled circle.

Gloria Steinem Drank Here

Until 1969, the Berghoff saloon was an all-male stronghold where no female dared set foot on its brass rail. Then, one November day that year, several women who belonged to the National Organization for Women (NOW) walked in, bellied up to the bar with the good old boys—and made history. Not long after, New York feminist Gloria Steinem came in for a much-publicized drink. Although the saloon has never been the same since, it has always been and still is a popular hangout, mostly for male Chicagoans.

- Taste from light to dark. Look first at the clarity. Wheat beers tend to be cloudy, whereas ales and lagers are clearer. Next, look at the color. Is is light, amber, or dark?

- Taste for weight and body. Is it light, or heavy and full?

- Taste for a hoppy bitterness or a malty sweetness. The Summer Solstice Wit Beer has a pronounced flavor of coriander on the front of the tongue. The Hefe Weizen has a banana flavor from the kinds of malted barley used. The Berghoff Lager beer offers heavy malty flavors, the ale a hoppy bitterness but it will seem lighter than the lager, and the Berghoff Genuine Dark will be sweetly bitter—like chocolate and coffee.

- Last, pour each guest a glass of his or her favorite brew. The ideal temperature for lighter-style beers is about 45°F; for stronger ales and beers, about 55°F. But no thirsty guest is going to take its temperature or refuse a cold beer.

A Bourbon Tasting

Third-generation Herman Berghoff held informal bourbon tastings every year to maintain the quality of his great-grandfather's private stock Kentucky bourbon. It always came from a small distiller who distilled and bottled to the restaurant founder's exacting standards. The tastings were so much fun that in the year 2000 he opened them to Berghoff's customers as a way to welcome the new millennium. Here's how it's done:

1. For the blind tasting, pick five bourbons, making sure that one of them is your gold standard (for example, Maker's Mark Bourbon).

2. Place the bottles in bags numbered 1 through 5.

3. Make tasting sheets for every guest. At the top, put the scale: 4 stars (outstanding); 3 stars (excellent); 2 stars (very good); 1 star (good).

Berghoff's bar in the 1930s with rattan stools and brass spittoons.

4. On the left side, write numbers 1 through 5 to correspond to the bourbons. Next to each leave two spaces, one for a first score, and the other for a second score. Leave a space for individual tasters' notes. And on the far right, list the quality criteria on which the bourbons are to be judged, each on a scale of 1 through 4:

Nose	Initial taste
Mid taste	Body
Balance	After taste
Drinkability	Overall satisfaction

5. On a separate $8^1/2$ by 11-inch sheet of paper, draw five circles the size of the base of a glass. Place each glass on a circle to correspond with the bourbon numbered in the bag.

6. Then taste each bourbon twice, rating it each time.

7. At the very end of the tasting, add up the scores and reveal the names of the bourbons.

CHEF MATT'S SPINACH DIP

Makes 3 cups | *Our creamed spinach was already famous when Matt Reichel become Berghoff's chef in 1995. But he created another spinach dish, the dip that follows, that became almost as popular, proving too much of a good thing is never enough. This can be used as a dip or a stuffing and is best made one day ahead.*

2 large red bell peppers

Oil, as needed

2 (10-ounce) packages frozen chopped spinach, defrosted and squeezed dry

1 cup prepared ranch dressing

1 cup sour cream

1 cup chopped water chestnuts

2 teaspoons prepared teriyaki sauce

1 teaspoon Maggi seasoning sauce

1 teaspoon minced garlic

$1/2$ teaspoon ground nutmeg

Between your hands, lightly rub the peppers with oil. Using long-handled tongs, place them on an open flame or rack set over an electric burner on high heat, turning them until their skins are blackened, 4 to 6 minutes per side. Transfer the peppers to a heatproof bowl and let stand, covered, with plastic wrap, until cool enough to handle. Keeping the peppers whole, peel them, cut off their tops, and scoop out and discard their seeds and ribs. Dice the peppers, reserving $1/2$ cup for the dip. Wrap and refrigerate any remainder for future use.

In a medium-size bowl, combine the reserved $1/2$ cup of roasted pepper with the other ingredients; mix well. Place in a covered container and refrigerate at least one day before needed.

GRILLED PORTOBELLO MUSHROOMS
MARINATED in BALSAMIC VINAIGRETTE

Serves 8 | *Jan put this on the menu in 2000, and it was an instant success. Vegetarians love it, and so do meat eaters.*

BALSAMIC VINAIGRETTE MARINADE

> 1 cup Balsamic Vinaigrette (page 92)
>
> 1 cup thinly sliced scallions
>
> 1/2 cup chopped fresh basil
>
> 1 tablespoon brown sugar
>
> 1 teaspoon chopped garlic
>
> 1 teaspoon salt
>
> 1 teaspoon ground black pepper
>
> 1/2 cup olive oil

MUSHROOMS

> 8 large portobello mushrooms, stems removed, brushed clean
>
> Shredded lettuce, for garnish

Make the marinade: In a large bowl, whisk together all the marinade ingredients except the olive oil. Whisk in the oil slowly until incorporated. Let the marinade stand for at least 2 hours before using. Store in covered container in the refrigerator for up to one week before using as directed. Bring to room temperature before using.

Make the mushrooms: Pour 1 1/2 cups of the marinade into a large bowl, reserving the rest for serving as a dressing. Add the mushrooms and toss to coat. Cover and let stand for at least 2 to 3 hours before cooking, tossing often.

Heat an outdoor or indoor grill. Place the mushrooms on the grill, cooking on both sides until tender, 2 to 3 minutes; turn constantly to ensure they do not burn. Discard all leftover marinade.

To serve: Set the mushrooms on a bed of shredded hearty lettuces, and accompany with the extra 1/2 cup of vinaigrette if desired.

BEER-BATTERED VEGETABLES
with TERIYAKI SAUCE

Serves 12 | *For decades, Berghoff's menu offered chopped steak. A platter of Pan-Fried Chopped Sirloin, French-Fried Potatoes, and Chef's Salad went for seventy-five cents in 1944. The chopped steak was garnished with a customer favorite: beer-battered French-fried onion rings. When the chopped steak finally left the menu, people missed those onion rings. So we brought them back—with good company.*

VEGETABLES

1 head broccoli, cut into florets

16 small white button mushroom caps

1 medium-size Spanish onion, cut into 1-inch pieces

1 medium-size carrot, cut into ¼-inch-thick slices

1 red bell pepper, cored, seeded, and cut into 1-inch-square pieces

1 yellow bell pepper, cored, seeded, and cut into 1-inch-square pieces

Vegetable oil for deep-frying, as needed

BATTER

2½ cups light Berghoff beer

2½ cups all-purpose flour

1½ teaspoons baking powder

1 teaspoon kosher salt

TERIYAKI SAUCE

¾ cup prepared low-sodium teriyaki sauce

½ cup chicken stock

¼ cup dry white wine

3 tablespoons sugar

1½ teaspoons minced white onions

1½ teaspoons prepared hoisin sauce

1½ teaspoons fresh lemon juice

½ teaspoon ground or grated fresh ginger

¼ teaspoon minced garlic

Pinch of crushed red pepper flakes

2 tablespoons cornstarch slurry (see Note)

1 scallion, curled, for garnish (see Note)

Seasonal edible uncooked baby vegetables, for garnish

Make the batter: In a large bowl, mix the beer, flour, baking powder, and salt. Set aside for at least 10 minutes before using as directed.

Make the sauce: In a medium-size saucepan, bring all the sauce ingredients except the cornstarch slurry to a boil; decrease the heat and let simmer for 30 minutes. Thicken with the cornstarch slurry, stirring until the sauce coats the back of a spoon thickly.

Make the vegetables: In a deep-fryer or heavy, deep pot, preheat the vegetable oil to 365°F. Making sure they are absolutely dry before dipping, so the batter will cling properly, dip the vegetables into the batter, coating well. Carefully place the vegetables into the hot oil, taking care not to crowd them. Fry in batches for 3 to 5 minutes, or until the battered vegetables are golden brown and crisp. Remove from the oil and drain well on paper towels before serving with the sauce for dipping.

Garnish the battered vegetables with the scallion curls and uncooked baby vegetables.

Note: A cornstarch slurry is made by mixing equal amounts of cornstarch and cold water, and stirring. As it sits, it tends to settle, so stir right before using.

To make scallion curls, trim the scallion top and bottom, then slice into fine julienne strips. Put the strips in a bowl of ice water, where they will curl.

GERMAN CHEESE, MEAT, and FRUIT BOARD

Almost since the beginning at the Berghoff Restaurant, cheese has occupied a prominent place on the menu. And it's never missing from family parties, either. It's nice to add to a cheese board cold meats, dried and fresh fruits, and sweet and savory condiments, along with a selection of carefully chosen breads and crackers.

To calculate how much you will need, plan on one ounce each of cheese and meat per guest. Cut the cheeses into different shapes to add interest. For example, cut soft and crumbly cheeses in wedges, and slice or cube firm cheeses. It's okay to plan on a little more per guest for a smaller party so your platter looks full. You can always recycle leftovers for sandwiches or salads.

Select at least four different cheeses—one blue, one soft or semisoft, one semifirm, and one hard. Select at least two dried and two fresh fruits, and three varieties of cold meats. Offer two mustards, one Dijon and one whole-grain, and two fruit preserves or chutneys.

Cheeses: Roquefort, Cambozola (a German blue-veined cheese), Muenster, Emmenthaler, Austrian Gruyère, aged Cheddar, Camembert, Liederkranz, and Limburger.

Meats: Pâté, Black Forest ham, boiled ham, hard salami, and liverwurst.

Fruits: Dried apricots, cherries, dates, and figs; fresh strawberries, blueberries, and sliced whole fruits.

Condiments: Whole-grain mustards, cornichons, lingonberry preserves, fruit chutneys, dried fig or cherry or apricot or cranberry preserves.

Presentation: Serve soft breads (sliced breads and small rolls) in woven reed baskets or contemporary woven wire baskets, lined with colorful napkins. Serve crackers and flatbreads in separate baskets to preserve crispness.

Sliced cheeses can be shingled in a circle on a large round plate with a pot of mustard in the middle, or else shingled in a spiral on a large rectangular platter with a pot of mustard and a pot of tapenade or aioli set in each of the S-curves.

Cubed cheeses look nice on a plate or platter lined with baby spinach leaves (see page 257); offer a container of disposable wooden picks for easy eating.

Cheese wedges need to be served with cheese knives on flat surfaces, making cutting easy. Try wooden or glass trays, and garnish with little dishes of dried fruits, nuts, or olives.

Glass bowls or plates let the natural beauty and color of fresh berries and sliced fruits show through. Fruit preserves also look pretty in small round or square glass dishes; be sure to serve upon another glass plate (in case of spills), with a small spoon for serving.

Pâtés can be served in white or earthenware crocks or pots, with butter knives for spreading; use matching bowls or crocks of mustard and cornichons.

Sliced ham can be rolled and the rolls set on platters lined with woven cucumber or carrot strips (see page 257). Slice salami as thinly as possible, and cut the liverwurst into even slices about $1/8$ inch thick. Shingle in rows on white platters and place sprigs of fresh rosemary, thyme, or any other green herb that doesn't wilt quickly, in between the rows.

The Cheese Menu

As early as 1914, cheese had its own section on the restaurant's menu. The offerings were Swiss, American Roquefort, and Limburger for 35 cents each; Fromage de Brie, 35 cents; and Pimiento Cheese, 20 cents. ("One order served for two, 10 cents extra.") By 1932, Limburger, Brie, Roquefort, American, and Pimiento had been joined by Liederkranz, Camembert, Downsville Cream Cheese, and Imported Swiss. The menu prices had risen by about five cents per cheese, except for the Swiss that was sold for a whopping price of fifty cents. Among the cheeses listed on the early Berghoff's menus were three distinctly American cheeses: cream cheese (invented by American cheese makers in 1872); Liederkranz (invented here by Emil Frey to recreate German Schlosskäse); and American cheese (plus that variation on American: pimiento cheese).

MUSHROOM STRUDEL

Serves 8 | *For the past five years, Mushroom Strudel has been one of the most popular appetizers on Berghoff's menu. We serve this often at home for family dinner parties because the filling can be made a day ahead and refrigerated, and the strudel is easy to assemble and bake. Once it's baked, it keeps well. What's not to like?*

FILLING

2 tablespoons canola oil

$^1/_3$ cup chopped white onion

$^1/_3$ cup chopped celery

4 cups sliced portabello mushrooms (12 ounces)

3 cups coarsely ground white button mushrooms (9 ounces)

2$^1/_2$ cups sliced shiitake mushroom caps (7$^1/_2$ ounces)

4 tablespoons ($^1/_2$ stick) butter

$^1/_4$ cup all-purpose flour

1 cup Madeira

$^2/_3$ cup chicken broth

2 large eggs, beaten

1 cup dry bread crumbs

1 cup thinly sliced scallions

2 tablespoons chopped fresh basil

TO ASSEMBLE

4 sheets frozen phyllo dough, defrosted (see Note)

$^1/_3$ cup (5 tablespoons plus 1 teaspoon) unsalted butter, melted

2 cups shredded Monterey Jack cheese ($^1/_2$ pound)

Oregano or other green herb, for garnish

Edible uncooked mushrooms, for garnish

Make the filling: In a large skillet, heat the oil, add the onions and celery, and sauté over medium heat for 3 minutes. Add all the mushrooms and sauté for 5 more minutes, stirring often. Stir in the 4 tablespoons of butter until it is melted, and then add the flour; mix until the mushrooms are well cooked, about 3 minutes. Do not allow to burn. Stir in wine and let simmer for 5 minutes. Then add the stock and simmer for 10 minutes more, stirring often. Remove from the heat. Cool to room temperature, cover, and refrigerate.

When cold, mix in the eggs, bread crumbs, scallions, and basil. Adjust the seasonings. This recipe makes approximately 5 cups of filling.

Preheat the oven to 350°F.

Assemble the strudel: On a clean, flat surface, lay out one sheet of phyllo dough and brush with the melted butter. Place another sheet on top and brush with the melted butter. Repeat this process with the remaining two sheets of phyllo, saving some butter for the top of the strudel.

Spoon the mushroom filling lengthwise down center of the stacked phyllo sheets and sprinkle evenly with the cheese. Roll up securely and place the strudel roll, seam side down, on a baking sheet. Seal the ends tightly by crimping together. Brush the top of the roll with melted butter and bake for 30 to 35 minutes, or until golden brown and heated through. Remove from the oven and let stand for 15 minutes before slicing.

Slice the phyllo roll into eight thick slices. Serve warm or at room temperature. Garnish with green herbs and/or edible uncooked mushrooms.

Note: Frozen phyllo is widely available in 1-pound boxes. Three common sizes are 12 by 17 inches (usually twenty-eight sheets of phyllo per pound); 14 by 18 inches (twenty sheets per pound); and 9 by 14 inches (forty sheets per pound). Defrost the phyllo in its box in the refrigerator for 8 hours. When working with phyllo, always keep the sheets not being used well covered with a clean, damp kitchen towel, to prevent them from drying out.

SWEET POTATO CHIPS with GREEN ONION DIP

Serves 6 | *Carlyn will never forget the day fifteen years ago when the chef at her catering company brought her a basket of these crisp, deep-fried sweet potato chips. Sweet potatoes are one of her least favorite vegetables, but these were love at first bite. You can freeze these and reheat them, and they keep very well. They have only one "enemy": high humidity. So best save making these for dry days during the fall, winter, and spring.*

GREEN ONION DIP

³/₄ **cup sour cream**

¹/₃ **cup sliced scallions**

1 tablespoon fresh lemon juice

¹/₄ **teaspoon salt**

¹/₈ **teaspoon ground white pepper**

¹/₈ **teaspoon hot red pepper sauce**

SWEET POTATO CHIPS

4 sweet potatoes or yams, washed (about 3 pounds)

Vegetable shortening or oil for deep-frying, as needed

1 tablespoon popcorn salt or fine-grained salt

1 teaspoon ground cinnamon

Make the dip: In a bowl, combine all the ingredients; mix well. Place in a covered container and refrigerate at least overnight before serving. This recipe makes ¹/₂ cup of dip.

Fry the potatoes: With a mandoline (see Note) cut the potatoes into paper-thin slices. Fill a deep-fryer or deep, heavy pot with shortening or oil to 4-inch depth; heat to 325°F. Fry the potato slices in batches, turning them with tongs or a slotted spoon until they are golden brown. Transfer the chips with a slotted spoon to paper towels, to drain. Mix together the salt and cinnamon, and sprinkle the chips with the mixture while still hot. If the sweet potato chips do not crisp up, place on a baking sheet in a single layer and bake in a preheated 375°F oven for 5 minutes before serving at room temperature.

To serve: Place the chips in a napkin-lined basket, with a bowl of Green Onion Dip served on the side.

Note: A mandoline, a slicing device used by professional chefs in a restaurant kitchen, is an expensive, heavy, large piece of manual equipment. But inexpensive, lightweight, small versions are available at culinary equipment stores and many Asian food markets. They do just as good a job at paper-thin slicing and are better suited to the home kitchen.

SALTIMBOCCA SKEWERS with PESTO CREAM DIP

Makes 12 skewers/4 servings | *Like the Brie Chicken Skewers, this can also be an entrée if not sliced and skewered. And like the Brie Chicken, this can be prepared in advance and frozen. Simply defrost and cook when ready to serve.*

PESTO CREAM DIP

> ¹⁄₂ **cup sour cream**
>
> **2 tablespoons prepared basil pesto**

SALTIMBOCCA SKEWERS

> **2 (6-ounce) skinless, boneless chicken breasts**
>
> **1 tablespoon fresh lemon juice**
>
> **Salt and ground black pepper**
>
> **4 thin slices prosciutto**
>
> **4 fresh sage leaves**
>
> **2 (¹⁄₂ by 3-inch) strips fontina cheese**
>
> **All-purpose flour, for dusting, as needed**
>
> **1 tablespoon olive oil**
>
> **Romaine lettuce leaves, for garnish**
>
> **12 (6-inch) bamboo skewers, soaked in water for 30 minutes**

Make the dip: In a small bowl, whisk together the dip ingredients. Place in a covered container and refrigerate at least overnight, or until ready to serve. Serve in a small dip bowl. This recipe makes ¹⁄₂ cup of dip.

Preheat the oven to 350°F.

Make the skewers: Butterfly the chicken breasts (split down the center, cutting almost, but not completely through) and lay between two pieces of plastic wrap or waxed paper. Lightly pound with a meat mallet or the bottom of a small skillet until evenly thin. The breast should be doubled in size.

Lightly brush each chicken breast with lemon juice, and season with salt and pepper. In the center of each breast, arrange two slices of prosciutto, one slice of fontina cheese, and two sage leaves. Roll up each breast into a log; wrap each roll in plastic wrap, tightly twisting the ends to keep the roll firm. Place the chicken rolls in the freezer for at least 2 hours.

Remove the chicken rolls from freezer and remove the plastic wrap. Lightly dust each roll with all-purpose flour. In an 8-inch skillet, heat the olive oil until it begins to smoke lightly; sauté the chicken rolls until golden brown on all sides. Remove the rolls from the skillet and poke six bamboo skewers equal distances apart along the length of each roll, all the way through the chicken so that they protrude equally on each side of the roll. Place the rolls on a lightly greased baking sheet and bake for 10 minutes. Remove the rolls from the oven and let stand for 5 minutes before slicing between each skewer to produce filled chicken spirals.

Arrange on a serving platter lined with romaine lettuce leaves, and serve with Pesto Cream Dip in a bowl in the center.

BRIE CHICKEN SKEWERS with CANDIED PECANS and APPLE CHUTNEY

Makes 12 skewers/4 servings | *When you're in the catering business, you learn that all brides love Brie. And the 1990s were the beginning of Brie madness. This was created as an appealing and appetizing way to serve Brie. It's easy to prepare and cook, and above all, pretty to serve. And you can make it up to three months in advance and freeze it. The better and tighter you wrap the rolls, the better it will keep. This can also be served as an entrée if you don't cut and skewer the rolls after baking.*

APPLE CHUTNEY

> **2 Granny Smith apples, peeled, cored, and chopped**
>
> **1 small white onion, diced (¹⁄₂ cup)**
>
> **¹⁄₂ cup apple cider vinegar**
>
> **¹⁄₂ cup light brown sugar**
>
> **1 tablespoon fresh chopped ginger**
>
> **1/8 teaspoon ground allspice**

CHICKEN SKEWERS

> **2 (6-ounce) skinless, boneless chicken breasts**
>
> **1 tablespoon fresh lemon juice**
>
> **Salt and ground black pepper**
>
> **2 (¹⁄₂ by 3-inch) strips Brie cheese**
>
> **¹⁄₄ cup Candied Pecans, lightly chopped (page 80)**
>
> **2 teaspoons chopped fresh tarragon**
>
> **All-purpose flour, for dusting, as needed**
>
> **1 tablespoon olive oil**
>
> **Romaine lettuce leaves, as needed**
>
> **12 (6-inch) bamboo skewers, soaked in water for 30 minutes**

Make the chutney: In a 2-quart saucepan, over low heat, combine all the chutney ingredients; simmer until the liquid evaporates and the apples are tender. Remove from the heat. When the chutney is cool enough to handle, pulse in a blender or food processor until smooth. Place in a covered container and refrigerate at least overnight, or until ready to serve. This chutney can be stored in an airtight container in the refrigerator for up to one week. Serve warm or chilled in a small dip bowl. This recipe makes 1 cup of chutney.

Preheat the oven to 350°F.

Make the chicken: Butterfly the chicken breasts (split down the center, cutting almost, but not completely through) and lay between two pieces of plastic wrap or waxed paper. Lightly pound with a meat mallet or the bottom of a small skillet until evenly thin. The breast should be doubled in size.

Lightly brush each chicken breast with lemon juice, and season with salt and pepper. In the center of each breast, arrange 1 slice of Brie cheese, and sprinkle with chopped Candied Pecans and tarragon. Roll up each breast into a log; wrap each roll in plastic wrap, tightly twisting the ends to keep the roll firm. Place the chicken rolls in the freezer for at least 2 hours.

Remove the chicken rolls from freezer and remove the plastic wrap. Lightly dust each roll with all-purpose flour. In an 8-inch skillet, heat the olive oil until it begins to smoke lightly; sauté the chicken rolls until golden brown on all sides. Remove the rolls from the pan and poke six bamboo skewers equal distances apart along the length of each roll, all the way through the chicken so that they protrude equally on each side of the roll. Place the skewered rolls on a lightly greased baking sheet and bake for 10 minutes. Remove the rolls from the oven and let stand for 5 minutes before slicing between each skewer to produce filled chicken spirals.

Arrange on a serving platter lined with romaine lettuce leaves, and serve with the chutney.

Coins in their Aprons

Until 1980, Berghoff waiters—whose no-nonsense demeanor was legendary—operated on the old German system of coins. The waiters were independent contractors and, at the beginning of each shift, purchased metal coins from the restaurant (sold in bags at the cigar counter). These coins were used to buy food and beverage from the house to fulfill their customers' orders. The customers paid in cash. At the end of the day, all the waiters' checks were audited and each waiter was expected to "zero out." Cash tips were their bread and butter. In 1980, computers, credit cards, and the new automated ordering and billing systems instantly eradicated a century-old way of doing business.

CREAMED SPINACH STUFFED MUSHROOMS

Makes 24 stuffed mushroom caps/8 servings | *Oh, that Berghoff creamed spinach! Customers kept asking for it to be served in a different way. The customer is always right, so we invented both another way to serve it and another way to stuff mushrooms.*

24 large white mushrooms
(2–2¹/₂ inches in diameter)

2 tablespoons olive oil

¹/₂ teaspoon salt

¹/₄ teaspoon ground black pepper

2¹/₂ cups Creamed Spinach (¹/₂ recipe, page 170) (see Note)

¹/₄ cup grated Parmesan cheese

Preheat the oven to 375°F, and lightly oil a large, shallow baking pan.

To create space for the stuffing, pull off the stems from the mushroom caps (trim and use the stems in other dishes). Brush the caps with the 2 tablespoons of oil, and season with salt and pepper. Put the mushroom caps, bottom down, in the prepared baking pan and bake until they release their liquid, 5 to 7 minutes; remove from the oven. Turn over the mushrooms, and gently fill the inside of each cap completely with the spinach mixture (there may be some filling left over). Sprinkle with Parmesan. Bake in the middle of the oven until the mushrooms are tender and the cheese is golden brown, about 10 minutes.

Note: To keep the stuffing from becoming runny from the moisture in the mushrooms, increase the butter and the flour in the creamed spinach recipe by ¹/4 cup each.

The Berghoff kitchen slide.

DILLED SHRIMP CUCUMBER CUP
with BOURSIN CHEESE

Makes 24 cucumber cups/8 servings | *This recipe takes a little work, but it's worth it. It's a refreshing summer hors d'oeuvre, an unexpected seafood appetizer for a wedding, and a showstopper when you want to wow guests.*

1 tablespoon olive oil

1 tablespoon chopped fresh dill

12 large cooked, peeled, and deveined shrimp, split in half lengthwise

2 English (seedless) cucumbers

2 (5-ounce) packages Boursin cheese or other soft herbed cheese spread

In a medium-size bowl, stir together the olive oil and chopped dill; add the shrimp, cover, and refrigerate for at least 1 hour.

Meanwhile, cut the cucumber widthwise into twenty-four $^{1}/_{2}$-inch sections. With a melon-baller, scoop out the central seeded area from one side of each section to create a cup.

Using an electric mixer fitted with the paddle attachment, whip the Boursin cheese to soften it. With a teaspoon, fill each cucumber cup with Boursin cheese; top each with one shrimp half. Garnish each cup with a dill sprig, and serve.

Note: Boursin cheese has a smooth and buttery texture, and is versatile to use. The version found in grocery stores is often flavored with herbs, garlic, or cracked pepper.

HAZELNUT QUESADILLAS with CHIHUAHUA CHEESE and RED PEPPER SAUCE

Serves 6 | *Chihuahua cheese, widely available in supermarkets these days, is a pale yellow semisoft cow's milk Mexican cheese originally from the northern Mexican state of Chihuahua. What Carlyn likes about it is its flavor—different from Monterey Jack. She chose it for this appetizer that's easy to assemble in advance and cook in a skillet to order. Her kids love it, and so do her clients at catered events.*

RED PEPPER SAUCE

1/2 **cup sour cream**

1/4 **cup mayonnaise**

1/2 **tablespoon fresh lime juice**

1/8 **teaspoon salt**

Pinch of ground white pepper

1 large roasted red pepper, skinned, seeded, and pureed (page 109)

HAZELNUT QUESADILLAS

4 (10-inch) flour tortillas

2 cups shredded Chihuahua or Monterey Jack cheese

3 tablespoons toasted chopped hazelnuts

2 tablespoons chopped fresh cilantro

2 tablespoons unsalted butter, melted

Make the sauce: In a large mixing bowl, combine the sour cream, mayonnaise, lime juice, salt, and pepper; mix until well blended. Stir in the red pepper puree and adjust the seasonings. The sauce can be made several days in advance and stored, covered, in the refrigerator. This recipe makes 1 cup of sauce.

Preheat the oven to 350°F.

Make the quesadillas: Spread out the tortillas on a clean surface. Sprinkle 1/2 cup of cheese evenly over half of each tortilla. Sprinkle hazelnuts and cilantro evenly over the cheese. Fold each tortilla in half over the cheese mixture. Brush the folded tortillas lightly on both sides with melted butter.

Brush a large, heavy skillet with more melted butter; set over medium-high heat. Working in batches, cook the quesadillas on both sides just until brown spots appear, approximately 2 minutes on each side. Continue to brush the skillet with butter between batches.

Transfer the quesadillas to a large baking sheet. Bake until the quesadillas are golden and the cheese melts, about 5 minutes.

Transfer the quesadillas to a clean work surface and cut each into six triangles. Arrange on a platter and serve with the sauce.

BRUSCHETTA with PEARS, GORGONZOLA, and WALNUTS

Serves 6 | *The Italians invented bruschetta, and Italian restaurants made it popular some time ago. But bruschetta can be more than just tomatoes and basil. This Artistic Events original can be made in advance and served hot or cold, or at room temperature.*

12 (½-inch-thick) slices
  French bread

3 tablespoons olive oil

Salt and ground black pepper

¼ pound Gorgonzola cheese,
  crumbled and softened (1 cup)

1 fresh ripe pear, peeled, cored,
  and diced

3 tablespoons chopped toasted
  walnuts (chop as uniformly as
  possible)

Preheat the oven to 350°F.

Brush the bread with the olive oil and season with salt and pepper. Place on a baking sheet and bake until golden brown on both sides. Remove from the heat and cool to room temperature.

Spread the Gorgonzola cheese evenly on all the toasted bread slices. Fan the pear slices over the cheese and garnish evenly with the chopped walnuts.

PESTO CHEESECAKE

Makes one 10-inch cake/Serves 8 to 12 | *This original Carlyn Berghoff recipe goes back twenty years, but it's still a family and customer favorite. It's inexpensive to make and a great buffet item that looks good, tastes good, and holds up well. It can be made in advance and refrigerated for a week.*

Nonstick cooking spray, as needed

2 tablespoons dry bread crumbs

1 tablespoon olive oil

1 small diced white onion (1/2 cup)

1 tablespoon chopped garlic

1 tablespoon cracked black pepper

4 1/2 pounds cream cheese, at room temperature

1/3 cup prepared basil pesto

2 large eggs

2 tablespoons fresh lemon juice

1 tablespoon all-purpose flour

1/2 teaspoon salt

1 1/2 cups shredded fontina cheese

Preheat the oven to 325°F. Spray a 10-inch springform cake pan with nonstick cooking spray. Sprinkle the bread crumbs evenly over the bottom of the pan.

In a small skillet, heat the olive oil. Add the onion, garlic, and pepper, and sauté for 4 minutes, stirring often. Remove from the heat and let cool completely.

Using an electric mixer fitted with the paddle attachment, gently mix the cream cheese, pesto, eggs, lemon juice, flour, and salt until smooth. Gradually fold in the fontina cheese and the onion mixture, and mix until blended. Pour the mixture into the prepared springform pan and smooth the top with a metal spatula. Bake for 50 to 60 minutes, or until slightly golden on top and set. Remove from the oven and allow to cool to room temperature before loosely covering and placing in the refrigerator to chill until ready to serve.

To serve: To add some pizzazz to your cake, decorate it with sliced seedless red or green grapes, chopped and seeded plum tomato confetti, fresh chopped herbs, or any other colorful vegetable. Leave the cake whole and serve on a cake stand or decorative plate. This makes a great accompaniment to sliced baguettes, crackers, or flatbread. Serve at room temperature.

GRAPES ROLLED in GOAT CHEESE

Makes 24 rolled grapes/Serves 8 | *This is one of Paul Larson's greatest hits. Paul is the executive chef for Carlyn's catering company, Artistic Events. He created this in 2000, and it is a one-in-a-millennium recipe. The grapes are beautiful to behold and taste so good that they're hard to stop eating. They can be made six hours ahead and refrigerated. An attractive way to serve them is one per skewer. Stick the other end of the skewers in a flowerpot full of brown sugar for an amusing presentation.*

¹⁄₄ pound goat cheese, at room temperature

24 red or green seedless grapes, stemmed, rinsed, and patted dry

¹⁄₃ cup finely chopped toasted walnuts

¹⁄₄ cup minced chives

Divide the goat cheese into twenty-four equal-size balls. With your fingers, mold the cheese around each grape until the fruit is completely covered. Keep cold.

Mix the walnuts and chives together in a small mixing bowl. Roll each coated grape one at a time in walnut mixture until covered. Place in a single layer in a low, flat dish, cover, and refrigerate until ready to serve. The grapes may be rolled up to 6 hours in advance.

CURRIED CHICKEN CRÊPE BITES
with PEANUT SAUCE

Makes 24 crêpe bites/8 servings | *These little crêpes are good cold, or can be served in larger portions for a luncheon entrée. The bite-size hors d'oeuvres can be dramatically presented on a plate or tray blanketed with black sesame seeds.*

PEANUT SAUCE

1/4 cup smooth peanut butter

1/4 cup low-sodium soy sauce

3 tablespoons fresh lime juice

3 tablespoons warm water

2 teaspoons brown sugar

1 clove minced garlic

1 1/2 teaspoons minced fresh ginger

1 tablespoon hot chile paste

CHICKEN CRÊPE BITES

1/2 pound boneless chicken breast

2 tablespoons curry powder, or as needed

1/4 teaspoon salt

1/4 teaspoon ground black pepper

3 tablespoons olive oil

1/4 cup mayonnaise

1 tablespoon fresh lemon juice

12 prepared 6-inch crêpes

Make the sauce: Place all the sauce ingredients in a food processor or blender, and lightly process until blended. Cover and let stand for at least 1 hour before serving. Serve as dipping sauce as directed. The recipe makes 1 cup of sauce.

Preheat the oven to 350°F.

Make the chicken crêpes: Season the chicken breast with curry powder, salt, and pepper. Heat the 2 tablespoons of olive oil in a 10-inch oven-proof skillet and brown the chicken on all sides. Place in the preheated oven for 10 minutes, and bake until cooked through. Remove from the oven and allow the chicken to cool completely.

Shred the cooled chicken and place in a medium-size bowl. Add the mayonnaise, lemon juice, and remaining tablespoon of olive oil, and toss well. Season the mixture with more curry powder, if desired. You will have about 1 1/2 cups of curried chicken salad.

Cut the crêpes in half, place a tablespoon of chicken salad on each half, and roll up into a cone shape. Place on serving platter until ready to serve. Continue rolling the crêpes until all the chicken salad has been used up. Serve with the sauce on the side, for dipping.

SHRIMP MARTINI

Serves 8 | *If Grapes Rolled in Goat Cheese is one of Paul Larson's biggest hits, this is his biggest claim to fame. When the mashed potato fad of the '90s was in full swing, and fine dining restaurants were serving skin-on lumpy mashed potatoes, this was his answer. At family parties, we serve it in plastic martini glasses.*

MASHED POTATOES

4 large Idaho potatoes

1/2 cup half-and-half

3 tablespoons salted butter, softened

1/2 teaspoon salt

1/4 teaspoon ground white pepper

WHITE WINE SAUCE

1 cup dry white wine

1/4 cup heavy whipping cream

12 tablespoons (1 1/2 sticks) salted butter, softened

Ground white pepper

SHRIMP

2 tablespoons olive oil

16 medium-size shrimp, peeled, deveined, and chopped, or lobster may be substituted

2 cloves garlic, chopped

2 tablespoons olive oil

2 tablespoons chopped fresh chives, for garnish

Make the mashed potatoes: Peel and dice the potatoes. Place in a medium-size saucepan, cover with cold water, bring to a simmer, and simmer until tender, 20 to 25 minutes. Remove from the heat and drain. Using an electric mixer, whip the potatoes to a thick puree with the half-and-half, butter, salt, and pepper. Set aside the potatoes in a warm place until ready to serve.

Make the sauce: In a 1-quart saucepan, heat the white wine over medium heat and simmer until reduced by two-thirds to 1/3 cup. Add the heavy cream and continue to simmer until reduced again by half to about 1/2 cup. Remove from the heat and gently whisk in the butter, a little at a time, until thickened. Season with white pepper, and set aside in a warm place until ready to serve. This recipe makes about 1 cup of sauce.

Make the shrimp: In a 10-inch skillet, heat the olive oil. Add the shrimp and sauté until tender and almost cooked through. Add the chopped garlic and sauté for another minute. Do not allow the garlic to brown or burn. Remove from the heat immediately.

Assemble the martinis: Divide the hot mashed potatoes among eight martini glasses. Place two cooked shrimp on top of the potatoes in each glass and drizzle each martini with 2 tablespoons of the wine sauce. Garnish with the chopped chives and serve immediately.

SOUPS

Bowls for All Seasons

Berghoff Classics

LENTIL SOUP	56
WHITE BEAN and CABBAGE SOUP	58
MUSHROOM SOUP	59
SPLIT PEA SOUP	60
CREAMY TOMATO BASIL SOUP	61
NEW ENGLAND CLAM CHOWDER	62
BEEF BARLEY SOUP	64
CHICKEN SOUP	65
CHICKEN BROTH	66
FISH BROTH	67

Carlyn's Favorites

CHILLED GRAPE GAZPACHO	68
BUTTERNUT SQUASH SOUP	70

SOUP HAS BEEN A FIXTURE ON THE MENU of the Berghoff Restaurant for as long as anyone can remember. Today, soup is our all-season solution to appetizing yet easy lunches and dinners for family or friends—meals that can please kids and grown-ups alike.

The kinds of soups we have served at the restaurant and enjoy at home have one thing in common: comfort. Our soups are satisfying and savory, and they're often the better half of a simple "soup and . . ." family meal.

On Fridays, a fish sandwich and a bowl of vegetable soup was great-grandfather Herman's favorite supper. He was a devout Catholic, but he enjoyed this meatless meal so much it never seemed like deprivation. His favorite Berghoff soup was lentil. And it's our favorite to this day. Our customers obviously shared this opinion because it was the restaurant's most popular soup and most requested recipe. Beef Barley was a close second.

Good soup is easy to make, provided you start with good ingredients. The soup pot is no place for leftovers or vegetables past their prime, but it's a great place for bits and pieces of perfectly good food that would otherwise go to waste, not to mention the stray stalk of celery or lone carrot. Soup allows you to use produce you may have overbought.

We often serve soup with salad in spring and summer, and soup and sandwiches year round. For informal family meals, we ladle the soup from the stove or a slow cooker, and put the sandwich makings on a platter with sliced bread, lettuce, garnishes, and condiments on the side—so everyone can make their own.

A Century of Soups

The earliest printed menu that our family has a copy of is from 1914. What it tells us about soup is two-fold: First, Berghoff's offered only two soups—Clam Chowder and Mexican Chili Con Carne, each listed at twenty-five cents. Second, the now-standard practice of serving two sizes of soup—cup and bowl—had not yet been introduced. In 1914, soup was served by the bowl.

By 1932, you could have Chicken Okra with Rice or Homemade Noodle Soup by the cup (15 cents) or the "large bowl" (20 cents). Unless, of course, you ordered the oyster stew by the bowl, with milk (40 cents), or with cream (50 cents).

Soup prices held steady until 1954, when they jumped to 20 cents per cup, and 25 cents per bowl.

And by 2000, a cup of soup at lunch cost $2.45, and a bowl $2.80; at dinner, the same soup was $2.50 per cup and $2.95 per bowl. The choices had increased tenfold, and soups had become more seasonal with the heavier soups, such as Beef Barley and White Bean and Cabbage, making their appearance in fall and winter.

The Berghoff Café, 1912.

Strange as it might sound at first, soup is a great gift to bring to someone's home—frozen and wrapped. Because soup is a big deal to make, you might as well make a double batch and freeze it. When you do, be sure to date and label it. Then take a frozen container to the host, who can simply pop it in the freezer—and enjoy to an easy lunch or supper at some future date.

You can simplify a sit-down meal by serving soup family style. Ladle the soup from a tureen, and serve with salads prepared in advance. And if you're making one of our hot sandwiches, such as a Reuben, or Black Forest Ham and Brie Panini (pages 100 and 106), assemble and cook the sandwiches and keep them warm on a sheet pan in a 200°F oven until ready to serve.

Our secret ingredient for soup is tomato paste. It's the miracle seasoning for broth-based soups. And while it doesn't appear in the recipes, feel free to add it to any broth-based soup that needs a flavor boost. Start with 1 tablespoon of tomato paste, and add more to taste.

Speaking of broths, there are recipes in this chapter for homemade chicken and fish broth. But if you're in a hurry (who isn't these days?) feel free to purchase stock in a can. Chicken broth is multipurpose; make sure it's salt free.

LENTIL SOUP

Makes 3 quarts/Serves 8 | *This was our founder Herman Berghoff's favorite soup; it is also our family's favorite soup, and it has remained a customer favorite for decades. The recipe has changed somewhat over the years, and the big fatty ham hocks of Herman's day have given way to leaner diced ham. But the flavor? It's as good as ever.*

1 tablespoon canola oil

1½ cups diced onion

1 tablespoon minced garlic

1½ cups diced celery

1½ cups diced carrot

9 cups chicken stock

2 cups dried lentils, rinsed and picked over

2 small bay leaves

⅛ teaspoon red pepper flakes

1½ cups diced ham

2 cups canned, diced tomatoes in juice

1 (6- or 7-ounce) bag baby fresh spinach, chopped

Salt and ground black pepper

Grated Parmesan cheese, for garnish

In a 4-quart saucepan, heat the oil; add the onion and sauté for 1 minute. Stir in the garlic and continue cooking for 1 minute. Add the celery and carrots, and continue to sauté for 1 minute.

Add the stock, lentils, bay leaves, and red pepper, and bring to a boil; decrease the heat and simmer for 1½ to 2 hours, or until the lentils are cooked to tender.

Stir in the ham and tomato, and continue to cook for 5 minutes. Add the spinach and adjust the seasonings; simmer for 5 more minutes. Remove from the heat and serve.

Ladle 1½ cups of soup per serving into soup plates or bowls, and sprinkle with grated Parmesan cheese, if desired.

WHITE BEAN and CABBAGE SOUP

Makes 3 quarts/Serves 8 to 12 | *This soup recipe dates back to Grandmother Carlyn. It was one of her favorites. She was big on ham hocks, and every time we visited it seemed she had a ham hock simmering in something.*

2 ¹/₂ pounds smoked ham hocks

3 quarts water

1 whole clove

1 medium-size white onion, peeled, left whole

1 cup dried great northern beans, soaked (see Note)

6 sprigs parsley

1 bay leaf

1 sprig fresh thyme

2 cloves garlic, finely chopped

1 pound Yukon Gold potatoes (3–4 medium-size)

1 pound green cabbage, cored and cut into ¹/₂-inch pieces (6 cups)

Salt and ground black pepper

Toasted rye croutons, for garnish

In a heavy 8-quart pot, over high heat, bring the ham hocks and water to a boil; decrease the heat and simmer covered, for 1 hour, skimming off the froth often.

Stick the clove into the onion. In the pot with ham hocks, add clove-studded onion, beans, parsley, bay leaf, thyme, and garlic; simmer, uncovered, stirring occasionally, until the beans are almost tender, 40 to 50 minutes.

When the beans are close to being done, peel the potatoes and cut into 1-inch pieces. Add the potatoes and cabbage to the beans. Simmer, uncovered, until the vegetables are very tender, 20 to 25 minutes.

Remove the ham hocks from the soup. When cooled enough to handle, discard the skin and bones, and cut the meat into bite-size pieces. Stir ham pieces into soup. Discard the bay leaf and onion. Season with salt and pepper.

Ladle 1 to 1¹/₂ cups of soup into each soup plate and serve with toasted rye croutons.

Note: Soak the beans in 2 inches of cold water at room temperature at least 8 hours. Drain and rinse in a colander. Or use the quick-soak method: Cover the beans with 2 inches of cold water in a 5- to 6-quart pot; bring to a boil and boil, uncovered, for 2 minutes; remove from the heat and let stand, uncovered, for 1 hour.

MUSHROOM SOUP

Makes 1¹/₂ quarts/Serves 6 | *Berghoff's Mushroom Soup began as a way for the restaurant kitchen to use up the extra beef broth it produced in the early days for the restaurant's sauces, gravies, and stews. As the years went by and the trend toward lighter food emerged, the broth in the mushroom soup was changed to chicken. This soup is nothing sexy—but oh, so good.*

**4 tablespoons (¹/₂ stick)
   unsalted butter**

**1 medium-size white onion,
   thinly sliced**

**1 pound white button mushrooms
   (quartered if large)**

4 cups chicken broth

2 sprigs flat-leaf parsley

2 tablespoons roux (see Note)

1 cup heavy cream

¹/₂ cup Marsala

Salt and ground white pepper

Crispy onion rings, for garnish

In a heavy 4-quart saucepan, melt 2 tablespoons of the butter; add the onions and sauté over medium heat until soft and translucent, 3 to 4 minutes. Add the mushrooms and remaining 2 tablespoons of butter and simmer over low heat for 8 minutes, taking care not to brown the onions. Stir in the chicken broth and parsley, and bring to a boil. Immediately decrease the heat to low and simmer, uncovered, for approximately 45 minutes.

Remove from the heat; remove and discard the parsley sprigs. Allow the soup to cool for 15 minutes. Transfer the soup to a blender, in batches, and blend at high speed until smooth.

Return the soup to the pot. Bring to a boil and whisk in the 2 tablespoons of the roux. Reduce the soup to a simmer, and add the cream and wine. Simmer the soup over low heat for another 10 to 15 minutes. Remove from the heat. Adjust the seasonings.

Serve in bowls, 1 cup per serving, with crusty French bread. Garnish with a crispy onion ring if desired.

Note: Roux is a mixture of fat and flour that is used to thicken soups and sauces. It is cooked over low heat for a few minutes, stirring (do not brown). It can be made in advance using these proportions of butter and flour, and used as needed:

**4 tablespoons (¹/₂ stick) unsalted
   butter**

¹/₃ cup all-purpose flour

SPLIT PEA SOUP

Makes 2¹/₂ quarts/Serves 8 to 10 | *This was another one of Grandmother Carlyn's "ham hock soups." We remember her kitchen as the little lady's with the big pot. Her soup pot was enormous, but she stood only four feet ten inches tall.*

2 tablespoons vegetable oil

1 cup diced onions

1 cup diced celery

8 cups chicken broth (page 66) (see Note)

2 cups dried split peas

1¹/₂ cups diced smoked ham

2 bay leaves

Kosher salt and ground black pepper

Croutons, for garnish

Heat the oil in a stockpot. Add the onion and celery, and sauté for 5 minutes. Add the chicken broth, split peas, ham, and bay leaves, and bring to a boil. Decrease the heat and simmer the soup for 1¹/₂ to 2 hours, stirring occasionally, until the peas are completely cooked (add more broth as needed). Remove and discard the bay leaves. Season with salt and pepper.

Ladle 1 to 1¹/₂ cups of soup into each bowl and garnish with croutons, if desired.

Note: Add broth as needed to keep the soup at the desired consistency. This soup will thicken overnight when stored in the refrigerator, and so may need more liquid added to it when reheated.

CREAMY TOMATO BASIL SOUP

Makes 1¹/₂ quarts/Serves 6 | *Berghoff's chef Matt Reichel says this is his favorite soup to make for his kids. It's so much better than canned cream of tomato soup, and almost as easy to make as is opening a can.*

1 tablespoon vegetable oil

1 tablespoon unsalted butter

¹/₂ cup diced sweet onion

¹/₂ cup diced celery

¹/₂ tablespoon finely chopped garlic

2 tablespoons all-purpose flour

1 quart tomato-vegetable juice

2 bay leaves

1 cube chicken bouillon

1 cup heavy cream

1 tablespoon sliced fresh basil (sliced crosswise into ¹/₄-inch strips), plus extra for garnish (optional)

1 cup diced, seeded tomato

Salt and ground black pepper

In a heavy 4-quart saucepan, heat the oil and butter. Add the onion, celery, and garlic, and sauté over medium heat for 3 to 4 minutes. Add the flour and cook for 2 minutes, stirring often.

Add the juice, bay leaves, and bouillon cube, and bring to a boil. Decrease the heat and simmer the soup for 20 to 25 minutes. Remove the bay leaves.

Stir in the heavy cream, tablespoon of basil, and tomatoes, and simmer for 5 more minutes. Season with salt and pepper.

Serve hot or cold. Ladle the soup into individual bowls, 1 cup per serving, garnishing with an extra sprinkling of sliced basil, if desired.

NEW ENGLAND CLAM CHOWDER

Makes 3 quarts/Serves 8 to 12 | *New England Clam Chowder appeared on Berghoff's 1914 menu. Was it made the same way as we make it today? No way. While today's recipe uses heavy cream—1¹/₂ cups for 3 quarts of soup, not too bad—the biggest part of the liquid is clam juice or homemade fish broth. In the good old days, it was all cream. And the oyster stew on the same menu could be ordered made with milk or cream. And customers could even order a side of a bowl of cream.*

3 tablespoons vegetable oil

1 cup diced onion

1 cup diced celery

1 medium-size leek, split, cleaned, trimmed, and sliced thinly

3 tablespoons all-purpose flour

6 cups clam juice or fish broth (page 67)

2 sprigs fresh thyme

2 bay leaves

2 cups chopped clams

2 cups diced potatoes

1¹/₂ cups heavy cream

Salt and ground white pepper

Oyster crackers, for garnish

Fresh thyme, for garnish

Hot red pepper sauce (optional)

In a heavy 4-quart saucepan, heat the oil; add the onions, celery, and leeks, and sauté for 3 to 4 minutes. Add the flour and cook for 1 to 2 minutes, stirring often.

Add the clam juice, thyme, and bay leaves, and bring to a boil. Add the chopped clams and diced potatoes, decrease the heat, and simmer the chowder for 35 to 40 minutes, or until the potatoes are tender. Remove the bay leaves.

Add the heavy cream to the soup. Season with salt and pepper.

To serve: Ladle the soup into individual bowls, 1 to 1¹/₂ cups per serving, and garnish with oyster crackers and fresh thyme. Serve with hot pepper sauce, if desired.

BEEF BARLEY SOUP

Makes 2¹/₂ quarts/Serves 8 to 10 | *Ever since Carlyn was a little girl, Beef Barley Soup has been her favorite—at home or in the restaurant. When the restaurant closed in 2006, this was its second-most-requested recipe.*

2 tablespoons vegetable oil

1 cup diced onion

1 cup diced celery

1 cup diced carrot

1 tablespoon chopped garlic (3 cloves)

³/₄ cup pearl barley

¹/₈ teaspoon crushed red pepper flakes

8 cups beef broth

2 bay leaves

2 cups diced cooked roast beef (about ³/₄ pound)

1 cup diced, seeded tomato (1 large)

2 scallions, sliced thinly

Salt and ground black pepper

2 tablespoons chopped fresh parsley, plus extra for garnish (optional)

In a heavy 4-quart saucepan, heat the oil; add the onion, celery, carrot, and garlic, and sauté for 5 minutes. Stir in the barley and red pepper flakes, and sauté for another minute. Add the beef broth and bay leaves, and cook over medium heat, uncovered, for 1 hour.

Add the beef, and simmer for another ¹/₂ hour (until the barley is tender). Stir in the tomato and scallions, and cook for 5 more minutes. (At this point it may be necessary to add more beef broth.) Remove the bay leaves.

Season with salt and pepper, and stir in the parsley.

Ladle the soup into individual bowls, 1 to 1¹/₂ cups per serving, and garnish with additional chopped parsley if desired.

CHICKEN SOUP

Makes 3 quarts/Serves 10 to 12 | *Who doesn't like chicken soup? It's easy to make—so easy that Carlyn has cooked this with her kids as soon as they were old enough to start helping in the kitchen. And Jan makes this soup with and for her grandchildren when she's babysitting.*

2 tablespoons canola oil

1 cup diced onion

1 cup diced celery

1 cup diced carrot

8 cups chicken broth (page 66)

1/4 teaspoon crushed red pepper

2 bay leaves

2 cups pulled cooked chicken
(page 66)

3 cups cooked long, medium-wide
egg noodles

3 tablespoons chopped parsley, plus
extra for garnish (optional)

Salt and pepper

In a heavy 4-quart saucepan, heat the oil. Add the onions, celery, and carrots, and sauté for 5 minutes. Add the broth, red pepper flakes, and bay leaves, and simmer, uncovered, for 45 minutes. Remove the bay leaves.

Add the chicken and egg noodles, and simmer for 10 minutes. Stir in the parsley, salt, and pepper.

Ladle into individual bowls, 1 to 1$^{1}/_{2}$ cups per serving, and garnish with extra chopped parsley, if desired.

CHICKEN BROTH

Makes 2¹/₂ to 3 quarts | *This recipe can be doubled and frozen in containers suitable in size for defrosting one at a time, as needed.*

4 quarts water

1 (3¹/₂–4 pound) roasting chicken, cut into pieces

1 cup chopped onion

1 cup chopped celery

1 cup chopped carrot

2 bay leaves

3 sprigs fresh parsley

2 teaspoons kosher salt

1 teaspoon red pepper sauce

Place all the ingredients in a heavy 8- to 10-quart stockpot. Bring to a boil, decrease the heat to a simmer, and cook, uncovered, for 2 hours. Skim off any froth as it accumulates. Remove the pot from the heat. Remove the chicken and let it cool, then pull for another recipe or freeze for later use (see Note). Pour the stock through a fine-mesh sieve into a large, clean pot and discard all solids. Cover and refrigerate. When cold, skim off and discard the fat. Use as directed in our recipes. The broth will freeze well for up to three months.

Note: Pulled chicken has a different texture from sliced or chopped chicken, and we use it in several recipes in this book. To pull chicken, first cook, then skin the chicken pieces and discard the skin. Then, using two forks, shred the meat into strands. You can also do this by hand, wearing disposable plastic gloves for food safety.

FISH BROTH

Makes 1¹/₂ quarts | *This is another recipe that can be doubled and frozen.*

1 quart fish bones and heads (best made from sole, flounder, halibut, and/or cod)

1¹/₂ quarts cold water

2 cups diced onions

2 cups diced celery

2 bay leaves

2 sprigs fresh parsley

2 sprigs thyme

1 bay leaf

¹/₄ teaspoon crushed red pepper flakes

Rinse the fish bones and heads, and place in a large saucepan with all the other ingredients. Bring to a boil, decrease the heat, and simmer for 45 minutes. Skim off any foam as it accumulates. Strain the broth though a fine-mesh sieve to remove all solids, which should be discarded. Cover the broth and refrigerate until ready to use. Or, freeze for up to three months.

Soup in Minutes

Several years ago it occurred to us that as long as we were making soup or stock at home—a time- and labor-intensive process—we might as well double the recipe and freeze half of it. And we have been doing that ever since. This simple process, so often overlooked, creates a stockpile of wonderful lunch and dinner dishes that are truly "heat and eat."

Be sure to bring the hot soup to room temperature by placing the soup pot in an ice-water bath and stirring until it has cooled. Then place in freezer containers and label with type and date. Freeze soup for up to three months.

CHILLED GRAPE GAZPACHO

Makes 1 quart/Serves 8 | *In the early '90s, our good family friend Bill Reynolds (who later became the provost at Washburn Culinary Institute in Chicago) gave a cooking class at a benefit for a local charity. He made a version of cold grape gazpacho that was the inspiration for this recipe.*

1 pound green seedless grapes, stemmed

1 seedless cucumber, peeled and chopped

1 cup half-and-half or light cream

1/2 cup vanilla-flavor low-fat yogurt

2 tablespoons reduced-fat cream cheese

2 tablespoons rice wine vinegar

1/4 teaspoon kosher salt

Pinch of ground red pepper

2 teaspoons chopped fresh dill

1/4 cup toasted sliced almonds, for garnish

In a blender or food processor, combine all the ingredients except the almonds and half of the dill; blend until smooth. With a strainer or colander, strain the soup into a large bowl. Cover and chill for 4 to 6 hours. If the soup separates, stir before serving.

Pour 1/2 cup of soup into individual small bowls or cups. Garnish with the remaining dill and the sliced almonds. For an interesting twist, the soup can be served in demitasse mugs, shot glasses, or martini glasses.

A Shot of Soup

One of Carlyn's favorite ways to serve soup is two or three at a time, in two-ounce shot glasses, or demi mugs. One selection might be a shot glass or demi mug each of hot Butternut Squash Soup, Creamy Tomato Basil, and Chilled Grape Gazpacho. Served this way, even soup can make a splash at a cocktail party.

Mini soup trio. *Left to right:* Butternut Squash Soup, Chilled Grape Gazpacho, and Creamy Tomato Basil.

BUTTERNUT SQUASH SOUP

Makes 3 quarts/Serves 8 to 12 | *Butternut Squash Soup is the number one best-seller at Artistic Events catered parties. When Carlyn serves this at home for the family, she ladles it into big bowls. But when company comes, she serves it in hollowed-out acorn squash bowls. These are easily created by cutting a small slice off the bottom of the squash, just enough to level it. Brush or spray the outside with oil and bake in a 450°F oven until cooked through, about 45 minutes. Remove from the oven and cool. Cut off the top and hollow out the squash just enough to make a bowl.*

2 tablespoons vegetable oil

2 cups thinly sliced white onions

2 leeks, split, cleaned well, and chopped coarsely

1 tablespoon minced fresh ginger

$^1/_2$–1 teaspoon ground cinnamon, plus extra for garnish

2 butternut squash (about 4 pounds), peeled and cubed (see Note)

6 cups chicken broth (page 66), plus extra for thinning

2 tablespoons light brown sugar

Salt and ground white pepper

Sour cream, for garnish

Heat the oil in a heavy 4-quart saucepan over medium heat. Add the onions, leeks, ginger, and cinnamon, and decrease the heat to medium. Cover the pot and simmer until the onions are tender, about 15 minutes.

Add the squash and continue to cook, covered, for another 10 minutes, until the squash and onions begin to caramelize (they should liquefy slightly and become brownish in color). Add the chicken broth and brown sugar, and bring to a boil. Decrease the heat to medium-low, cover the pot, and simmer for 10 minutes.

When cooled enough to handle, working in batches, puree the soup in a blender or food processor, or with an immersion blender. Cool the purée slightly, cover, and refrigerate. This step may be done one day prior to serving.

When ready to serve, return the soup to the pot and bring to a simmer, until heated through. Thin the soup with more broth if necessary, to reach the desired consistency. Season with salt and pepper.

Serve hot or cold. Ladle the soup into individual bowls, $1^1/_2$ cups per serving. Garnish with a dollop of sour cream and a sprinkling of cinnamon.

Variations: Add heavy cream, light cream, half-and-half, or coconut milk to the soup, to increase the richness and enhance the texture.

Note: Butternut squash already peeled, trimmed, and cut up for your convenience may be purchased in packages at specialty grocery stores.

OYSTERS

Blue Points, Half Doz. . . . 35
Blue Points, Doz. 60
Cotuits, Half Doz. 45
Cotuits, Doz. 80
Raw Select, Half Doz. . . 30
Fried, Half Doz. 45
Fried, Doz. 80
Milk Stew 40
Cream Stew 50
Oyster Cocktail 30

COLD MEATS
(Including Potato Salad)

Kassler Ribs 60
Roast Veal 60
Corned Beef 60
Prime Roast Beef, Lettuce . 70
Cold Chicken 80
Salami Sausage 60
Steak a la Tartar 60
Pickled Lamb Tongue . . 50
Roast Pork 50
Liver Sausage 45
Boiled Ham 50
Boiled Tongue 60
Westphalian Smoked Ham . 75
Assorted Meats 60

SALADS

Lobster 65
Shrimp 55
Salmon 50
Chicken 65
Combination 30
Potato 15
String Beans 15
Lettuce 20
Crabmeat 65
Thousand Island Dressing 15

RELISHES

Sliced Tomatoes 20
Sliced Cucumbers 20
Young Green Onions . . . 15
Radishes 15
Celery 15
Queen Olives 20
Ripe Olives 20
Chow Chow, C. & B. . . . 25
Asparagus, Vinaigrette Sce. 45
Cold Slaw, Green Peppers . 15
Dill Pickles, per order . . 10

DELICACIES
(Including Potato Salad)

Imported Sardellen in Oil . 35
Bismarck Herring 40
Filets of Anchovies, Capers 35
Fresh Shrimps 50
Marinated Herring . . . 40
Eel in Gelee 50
Tunafish 50
Marie Elizabeth Imported
Sardines, quarter 45
Genuine Brisling Smoked
Sardines, quarter 50
Imported Boneless Sardines 50
Caviar 80

EGGS
(Including Potatoes)

Scrambled Eggs 35
Boiled Eggs (3) 35
Fried Eggs (3) 35
Poached Eggs on Toast . . 35
Ham and Eggs 45
Bacon and Eggs 45
Omelette, Plain 35
  "   Ham 45
  "   Parsley . . . 45
  "   Cheese . . . 45
  "   Mushrooms . . . 50

OPEN EVERY DAY—9 A. M. TO MIDNIGHT

Berghoff
RESTAURANT

17 to 23 West Adams Street
Phone Webster 0118

Sunday, January 10, 1932

Fresh Shrimp Cocktail 30
Oyster Cocktail 30 Crabmeat Cocktail 35
Sauerkraut Juice, per glass 10
Grein's Tomato Juice 10

SOUPS

Chicken Okra with Rice 15; large bowl 20
Home-made Noodle Soup 15; large bowl 20
Oyster Stew with Milk 40; with Cream 50

ENTREES

Soup Served with all Entrees and Roast
Idaho Baked Potato (Large Size) 15
Boiled Smoked Pork Butts, Red Cabbage 55
Breaded Veal Cutlet, Tomato Sauce,
California Jumbo Asparagus 60
Braised Sweetbreads on Toast, Mushroom Sauce 60
Broiled Lamb Chops, Spiced Crabapples,
French Fried Potatoes 70
Fresh Pork Shank and Sauerkraut, Boiled Potatoes 50
Broiled Beef Tenderloin Steak, Sliced Tomatoes,
Mushroom Sauce 80
Chicken Fricassee with Rice, Boiled Potatoes 75
English Beef Stew with Vegetables en Casserole 55
Broiled Fork Tenderloin, French Fried Potatoes,
Brussels Sprouts 55
Smoked Thueringer Sausage, Red Cabbage, Boiled Potato 50
Pickled Pork Shank, Cole Slaw or Potato Salad 50
Domestic Frankfurter with Sauerkraut or Potato Salad 35
Fresh Thueringer Sausages and Boiled Potato 50

ROASTS

Roast Sugar Cured Ham, Navy Beans, Candied Sweet Potato 50
Roast Young Turkey, Cranberry Sauce, Celery, Mixed Olives 80
Roast Watertown Goose, Apple Sauce 65
Roast Young Chicken, Endive Salad 75
Roast Loin of Pork, Apple Sauce, Parsley Potatoes 50
Roast Stuffed Breast of Veal, Stewed Prunes 55
Roast Prime Ribs of Beef 65; extra cut 90

STEAKS AND CHOPS

Special Steak 60   Sirloin Steak 85   Extra Sirloin 1.25
Hamburger 60 Mushrooms 25 Fried or Grilled Onions 15
Pork Chops (2) 55   Tenderloin Steak 90   Lamb Chops (2) 70
Veal Chop Breaded 60   Broiled Ham or Bacon 50

VEGETABLES

Spinach 15   New Brussels Sprouts 15   Buttered Beets 15
Apple Sauce 15   Pickled Red Beets 15   Sauerkraut 10
String Beans 15   Cauliflower 15

POTATOES

Boiled or American Fried 10   Shoestring or Cottage Fried 25
Au Gratin 30   French Fried, Hashed Brown or Lyonnaise 15

35c—PLATE DINNER—35c
From 11 a. m. to 11 p. m.
Home-made Head Cheese, Potato Salad
Fresh Thueringer Sausage, Boiled Potatoes and Sauerkraut
English Beef Stew, Spring Vegetables, Mashed Potatoes
Roast Loin of Pork, Apple Sauce
Roast Stuffed Breast of Veal, Carrots and Peas

PASTRY

PIES—Apple, Cherry or Raisin 10   Hot Mince Pie 10
Blueberry Pie 10   French Pastry 10   Cheese Cake 10
Peach Pie 10   Pumpkin Pie 10   Lemon Meringue Pie 10
Coffee Cake 10   Apple Strudel 15   Almond Coffee Cake 10

COFFEE
Coffee 10   Iced Coffee 10   Tea 10   Iced Tea 10

CHEESE
Downsville Cream 20   Liederkranz 25   Pimento 25
American 35   Imported Swiss 50   Limburger 35
Fromage de Brie 35   Camembert 25   Roquefort 25
One Order served for two 10c extra
No Charge for Bread and Butter with Meat or Fish Orders

BEVERAGES

Berghoff, Light per Glass . 10
Stein 15

Berghoff Dark, per Glass . 15
Stein 20

Berghoff Light, Bottle . . 15
Berghoff Dark, Bottle . . 15
Berghoff Malt Tonic . . 15
Berghoff Ginger Ale . . . 15
Berghoff Lime Rickey . . 20
Apple Cider, per Schoppen 10
Ginger Ale, glass 10
Soda 10
Root Beer, glass 10
Grape Juice 10
Schlitz, bottle 20
Budweiser, bottle 20
Canada Dry Ginger Ale . . 25
Hadden Hall Ginger Ale,
bottle 25
Busch Ginger Ale . . . 25
Germania Sparkling Water,
split 15

MILK, CREAM

Milk, per bottle 10
Cream and Milk, glass . . 15
Buttermilk, glass 10
Small bowl of Cream
and Milk 15
Small bowl of Cream . . . 20

SANDWICHES

Club House 50
Hot Corned Beef 20
Chopped Beef 20
Fried or Boiled Egg . . . 10
Hot Frankfurter 20
Combination Ham and
Cheese 30
Roast Veal 20
Corned Beef 15
Hot Roast Beef 20
Roast Pork 20
Beef Tongue 20
Fried Ham 20
Baked Ham 20
Boiled Ham 15
Roast Beef (Cold) . . . 35
Westphalian Ham . . . 30
Liver Sausage 15
Salami 20
Cervelat 20
Sardine 20
Sardellen 20
Caviar 40
A la Tartar 40
Chicken 35
Imported Swiss 20
American Cheese 15
Pimento Cheese 15
Limburger Cheese . . . 15
Brie Cheese 20
Tomato 20
Lettuce and Tomato . . . 20
Ham and Egg 20
Minced Ham 15
Minced Tongue 15

180

Berghoff menu, 1932.

SALADS

Main Dish and Side Salads

Berghoff Classics

BERGHOFF STEAK SALAD 76

CHICKEN WALDORF SALAD 78

CAJUN SALMON SALAD 79

ASIAN PEAR and CHICKEN SALAD 80

GERMAN POTATO SALAD 81

PANKO-CRUSTED GOAT CHEESE SALAD with
CHERRY BALSAMIC DRESSING 82

COBB SALAD with BERGHOFF BLUE CHEESE DRESSING ... 84

Carlyn's Favorites

BABY SPINACH SALAD with PANCETTA and
ROASTED SHALLOT VINAIGRETTE 86

BLUE CHEESE TERRINE 88

ROASTED VEGETABLE PASTA SALAD 89

SALAD CAPRESE 90

MIXED GREENS with BEET and GOAT CHEESE TOWER 91

Dressings

BERGHOFF'S BALSAMIC VINAIGRETTE 92

BERGHOFF'S CREAMY RANCH DRESSING 92

CARLYN'S FRESH HERB VINAIGRETTE 93

CARLYN'S LEMON-DIJON VINAIGRETTE 93

IN THE BEGINNING, SALADS AT BERGHOFF'S were anything but green. In 1914, on our earliest preserved menu, the concession to green was a twenty-cent salad simply called "Lettuce." We're certain the lettuce was iceberg. Things didn't change much until around 1944, when composed salads became popular, such as tomatoes stuffed with lobster, chicken, or shrimp salad. These were still protein heavy and substantial, not leafy and green. The only lettuce on the menu was under "steak": Berghoff Steak Salad, which was and remained the number one best-selling salad.

The greening of Berghoff's happened in 1986, shortly after Jan and Herman had taken over the restaurant from Herman's cousins. Jan says, "In a world of corned beef, we needed to make room for a piece of lettuce." So one day she and executive chef Mohammed Hussein put their heads together and came up with recipes for some salads—Waldorf, Cobb, and Tuna—all made with greens. "We made forty of those salads the first day we put them on the menu— and we sold them all within forty minutes," says Jan. From that day forward, the salads section of the menu grew. The Steak Salad was officially joined by Cobb Salad and Chicken Waldorf Salad, and these three remained on the menu until 2006. But of course, the Berghoff Restaurant put its own spin on the classics, as shown in the recipes that follow.

Ready and waiting: Berghoff's waiters in the 1950s.

In our family, as in the restaurant, we tend to think of salads as main dishes. Salads are a lot of work to prepare—all the washing, drying, cutting, and chopping. And mixed salads have a short shelf life. Sometimes, at home, we simply cut up the greens, put them in a bowl, and place all the other ingredients on the side. That way we have a variety, and everyone—especially the kids, whom we want to encourage to eat salads—can mix their own.

When you are entertaining, if salads are just one of the items offered, people will eat less. But if a salad bar is your main event, count on guests coming back for seconds and thirds. The Chicken Waldorf Salad, Cobb Salad, Salad Caprese, and Roasted Vegetable Pasta Salad all make great buffet items.

The following salad recipes are designated as main dishes, or can be served as sides. Many of the side dishes can also double as appetizers.

Salad Days

Berghoff's surviving printed menus, beginning with one from 1914, tell an evolutionary tale about salads. In 1914, ten salads were listed, among them: lobster, 50 cents; shrimp, 40 cents; chicken, 45 cents; potato, 15 cents; and the rather minimal lettuce, 20 cents. By 1932, salmon, 50 cents; and crabmeat, 65 cents; had displaced 1914's tomato, 15 cents; and cucumber, 20 cents. By 1944, cole slaw had joined the menu, 15 cents; and composed salads had become more substantial. Tomato stuffed with lobster salad accompanied by julienned potatoes sold for 65 cents; and, for 5 cents less, the same salad and potatoes could be had with chicken or shrimp stuffing. By 1944, Berghoff's kitchen had its own salad spinner for lettuce. It was the size and shape of an old-fashioned washing machine.

BERGHOFF STEAK SALAD

Serves 8 | *This main dish salad, introduced in 1955, was long the "green" on Berghoff's menu. It became and remained the restaurant's number one best-selling salad. It contains not only steak but cantaloupe, strawberries, tomatoes, and carrots.*

MARINADE

⅓ cup canola oil

2 tablespoons chopped fresh garlic

2 teaspoons minced fresh oregano

2 teaspoons chopped fresh basil

2 teaspoons kosher salt

1 teaspoon ground black pepper

DRESSING

1½ cups mayonnaise

1 (10-ounce) box frozen chopped frozen spinach, thawed and squeezed dry (¾ cup)

½ cup prepared sour pickle relish, drained

1 tablespoon Worcestershire sauce

¼ teaspoon Tabasco sauce

SALAD

2½ pounds beef tenderloin tip meat, cut into pieces approximately 1 by ½ inch thick

Oil, as needed, to sauté

16 cups baby lettuce (16 ounces)

1 cantaloupe, peeled, seeded, and cut into 16 wedges

1 pint strawberries, washed, stemmed, halved lengthwise

2 cups grape tomatoes

1 small red onion, halved and then sliced thinly

1 cup shredded carrots

Make the marinade: Combine all the marinade ingredients and mix well. Cover and let stand for at least 2 hours before using as directed. This recipe makes ½ cup of marinade.

Make the dressing: Combine all the dressing ingredients and mix well. Cover and refrigerate at least 2 hours, so the flavors have a chance to meld. This recipe makes 2 cups of dressing.

Marinate and cook the steak: Place the meat in a large zippered plastic bag; pour in the marinade, toss to coat, and let marinate, refrigerated, for 2 to 3 hours before cooking. Remove the meat from the bag (discard the used marinade) and sauté in a skillet for 4 to 5 minutes, stirring often. Remove from the heat and set aside until ready to serve.

Assemble the salad: For each serving, place 2 cups of lettuce on a large, chilled plate and arrange on the greens two wedges of cantaloupe, three to four sliced strawberries, four to five tomatoes, several onion slices, and 2 tablespoons of shredded carrots. Top each dish with ¼ pound of cooked beef, and drizzle with ¼ cup of dressing.

CHICKEN WALDORF SALAD

3 quarts salad/Serves 8 | *Our Chicken Waldorf Salad can be served either as a side dish (use half the amount) or as a satisfying main dish salad. It is, of course, a variation of the famous Waldorf salad, which contained apples, celery, walnuts, and mayo on a bed of lettuce leaves. It was invented by the famous Oscar Tschirky ("Oscar of the Waldorf") at the Waldorf-Astoria, which opened in 1898—the same year as Berghoff's. Oscar, who was hired originally as a busboy, was the maître d' of Waldorf's dining room from 1893 until 1943.*

CHERRY REDUCTION

> 1 cup dry red wine
>
> $^3/_4$ cup sugar
>
> $^1/_2$ cup dried cherries

DRESSING

> $1^1/_2$ cups mayonnaise
>
> 1 tablespoon lemon juice
>
> $^1/_4$ cup Cherry Reduction

SALAD

> 1 quart pulled cooked chicken meat (page 66)
>
> 3 cups cored, diced, but unpeeled Red Delicious apples (2 large)
>
> 3 cups cored, diced, but unpeeled Granny Smith apples (2 large)
>
> 2 cups sun-dried cherries
>
> $1^1/_2$ cups diced celery
>
> $^1/_4$ cup diced sweet onions
>
> 8 large red lettuce leaves
>
> $^1/_2$ cup toasted, slivered almonds, for garnish

Make the Cherry Reduction: In a medium-size saucepan, bring all the Cherry Reduction ingredients to a boil over high heat. Decrease the heat and let simmer until reduced by two-thirds. Cool, cover, and refrigerate until ready to use as directed. This recipe makes $^1/_2$ cup of Cherry Reduction.

Make the dressing and salad: In a large bowl, combine the mayonnaise, lemon juice, and $^1/_4$ cup of Cherry Reduction. Gently fold in the chicken, apples, cherries, celery, and onions. Cover and refrigerate at least 2 hours, or until ready to serve.

To serve: For each salad, lay a large lettuce leaf on a chilled salad plate. Top with $1^1/_2$ cups of prepared chicken salad. Garnish the top of each salad with 2 teaspoons of the remaining Cherry Reduction, and 1 tablespoon of almonds.

CAJUN SALMON SALAD

Serves 8 | *In the 1980s, Louisiana chef Paul Prudhomme made Cajun cookery famous, and blackening swept the nation. Not to be left out, Berghoff's created this Cajun Salmon Salad using his signature seasoning mix, and it became one of our most popular entrée salads.*

DRESSING

³/₄ **cup prepared Italian dressing**

³/₄ **cup prepared honey-mustard dressing**

SALMON

2 tablespoons vegetable oil

8 (6-ounce) Atlantic salmon fillets, skinned and boned

¹/₂ **cup Cajun spice mixture (try Paul Prudhomme's Blackened Redfish Magic Seasoning)**

SALAD

16 cups baby lettuce (16 ounces)

1 cantaloupe, peeled, cut into 16 small wedges

1 pint strawberries, washed and stemmed

1 pint blueberries

1 pint raspberries

¹/₂ **cup thinly sliced red onion**

32 grape or teardrop tomatoes (1 pint)

Make the dressing: In a bowl, whisk the two prepared dressings together. Place in a covered container and allow to stand at room temperature for at least 2 hours before using as directed.

Make the salmon: Brush the salmon with oil and sprinkle one side of each fillet with Cajun seasoning. (Sprinkle both sides for spicier fish.) In a large, heavy skillet, heat the oil. Place the salmon in the pan, seasoned side down, and cook to blacken, approximately 2 minutes. Turn over and cook other side for 3 to 4 minutes, or until cooked through. (If the fillet is very thick, lower the heat, cover the skillet, and continue cooking until it flakes with a fork.) When the salmon is completely cooked, remove from the skillet. Keep warm until ready to serve.

Assemble the salads: Top eight luncheon plates with 2 cups of lettuce leaves per plate. Using two forks, gently pull the cooked salmon fillets apart into tablespoon-size pieces, and place on top of salad greens. Arrange the fruit, onion, and tomatoes evenly among the salads. Drizzle each salad with 3 tablespoons of dressing before serving.

ASIAN PEAR and CHICKEN SALAD

Serves 8 | *This colorful entrée salad is one of our very latest. It joined the menu in the twenty-first century, making use of a fruit that then became popular and widely available—the Asian pear. The fruit has the texture of a crisp pear, and a sweet apple-pear flavor—and is very juicy.*

CANDIED PECANS

> 1 cup pecan halves
>
> 2 tablespoons light corn syrup
>
> 1 tablespoon sugar

SALAD

> 4 cups pulled cooked chicken meat (page 66)
>
> 1½ cups mayonnaise
>
> 2 tablespoons sugar
>
> 4 cups cored, diced, unpeeled Asian pears (3 pears), plus 2 more Asian pears, cored, quartered lengthwise, and sliced thinly
>
> 1 cup cored, diced, unpeeled Granny Smith apples
>
> 1 cup diced celery
>
> 1 cup dried cherries
>
> 2 tablespoons diced white onions
>
> 8 cups baby lettuce greens (8 ounces)
>
> ¼ cup Candied Pecans
>
> 2 ounces shaved prosciutto
>
> 1 tablespoon orange zest
>
> 1 tablespoon lemon zest
>
> ½ cup Cherry Reduction (page 78)

Make the Candied Pecans: Preheat the oven to 350°F. Combine the pecans, corn syrup, and sugar in a large mixing bowl. Stir to coat the nuts evenly. Place on a nonstick baking sheet and bake for 10 minutes, until the sugar is melted and the nuts are golden brown. Remove from the oven and cool completely before using as directed.

Make the salad: In a large bowl, toss together the chicken, mayonnaise, and sugar. Gently fold in the diced pears, apples, celery, cherries, and onion.

Place the lettuce greens on eight chilled plates. Top each plate with 1 cup of chicken salad. Fan out a quartered, sliced pear on top of each salad, and arrange with several slices of prosciutto, 2 tablespoons of Candied Pecans, and a sprinkling of lemon and orange zest. Drizzle each salad with 1 tablespoon of Cherry Reduction. Serve with breadsticks.

GERMAN POTATO SALAD

Makes 8 cups/Serves 8 | *German potato salad has been on Berghoff's menu as far back as anyone can remember and was a customer favorite. The secret to its great taste is the advance preparation that allows the flavors to mellow. We like to serve it warm or at room temperature. This makes a great side salad for sandwiches, hearty meats, grilled poultry—and a wonderful buffet dish.*

DRESSING

- 1¼ cups cider vinegar
- ½ cup minced sweet onion
- ⅓ cup vegetable oil
- 1 teaspoon salt
- 1 teaspoon ground white pepper

SALAD

- 8 large white potatoes, peeled, boiled, and sliced ⅛ inch thick (about 4 pounds)
- 1 cup cooked, chopped applewood-smoked bacon (3 ounces)
- 1 cup chopped scallions

Prepare this salad 4 to 6 hours, or one day, ahead of serving, for its flavors to blend optimally.

Make the dressing: In a small bowl, combine all the dressing ingredients and whisk to mix well. Cover and let stand for at least 2 hours before using as directed. This recipe makes 1⅔ cups of dressing.

Make the salad: Gently toss the hot, sliced potatoes with the bacon and chopped scallions. Stir in the dressing and toss gently to coat evenly. Refrigerate, covered, for at least 4 to 6 hours, or overnight. The salad can be reheated in the microwave if you wish to serve it warm.

To serve: Place the salad in a bowl.

PANKO-CRUSTED GOAT CHEESE SALAD
with CHERRY BALSAMIC DRESSING

Serves 8 | *This Berghoff's salad was especially popular with vegetarians. It began as Jan's way of getting the increasingly popular goat cheese on the menu in the late 1980s. Serve this as an entrée salad, or serve half as a side salad—or even as an appetizer.*

CHERRY BALSAMIC DRESSING

$2/3$ cup canola oil

$1/4$ cup Cherry Reduction (page 78)

2 teaspoons balsamic vinegar

Salt and ground black pepper

BALSAMIC REDUCTION

1 cup balsamic vinegar

2 tablespoons sugar

CHEESE PATTIES

4 cups fresh goat cheese

1 cup all-purpose flour

4 large eggs

3 cups panko

2 tablespoons finely minced scallions

$1/8$ teaspoon granulated garlic

$1/4$ teaspoon salt

$1/4$ teaspoon ground black pepper

4 cups vegetable oil (or enough to cover patties completely when frying)

SALAD

16 cups baby lettuce (16 ounces)

1 cup julienned red bell pepper

1 cup julienned yellow bell pepper

$1/4$ cup thinly sliced red onion

$1/2$ cup toasted sliced almonds, for garnish

16 grape tomatoes, halved, for garnish

Make the dressing: In a bowl, whisk together all the dressing ingredients; season with salt and pepper. Use as directed.

Make the Balsamic Reduction: In a small saucepan, bring the vinegar and sugar to boil over high heat; decrease the heat and simmer until reduced by two-thirds (20 to 30 minutes). Remove from the heat. Set aside until ready to use.

Make the cheese patties: Slice and shape the goat cheese into eight 4-inch patties. Place on a baking sheet, cover, and refrigerate at least 1 hour. Place the flour in a shallow dish. In a bowl, lightly beat the eggs. In another bowl, combine the panko, scallions, garlic, salt, and pepper. Dip the cheese patties into the flour and shake off excess. Then dip into the eggs, and last into panko. Pat on the crumbs to coat each patty evenly. Place the patties back on the baking sheet in one layer, cover, and refrigerate again, for 2 hours.

Right before serving as directed, heat the oil to 360°F in a deep-fryer or deep, heavy pot. Fry the cheese patties in batches for 1 to 2 minutes, or until lightly browned and crisp. Serve immediately.

To serve: In a large bowl, toss together the lettuce, peppers, and onion; mix well. Place 2 cups of salad on each of eight chilled salad plates. Gently drizzle each salad with 1 tablespoon of dressing and $^{1}/_{4}$ teaspoon of Balsamic Reduction. Top each salad with a hot cheese patty. Garnish each salad with four tomato halves and 1 tablespoon of toasted almonds. Serve immediately.

COBB SALAD with BERGHOFF BLUE CHEESE DRESSING

Serves 8 | *Our entrée version of the original Cobb salad (invented in 1936 at the Brown Derby Restaurant in Hollywood by the owner, Robert Cobb) has the Berghoff touch. Instead of the plain poached chicken breast from the original recipe, we marinate the chicken for extra flavor. And our salad is accompanied by hot blue cheese croutons.*

BERGHOFF BLUE CHEESE DRESSING

1 cup mayonnaise

$1/2$ cup crumbled blue cheese

$1/3$ cup sour cream

3 tablespoons white wine vinegar

1 teaspoon Worcestershire sauce

$1/4$ teaspoon ground black pepper

$1/8$ teaspoon Tabasco sauce

COBB SALAD

$1/2$ cup prepared teriyaki sauce

$1/4$ cup sherry

$1/2$ teaspoon Tabasco sauce

8 (5-ounce) skinless, boneless chicken breast halves

Nonstick cooking spray

$1^1/2$ cups chopped crisp-cooked bacon

$1^1/2$ cups sliced black olives

4 peeled large hard-boiled eggs, chopped or sliced

2 ripe plum tomatoes, cut into medium-size dices

1 cup crumbled blue cheese

3 ripe avocados, sliced ($2^1/2$ cups)

8 cups baby lettuce (8 ounces)

8 cups chopped romaine lettuce (8 ounces)

CROUTONS

1 sourdough baguette

$1/3$ cup ($5^1/3$ tablespoons) melted butter

$1/2$ teaspoon Tabasco sauce

1 cup crumbled blue cheese

Make the dressing: Combine all the dressing ingredients in a medium-size mixing bowl and stir well. Cover and refrigerate for at least 1 hour, or until ready to use as directed.

Marinate and cook the chicken: In a large bowl, combine the teriyaki sauce, sherry, and Tabasco. Add the chicken and toss to coat. Cover and marinate in the refrigerator for at least 2 to 3 hours, turning often. Remove from the marinade and drain; discard the used marinade. Spray the chicken with cooking spray and grill, on an outdoor or indoor grill, on both sides until cooked through, about 3 minutes per side. Remove from the heat and let cool completely. Slice into strips and set aside until ready to serve.

Make the croutons: Heat the broiler. Cut the sourdough baguette on a diagonal into eight $1/4$-inch slices. Brush one side of each slice with a mixture of melted butter and Tabasco. Place in one layer on a baking sheet. Toast under the broiler for 2 minutes on each side until golden and crisp. Sprinkle each slice evenly with cheese and place under the broiler just until the cheese is melted. Serve while hot, as directed.

To assemble the salad: In a large bowl, toss together the chicken strips, bacon, olives, eggs, tomatoes, and cheese. Gently fold in the avocado. In a separate bowl, toss together the two lettuces, to mix. Place 2 cups of the mixed lettuces on each of eight plates and top each with 2 cups of the chicken mixture. Drizzle each salad with 2 tablespoons of dressing and top with hot croutons.

TLC

Salad greens are perishable and require tender loving care. At the restaurant and at home, we cut romaine lettuce for speed, but we hand-tear butter, Bibb, and other tender lettuces. A word of caution: If you are buying any of the convenience mixes of salad greens, look not only at the expiration date on the package, but inside and especially at the bottom of the bag for signs of wilting or slime. And even though the bag says the contents have been washed and are ready to use, we recommend removing the salad from the bag, washing it in cold water, spinning it dry, and crisping it—in the fridge—in a bowl or a zippered plastic bag along with a clean paper towel to absorb any excess moisture.

What about iceberg? It may not be in fashion, but nothing beats iceberg for crisp texture in a salad mixed with other greens.

BABY SPINACH SALAD with PANCETTA and ROASTED SHALLOT VINAIGRETTE

Serves 6 | *Carlyn created this as a side salad on the menu of Artistic Events, for upscale catered parties. This light yet flavorful salad replaces traditional bacon with pancetta, crisped in a skillet. The dressing is made in the same skillet. Her inspiration came from her grandmother Carlyn's hot bacon dressing for the old-fashioned salad of young dandelion greens.*

6 slices pancetta

3 medium-size shallots, minced

2 fresh thyme sprigs

¼ cup olive oil

⅓ cup red wine vinegar

½ teaspoon salt

¼ teaspoon ground black pepper

12 cups baby spinach, well-washed and dried (12 ounces)

12 cherry tomatoes, halved, for garnish

¼ cup shredded Parmesan cheese, for garnish

Preheat the oven to 350°F.

In a 12-inch skillet, cook the pancetta over moderate heat until golden and crisp, about 8 minutes. Transfer the pancetta to paper towels to drain, and set aside. Do not clean the fat from the skillet.

Place the shallots and thyme in the skillet and sauté over medium heat for 4 minutes, until tender. Add the oil and vinegar, and mix; season with salt and pepper. Cover the dressing and set aside until ready to serve. Remove the thyme sprigs before serving.

In a large mixing bowl, toss the spinach leaves with the shallot vinaigrette.

To serve: Distribute equal amounts of dressed spinach salad among six chilled salad plates or bowls. Crumble one slice of pancetta over each salad, and garnish each with four cherry tomato halves and sprinkling of Parmesan cheese.

BLUE CHEESE TERRINE

Serves 8 | *We use this for entertaining at home, either as an appetizer or as a side dish at a dinner party. We sometimes omit the lettuce and spoon the blue cheese mixture into ramekins, and serve the terrine as a spread for cocktail parties.*

$3/4$ **pound blue cheese, softened**

$1/4$ **pound (1 stick) unsalted butter, softened**

2 tablespoons brandy

1 teaspoon ground white pepper

$1/8$ **teaspoon Tabasco sauce, or to taste**

16 cups mixed baby salad greens (16 ounces)

Any Berghoff salad dressing, as desired (pages 92–93)

Candied Pecans (page 80)

Using an electric mixer fitted with the paddle attachment, cream the blue cheese and butter together until soft and creamy. Add the brandy, white pepper, and Tabasco sauce, scrape the bowl with a rubber spatula, and continue to mix until smooth.

Place a sheet of waxed paper on a clean, flat work surface. Along the center of the waxed paper, using a spatula, form the cheese mixture into a log shape. Roll the cheese log into a paper-wrapped cylinder and twist the ends of the paper in opposite directions to tighten. Roll in plastic wrap and twist the ends. Place the roll in the freezer for about 1 hour. Remove from the freezer and unwrap. While it is still frozen, slice the

cheese into eight $1/2$-inch disks. (Instead of freezing, the log may be refrigerated until very firm for 4 hours or overnight, before using as directed.)

To serve: Top each salad plate with 2 cups of salad greens, and place a slice of terrine over the greens. Drizzle each salad with 2 to 3 tablespoons of your favorite Berghoff salad dressing. Sprinkle with Candied Pecans. Serve.

Over- or Underdressed?

How much salad dressing is enough? It's a personal choice. At the restaurant, we ladled three tablespoons of dressing on a salad that filled a seven-inch diameter salad plate. Hearty salads, such as the Steak Salad, require two ounces—or $1/4$ cup. But, at a customer's request, we would serve the salad undressed with a small side dish of dressing. And for customers who liked their salads drowned in dressing, we would dress the salad as usual and serve a separate side dish of dressing. We follow the same principles when entertaining at home.

ROASTED VEGETABLE PASTA SALAD

Serves 6 | *Popular on buffets or as a side dish salad, this is one of Carlyn's favorite picnic salads.*

**6 cups cooked penne pasta
(¹/₂ pound dried)**

**¹/₂ cup roasted/grilled and
large diced eggplant**

**¹/₂ cup roasted/grilled sliced yellow
squash**

¹/₂ cup roasted/grilled sliced zucchini

**¹/₂ cup roasted/grilled red onion
slices**

**¹/₂ cup roasted/grilled halved
asparagus**

**¹/₂ cup roasted/grilled bell pepper
strips (page 109)**

**¹/₂ cup frozen green peas, defrosted
and drained**

¹/₄ cup toasted pine nuts

2 tablespoons sliced scallions

**³/₄—1 cup any Berghoff salad dressing
(pages 92—93)**

¹/₄ cup chopped fresh basil

Salt and ground black pepper

Crumbled feta cheese, for garnish

**Pitted, sliced kalamata olives,
for garnish**

This salad can be made up to 4 hours ahead of time. In a large bowl, mix together the pasta, roasted vegetables, peas, pine nuts, and scallions. Toss with ³/₄ to 1 cup of your favorite Berghoff salad dressing. Stir in the basil and toss a bit more. Season with salt and pepper. Cover and refrigerate until ready to serve. Let stand at room temperature at least 1 hour before serving.

Just before serving, garnish the salad with the feta cheese and kalamata olives.

SALAD CAPRESE

Serves 6 | *This is Berghoff's and our family's most seasonal salad. We always use ripe tomatoes, usually from the farmers' market, and we love the heirloom varieties. Sometimes our Salad Caprese contains Green Zebra, Cherokee Purple, and Black Russian tomatoes—quite a show. This side salad makes a great buffet platter as well. Caprese salad takes its name from the Isle of Capri, in Campania, Italy, where this salad supposedly was created.*

½ **cup balsamic vinegar**

1 teaspoon minced garlic

1 teaspoon minced shallots

¼ **teaspoon sugar**

½ **teaspoon salt**

¼ **teaspoon cracked black pepper**

¼ **cup olive oil**

1 pound fresh buffalo mozzarella cheese, sliced ¼ **inch thick (see Note)**

1 large ripe red tomato, sliced ¼ **inch thick**

1 large ripe yellow tomato, sliced ¼ **inch thick**

1 large green or orange tomato, sliced ¼ **inch thick**

18 large fresh basil leaves, for garnish

In a small bowl, whisk together the vinegar, garlic, shallots, sugar, salt, and pepper; whisk in the oil. Let stand for at least 1 hour before using.

On a large serving platter, arrange the mozzarella slices alternately with the tomato slices. Drizzle with the vinaigrette. Garnish with basil leaves just before serving.

Note: Buffalo mozzarella is the highest quality of the fresh mozzarellas. The type found in the United States is made from a combination of water buffalo's milk and cow's milk. It can be found in specialty grocery stores or the gourmet aisle of traditional stores.

MIXED GREENS with BEET and GOAT CHEESE TOWER

Serves 6 | *This is labor-intensive and must be assembled just before serving. But it's a dramatic and delicious side salad or appetizer, and worth the effort.*

SHERRY VINAIGRETTE

- 3 tablespoons sherry vinegar
- 2 tablespoons Dijon mustard
- 1 tablespoon chopped shallots
- 1 tablespoon real maple syrup
- 1 tablespoon water
- $1/2$ teaspoon salt
- $1/2$ teaspoon ground black pepper
- 2 tablespoons olive oil

CANDIED WALNUTS

- 1 cup walnut halves
- 2 tablespoons light corn syrup
- 1 tablespoon sugar

TOWERS

- 10 ounces goat cheese, at room temperature
- 1 tablespoon chopped fresh chives
- 6 large roasted beets, peeled and sliced $1/4$ inch thick ($1^1/2$ pounds)
- 12 cups assorted mixed greens (12 ounces)
- Frizzled (julienned and deep-fried) onions or shallots, for garnish

Make the sherry vinaigrette: In a bowl, combine the vinegar, mustard, shallots, syrup, water, salt, and pepper. Slowly whisk in the oil to emulsify the dressing. Place in a covered container and let stand for at least 1 hour before using. This recipe makes $1/2$ cup of dressing.

Make the candied walnuts: Preheat the oven to 350°F. Combine the walnuts, corn syrup, and sugar in a large mixing bowl. Stir to coat the nuts evenly. Place on a nonstick baking sheet and bake for 10 minutes, until the sugar is melted and the nuts are golden brown. Remove from the oven and allow the nuts to fully cool.

Assemble the towers: Do this immediately before serving, or the beet juice will bleed into the goat cheese layer. Using an electric mixer with the paddle attachment, beat the goat cheese and chives until smooth. Place the mixture in a piping bag with a star tip. On a clean baking sheet, place a single layer of six beet slices. Pipe a round of the goat cheese mixture on top of each slice. Top each with a second layer of beet slices and a layer of goat cheese. Repeat, and top with a fourth beet slice.

In a bowl, toss the greens with the vinaigrette and place on six chilled plates. Place one beet tower on each, and sprinkle with 2 tablespoons of walnuts. Serve with frizzled onions , if desired.

Berghoff's Balsamic Vinaigrette

Makes about 1 cup | *The combination of chopped shallot, garlic, and fresh oregano gives this vinaigrette enough assertive flavors to balance the dominant balsamic vinegar.*

- $1/4$ cup balsamic vinegar
- 1 tablespoon minced shallot
- 1 tablespoon chopped fresh oregano
- 1 clove garlic, minced
- $1/4$ teaspoon kosher salt
- $1/4$ teaspoon fresh ground black pepper
- $3/4$ cup olive oil

In a small bowl, whisk all the ingredients except the oil; slowly whisk in the oil to make a vinaigrette. Let stand for at least 1 hour before using as directed. May be refrigerated, covered, for up to 1 week.

Berghoff's Creamy Ranch Dressing

Makes about $1^1/2$ cups | *This creamy dressing is wonderful over mixed greens or used as a dip with your favorite raw vegetables.*

- $1/2$ cup mayonnaise
- $1/3$ cup buttermilk
- $1/3$ cup sour cream
- 2 tablespoons minced fresh parsley
- 2 tablespoons minced fresh chives
- 1 clove garlic, minced
- 1 teaspoon fresh lemon juice
- $1/2$ teaspoon ground white pepper
- $1/2$ teaspoon salt, or to taste

In a small bowl, whisk all the ingredients together. Place in a covered container and refrigerate for at least 2 hours before serving. May be refrigerated, covered, for up to 1 week.

Carlyn's Fresh Herb Vinaigrette

Makes about 1 cup | *Toss or drizzle this lovely, light vinaigrette over your favorite mixed greens.*

- $1/4$ **cup white balsamic vinegar**
- **2 tablespoons minced shallots**
- **2 cloves garlic, minced**
- **2 tablespoons minced fresh thyme**
- **2 tablespoons minced fresh tarragon**
- $1/2$ **teaspoon kosher salt**
- $1/2$ **teaspoon freshly ground black pepper**
- $3/4$ **cup olive oil**

In a small bowl, whisk all the ingredients except the oil; slowly whisk in the oil to make a vinaigrette. Let stand for at least 1 hour before using as directed. May be refrigerated, covered, for up to 1 week.

Carlyn's Lemon-Dijon Vinaigrette

Makes about 1 cup | *Champagne vinegar is an ingredient worth looking for. It adds a fabulous flavor to this fresh, lively dressing.*

- $1/3$ **cup fresh lemon juice**
- **2 tablespoons champagne or white wine vinegar**
- **1 tablespoon Dijon mustard**
- $1/2$ **cup minced shallots**
- **2 tablespoons chopped fresh chives**
- **2 teaspoons (packed) grated lemon peel**
- $1/2$ **teaspoon kosher salt, or to taste**
- $1/2$ **teaspoon ground black pepper, or to taste**
- $3/4$ **cup olive oil**

In a small bowl, blend together the lemon juice, vinegar, and mustard. Whisk in all remaining ingredients except the oil; slowly whisk in the oil to make a vinaigrette. Let stand for at least 1 hour before using as directed. May be refrigerated, covered, for up to 1 week.

SANDWICHES

A Sandwich with Your Dime Stein of Beer

Berghoff Classics

CORNED BEEF SANDWICH 99

REUBEN on RYE 100

BRATWURST, KNOCKWURST, and SMOKED THURINGER 102

BERGHOFF BEER-BRAISED BRISKET 104

BERGHOFF ROASTED TURKEY BREAST SANDWICH 105

BLACK FOREST HAM and BRIE PANINI 106

BLACKENED SWORDFISH SANDWICH 108

BERGHOFF HOME RYE 110

OLIVE BREAD 112

BERGHOFF BEER BREAD 114

Carlyn's Favorites

CAPRESE SANDWICH 116

BRIE and RASPBERRY GRILLED CHEESE SANDWICH 117

SMOKED TURKEY WRAP 118

GRILLED VEGETABLE WRAP 120

SMOKED SALMON WRAP with CAPERS and DILLED CREAM CHEESE 121

TUNA SALAD 122

PESTO TURKEY SALAD 123

BLACK OLIVE TAPENADE with WALNUTS 124

BASIC AÏOLI 125

NECESSITY IS THE MOTHER OF INVENTION, said Plato. In the history of the Berghoff family, necessity has been the mother of creations that became traditions that have lasted for generations. Sandwiches became a tradition at the Berghoff Café in 1898. They were founder Herman Berghoff's inventive way of selling Berghoff beer. If customers bought a glass of beer it cost them five cents. But if they upgraded to a ten-cent stein, that came with a free sandwich—quite a deal. Sandwiches became a mainstay on Berghoff's menus—but not for free.

Sandwich night came into Carlyn's home several years ago, and by now it's an established tradition—one we wholeheartedly recommend. Often, over the weekend, Carlyn would grill a turkey breast or make a roast—and the family couldn't finish it. The kids would give her grief about eating the same meat again in the same form. So, to circumvent complaints and save the roasts, Carlyn had to reinvent the leftovers. Sliced turkey breast or beef roast were perfect for sandwiches and, diced, they made

extraordinary salads. So sandwich night chez Berghoff was born.

Sandwich night is a great way not only to use up leftovers but to take the pressure off the cook once a week. Sandwiches are also the answer to households with different schedules—once made, a sandwich keeps, ready to serve. And nothing lends itself to a buffet quite like sandwiches, unless it's a salad bar. We often serve the two together for a well-balanced, healthful meal.

When it comes to entertaining, a sandwich buffet can not only provide the host with a stress-free party (see page 259) but can captivate guests. Who doesn't love to pick and choose combinations of fillings?

Another informal meal that we find it hard to imagine without sandwiches is a picnic. And it's a meal occasion that can be just for family or a more festive party for friends. When Carlyn's children began to eat without needing a high chair, our family picnics got bigger. She still has the blanket that Jan bought her when she moved into her first apartment, and it has become the family's official picnic blanket. At a recent picnic for neighborhood friends, Carlyn's youngest son, Todd, was making conversation with a guest. "This blanket is twenty years old," he said, "and my mom has had it since she graduated from college." Carlyn is the family picnic fanatic, and her picnic season begins as soon as it is warm enough to eat outside (warm enough by whose standards?). But thanks to her, we have had some memorable picnic parties.

Recipes in this chapter include all the Berghoff's favorite sandwiches—including three famous Berghoff bread recipes reformulated for the home kitchen—and some unique sandwiches that Carlyn created for catering clients, which have now become family favorites. You will also find easy-to-make spreads to make your sandwiches special.

The Berghoff Saloon— Beer and Free Lunch

By 1914, the free lunch that the Berghoff Café offered in 1898 was only a memory. Before then, if a customer bought a dime stein of beer, it came with a choice of three sandwiches—corned beef, boiled ham, or a frankfurter—plus hard-boiled eggs and a pickle. By 1914, there were twenty-nine sandwiches on the printed menu. The original corned beef (now 15 cents), boiled ham (15 cents), and frankfurter (20 cents) were still listed. In those days, Herman hung out with Oscar Mayer, the founder of today's well-known cured-meat company. In 1914, a frankfurter was the original German sausage, highly flavored with a crisp, natural casing.

Among 1914's more unusual sandwiches were roast veal (15 cents), Westphalian ham (25 cents), and sandwich "à la Tartar," featuring raw minced beef (35 cents). One of the most expensive sandwiches on the 1914 menu was chicken (35 cents). Says third-generation Herman, "In those days, chicken was today's steak."

CORNED BEEF SANDWICH

Serves 8 | *In this recipe, we share our secret for moist corned beef, which has been on the menu since 1914. It's an essential element in our appealing "Eau de Berghoff": Berghoff's was famous for an appetizing aroma that hit the nose of patrons the moment they walked in the door—and started them salivating. It was a combination of corned beef cooking and roast beef roasting—made fresh every day.*

5 pounds lean, raw corned beef

1 tablespoon pickling spice

4 quarts water, or enough to cover the meat

Salt and pepper

^{1}/$_2$ cup Dijon or Düsseldorf mustard

16 slices rye bread

In a pot large enough to hold all the ingredients, place the corned beef, pickling spice, and water. Make certain the water completely covers the meat. Bring the mixture to a boil, then decrease the heat and let the meat simmer, covered, for 2^1/$_2$ to 3 hours. Insert a fork into the meat, and it should pull out easily when done. Remove the meat from the pot and let it cool, reserving the cooking liquid. Refrigerate the meat and liquid until completely cool, 3 to 4 hours.

After the meat is cool, remove the fat and slice the meat with the grain, on a slight angle. Slice about ^{1}/$_{16}$ inch thick. This should yield eight (5- to 6-ounce) portions of meat for each sandwich.

Reheat the cooking liquid to a boil; decrease the heat to a simmer, and season with salt and pepper. Dip the meat in batches into the liquid, using a heatproof strainer or small colander. Remove and let drain for 1 minute. Make eight sandwiches, distributing the corned beef among eight slices of rye bread spread with mustard, and topping each with another slice of rye bread. Cut in half to serve.

Opposite: One hundred years later, Berghoff's bar was still going strong, 2006.

REUBEN on RYE

Serves 8 | *Around the year 2000, Jan, Herman, and executive chef Matt Reichel started searching for new sandwiches for the downstairs café. Matt created this version of the famous Reuben sandwich, and it was an instant success. The original Reuben dates from 1914 or 1955, depending on two equally tall tales. The first: In 1914, New York delicatessen owner Arthur Reuben created it for Annette Seelos, the leading lady in a Charlie Chaplin film. The second: In 1955, Omaha grocer Reuben Kay invented it during a poker party. Years later it was entered in a national contest, and it won. Either way, it's a fabulous sandwich to make at home.*

DRESSING

1 cup mayonnaise

2¹/₂ teaspoons chile sauce

1 tablespoon ketchup

¹/₄ teaspoon Tabasco sauce

1 teaspoon lemon juice

1 teaspoon finely diced onion

1 teaspoon finely diced celery

2 teaspoons finely diced pickle

¹/₄ teaspoon Cajun spice mix

Pinch of red pepper flakes

¹/₄ teaspoon Worcestershire sauce

¹/₄ teaspoon chopped fresh parsley

SAUERKRAUT

1¹/₂ cup chopped applewood-smoked bacon

1 cup Berghoff Lager beer

6 cups bagged or canned sauerkraut, drained

¹/₂ tablespoon caraway seeds

¹/₄ pound (1 stick) butter

TO ASSEMBLE

16 slices rye bread

2 pounds thinly sliced corned beef (page 142)

16 slices Swiss cheese

Make the dressing: Combine all the dressing ingredients one day ahead, so the flavors can blend. Season with salt and pepper. Refrigerate, covered, until ready to use.

Make the sauerkraut: Sauté the bacon in a 12-inch skillet until crisp and drain off the fat. Add the beer to deglaze the pan. Add the sauerkraut, caraway seeds, and butter, and simmer for 45 minutes over low to medium heat, stirring occasionally.

Make the sandwiches: Lay out eight slices of bread. Layer each with one slice of Swiss cheese, the hot corned beef (reheated in hot beef stock; see page 142), the hot sauerkraut mix, the dressing, one more slice of Swiss cheese, and finally another slice of rye bread.

Grill in a panini machine following the manufacturer's instructions. (Alternative method: Cook on a griddle or in a skillet with butter, as you would a grilled cheese sandwich, until crisp and brown, about 5 minutes per side.)

BRATWURST, KNOCKWURST, and SMOKED THURINGER

Makes 24 servings, 8 of each kind of sausage | *The three timeless German sausages never fail to please (see "What's Brat, What's Not?" page 103). Bratwurst is usually sold uncooked, so it must be boiled, grilled, or otherwise cooked completely. Regardless of their cooking method or the type of sausage, all sausages should be cooked to an internal temperature of 165°F on a meat thermometer. Serve these sausages hot on buns with our German Potato Salad, Sauerkraut, and Smothered Onions. You and your guests will think they're at Berghoff's.*

8 (3-ounce) veal bratwurst

8 (3-ounce) knockwurst

8 (3-ounce) smoked Thuringer

1 (12-ounce) bottle Berghoff Red beer

6 cups chicken stock

1 (12-ounce) bottle Berghoff Lager beer

24 buns of choice

Düsseldorf mustard, as needed

German Potato Salad (page 81)

Sauerkraut (page 181)

SMOTHERED ONIONS

1 pound (4 sticks) butter

6 cups sliced onions

1 (12-ounce) bottle Berghoff Lager beer

Salt and pepper

Make the sausages: Preheat the oven to 350°F if it will be used to cook the bratwurst, which should be baked at 350°F or grilled until lightly browned, 12 to 15 minutes. Use tongs rather than a fork for turning, as piercing skin will release juices and cause the bratwurst to dry out.

In a large stockpot, heat to a boil the red beer and 3 cups of the chicken stock. Add the Thuringer to the pot and decrease the heat to a simmer. Cook for 8 to 10 minutes.

In a large stockpot, heat to a boil the lager beer with the remaining 3 cups of chicken stock. Add the cooked knockwurst to the pot and decrease the heat to a simmer. Cook for 8 to 10 minutes.

To make the Smothered Onions: In a deep 12-inch skillet, melt the butter over medium heat. Add the onions and cover, stirring occasionally. After the onions turn light brown, about 10 minutes, add the beer and simmer, uncovered, for 10 minutes. Season with salt and pepper.

Accompany the sandwiches with a pot of Düsseldorf mustard, and serve with German Potato Salad, Sauerkraut, and the Smothered Onions. You may omit the buns and serve the sausages on a plate with the onions, kraut, and potato salad.

What's Brat? What's Not?

Bratwurst is a German sausage tradition-ally made of pork and veal, which is highly seasoned. The spices include caraway and/or coriander, ginger, and nutmeg. Every sausage maker has a signature spice formula. Sometimes available precooked, the best bratwurst is fresh and should be completely cooked by boiling, grilling, or sautéing before eating.

Knockwurst sausage (sometimes spelled knackwurst) comes in short, fat links, redolent with garlic. This sausage is made of beef and pork. Although it's usually pre-cooked, boiling or grilling enhances knackwurst, which is often accompanied by sauerkraut. In German, "knack" means "crack" and "wurst," of course, means "sausage." When you bite into a good knockwurst, it makes a crackling noise.

Thuringer can be any one of a variety of fresh or smoked beef or pork sausage that originally came from Thuringia, a region in Germany, where it is known as Thüringerwurst. Coriander is an integral, often predominant, flavoring.

Mustard Muster

The saying to "cut the muster" (i.e., to "make the cut" and be mustered—enlisted as a soldier) has evolved into the expression "cut the mustard" (to be worthy of suc-cess). And mustard, right out of the jar, can indeed make a success of many a sandwich or sausage.

Prepared mustard is made from the ground seeds of two main varieties, white and brown (a third variety, black, has been replaced by brown in recent times, though it is still used as a spice in Far and Middle Eastern cuisine). Mustard spreads get their infinite vari-ety and texture in three different ways: how finely or coarsely the seeds are ground, what kind of seeds are used, and what additional seasonings and flavorings are added. Less pungent white mustard seeds are most often found in American-style yellow mustards, which tend to be simple in flavor and texture. The more pungent brown mustard seeds are traditional in English, European, and Chinese mustards. The French have made Dijon mus-tard famous; and German mustards range from mild and sweet to hot and tangy. Chinese mustards are the strongest of all.

BERGHOFF BEER-BRAISED BRISKET

Makes 8 sandwiches | *The best of both worlds—barbecue and beer—are combined in a beer-braised brisket that creates its own unique barbecue sauce. It's slow-cooked but perfectly simple to prepare, and it may make you as famous as it has made us.*

1 (3¹/₂–4-pound) boneless beef brisket, trimmed of excess fat

1 teaspoon kosher salt

1 teaspoon cracked black pepper

¹/₄ cup olive oil

2 pounds onions, sliced

1 bay leaf

1 (12-ounce) bottle Berghoff Lager beer

2 cups beef broth

1 cup prepared barbecue sauce

8 kaiser rolls or onion rolls, halved

Season the meat with salt and pepper. Heat the oil in a 6- to 8-quart wide, heavy pot over moderately high heat until hot but not smoking. Brown the meat well on all sides, about 10 minutes total. Remove from the pan and set aside, reserving the fat in the pot (do not clean the pot).

Sauté the onions with the bay leaf in the fat remaining in the pot over moderate heat until golden. Remove from the heat and transfer half of the onions to a bowl. Arrange the brisket over the onions remaining in the pot, then top with the remaining onions. Add the beer and broth,

(the liquid should come about halfway up the sides of the meat). Cover the pot and braise for 1¹/₂ to 2 hours, pour the barbecue sauce over the brisket, and continue to braise for 1 more hour. Remove the meat from the pan and let it rest for about 30 minutes. In a saucepan, reduce the braising liquid to a saucelike consistency.

Transfer the brisket to a clean cutting board. Slice the meat across the grain and distribute among the bottom halves of the buns, topping with the upper halves. Top with additional barbecue sauce, if desired.

BLACK FOREST HAM and BRIE PANINI

Makes 8 sandwiches | *In 2003, the downstairs Berghoff Annex was reborn as the Berghoff Café, and chef Matt Reichel created a whole new menu that kept the best of the old but added some new. This was one of his new sandwiches, which became and remained one of the most popular with guests. We serve it at home every chance we get. Available here in European delicatessens, Black Forest ham is sold very thinly sliced. Mild, creamy Brie complements the lean, smoked ham, and the kick of wasabi mayonnaise raises the flavor profile. Wasabi (Japanese green horseradish) is available in gourmet and health-food shops and Asian markets, in paste and powdered forms—both very pungent! Milder flavored versions, such as apricot wasabi and wasabi-flavored dressings, are also available.*

SPREAD

> **1 cup apricot wasabi**
>
> **¹/₄ cup mayonnaise**
>
> **2 tablespoons ketchup**

SANDWICH

> **16 slices sourdough bread**
>
> **³/₄ pound Brie cheese, sliced thinly**
>
> **2 pounds Black Forest ham, sliced thinly**
>
> **2–3 plum tomatoes, sliced thinly**
>
> **8 ounces baby lettuce**

Make the spread: Blend the apricot wasabi, mayonnaise, and ketchup together in a medium-size bowl. Cover and refrigerate until ready to use. The spread may be made up to 4 days in advance.

Make the sandwiches: Lay out eight slices of bread. Place a layer of Brie on each, then spread with 3 tablespoons of wasabi spread. Layer with the sliced tomatoes and lettuce. Top with the ham and another slice of bread. The sandwiches can be assembled up to 3 hours before grilling.

Grill in a panini machine, following the manufacturer's instructions. (Alternative method: Cook on a griddle or in a skillet with butter, as you would a grilled cheese sandwich, until crisp and brown, about 5 minutes per side.) Serve with Berghoff Chips (page 175) and a pickle.

BERGHOFF ROASTED
TURKEY BREAST SANDWICH

Serves 8 | *For decades, Berghoff's served turkey dinner as a regular menu item, not just on Thanksgiving. It was on the 1932 menu (Roast Young Turkey and Dressing, Cranberry Sauce, Celery, Mixed Olives, 80 cents) and on the 1975 menu (Roast Young Tom Turkey with Dressing, Cranberry Sauce, String Beans Julienne, Mashed Potatoes, $3.00). Years later, we still love turkey. The advent of fresh turkey breast gave us reason to celebrate with a sandwich. Never underestimate the tender juiciness of a fresh turkey breast; if you can't get your supermarket butcher to order it for you, go to a local butcher. When your turkey is tender and juicy, less spread and fewer condiments will be ample. But if you want to dress it up, serve it on Berghoff Olive Bread (page 112), spread with Basil Aïoli (page 125), and garnished with fresh basil leaves.*

5–6 pounds fresh turkey breast, skin on

1 teaspoon paprika

½ teaspoon kosher salt

½ teaspoon black pepper

½ teaspoon marjoram

16 slices rye bread, multigrain bread, or other hearty bread

Fresh basil leaves (optional)

Preheat the oven to 325°F.

Place turkey, skin side up, in a roasting pan.

Mix together the paprika, salt, pepper, and marjoram, and rub the mixture over the turkey breast. Place in the oven and roast until the internal temperature reaches at least 165°F, approximately 1 hour and 40 minutes, depending on the weight of the breast. Remove from the oven and let rest for 15 to 20 minutes. Slice the turkey into ¹/₁₆- to ¹/₈-inch-thick slices and place on the bread, spread with your choice of condiments, and serve.

BLACKENED SWORDFISH SANDWICH

Serves 8 | *The Berghoff Restaurant bought its swordfish headless but otherwise whole, and cut it into steaks for our popular sandwich. Swordfish is often described as "meaty" because of its firm texture and mild but appealing flavor (that is, not "fishy"). For this sandwich, it is coated on one side with a pre-pared Cajun seasoning mix and sautéed, for a less extreme version of Cajun blackened-style fish. Serve open-faced or as a regular sandwich, with sweet roasted peppers, sliced tomatoes, crisp lettuce, Monterey Jack cheese, and a Cajun spread.*

CAJUN SAUCE

- 1 cup mayonnaise
- 1/4 teaspoon Cajun seasoning
- 2 1/2 teaspoons chile sauce
- Pinch of crushed red pepper
- 1 tablespoon ketchup
- 1/4 teaspoon Worcestershire sauce
- 1/4 teaspoon Tabasco sauce
- 1/4 teaspoon chopped fresh parsley
- 1 teaspoon fresh lemon juice
- 1 tablespoon prepared horseradish, drained
- 1 teaspoon finely diced onion
- 1/2 tablespoon chopped cilantro
- 1 teaspoon finely diced celery
- Salt and pepper
- 2 teaspoons finely diced pickle

SWORDFISH

- 8 (5-ounce) center-cut swordfish fillets, rinsed and patted dry
- 1/2 cup Cajun seasoning mix
- 3 tablespoons canola oil

TO ASSEMBLE

- 16 slices Berghoff Beer Bread or other whole-grain bread (page 114)
- 3 Roma tomatoes, sliced
- 1 head romaine lettuce, or one 10-ounce bag baby lettuce
- 3 roasted red peppers, sliced (see Note)
- 16 slices Monterey Jack cheese

Make the sauce: Combine all the sauce ingredients in a medium-size bowl and mix well. This sauce can be made ahead and refrigerated, covered, until ready to use.

Make the swordfish: Dredge one side of the swordfish in the Cajun spice mix. Heat the oil in a medium-size skillet. Place the fish in the skillet, spice side down, and sauté for about 2 minutes. Turn over and cook the other side for 2 to 3 minutes. Depending on its thickness, the fish should be cooked in 5 minutes. Be careful not to overcook.

To assemble: While the fish is cooking, toast the bread and on eight of the slices layer the tomato, lettuce, pepper, and cheese. Spread the other slices with Cajun Sauce and top with the fish. Serve open-faced. Alternatively, place the fish atop the cheese, and top the second slice of bread, spread with Cajun Sauce, to create eight regular sandwiches.

Note: To roast red peppers, lightly coat whole peppers with canola oil and place them in a 400°F oven until their skins turn brown, about 20 to 30 minutes. Place them in a bowl, and cover it with plastic. After 20 minutes, remove the plastic, peel the skin, and remove the seeds and stems.

BERGHOFF HOME RYE

Makes 1 loaf | *The traditional Berghoff Rye Bread served at the restaurant was made on the premises by a professional baker and baked in steam-injected ovens. The bread started with a rye sourdough starter and rose twice. The result was a whopping three-pound loaf. We have adapted this recipe for the home cook. Yogurt provides the familiar tangy taste without the need for a sourdough starter. The recipe can be mixed by hand or made in a heavy-duty stand mixer. It's important to use rapid-rise active dry yeast (or bread machine yeast), rather than plain active dry yeast. Rapid-rise is a strain of yeast that is superactive and can be mixed in with the dry ingredients.*

2 cups all-purpose unbleached flour, plus extra for kneading

1 cup stone-ground rye flour, plus extra as needed

1 (¼-ounce) envelope rapid-rise active dry yeast or bread machine yeast

1 tablespoon sugar

1 tablespoon caraway seeds

1½ teaspoon salt

1½ cup whole-milk or low-fat plain yogurt (do not use fat-free), at room temperature

Oil, as needed, for bowl and bread pan

In the bowl of a standing mixer fitted with the paddle attachment, place the unbleached flour and 1 cup of the rye flour, and the yeast, sugar, caraway seeds, and salt. Mix on low speed.

Add the yogurt, and mix with the paddle until combined. Turn off the mixer. Scrape down the paddle with a rubber spatula, and remove. Replace with the dough hook. Using the dough

hook on low speed, knead for 10 minutes, adding additional rye flour by the tablespoon (anywhere from 2 to 8 tablespoons), until the dough is well formed and leaves the sides of the bowl.

Alternatively: Mix by hand in a 6-quart bowl, using a whisk to combine the dry ingredients and then a large, sturdy spoon to stir the dough. You may knead the dough by hand directly in the bowl, adding rye flour, until it becomes cohesive and leaves the side of the bowl.

Turn out the dough onto a surface lightly dusted with all-purpose flour, and knead to shape into a ball. Lightly oil a large bowl. Put in the dough, turning once so the oiled side is on top. Cover with plastic wrap and let rise in a warm (85°F) place until doubled, 1 hour 15 minutes to 1 hour and 30 minutes.

Turn out the dough onto a surface lightly dusted with all-purpose flour. Punch down, knead briefly, and shape into a rough rectangle. With a rolling pin, press the dough into a more even rectangle, about 12 by 8 inches.

Then, using your hands, roll up the dough into a tight cylinder, 8 inches long. Taper the ends. Set on a lightly oiled flat baking pan. Or, you may place the shaped dough in an oiled $8^1/2$-inch long by 5-inch wide by 3-inch deep metal or glass loaf pan.

Cover with a lint-free, clean kitchen towel that has been wetted and wrung almost dry. Let rise in a warm place until doubled, about 1 hour.

Preheat the oven to 400°F. With a sharp, serrated knife, horizontally slash across the top of the loaf in three places, and place in the oven. Bake for 35 minutes, until browned on top. Transfer from the pan to a metal rack. Let cool completely before slicing.

OLIVE BREAD

Makes 1 large round loaf or rectangular loaf | *Before Jan and Herman opened the Berghoff Café in 2003, they went to New York on a sandwich safari. Armed with a map of all New York's great sandwich shops, they went from place to place tasting breads. Then they came back and, with the help of a professional baker, developed this recipe, inspired by one of the olive breads they tasted. Happily, this bread is one of the easiest to make at home because it contains rapid-rise active dry yeast and pitted kalamata olives. A word of warning: Although the olives are prepitted, every batch may contain a pit or two. So do a quick simple check by squeezing each olive between your thumb and forefinger before stirring into the dough. Better safe than sorry.*

3 1/3 cups unbleached all-purpose flour, plus extra for kneading

2/3 cup whole wheat flour

1 (1/4-ounce) envelope rapid-rise active dry yeast or bread machine yeast

1/4 teaspoon salt

1 teaspoon dried thyme

1 1/2 cups water

1 (8-ounce) jar (or 5 ounces dry weight) pitted kalamata olives, drained and chopped coarsely

Oil, as needed, for bowl and bread pan

In the bowl of a standing mixer fitted with the paddle attachment, place the all-purpose flour, whole wheat flour, yeast, salt, and thyme. Mix on low speed.

Add the water and olives, and mix, using the paddle. Gradually add the remaining 1 cup of all-purpose flour, as needed, to form a cohesive dough. When the dough leaves the sides of the bowl, turn off the mixer. Using a rubber spatula, scrape down the paddle attachment and replace with the dough hook. With the dough hook, knead for 10 minutes, stirring in additional all-purpose flour, as needed, to achieve the desired consistency of dough. The dough should leave the sides of the bowl and cling to the dough hook.

Alternatively: Mix by hand in a 6-quart bowl, using a whisk to combine the dry ingredients and then a large, sturdy spoon to stir the dough. You may knead the dough by hand directly in the bowl, adding all-purpose flour, until it becomes cohesive and leaves the side of the bowl.

Turn out the dough onto a surface lightly dusted with all-purpose flour, and knead to shape into a ball. Lightly oil a large bowl. Put in the dough, turning once so the oiled side is on top. Cover with plastic wrap and let rise in a warm (85°F) place until doubled, 1 hour 15 minutes to 1 hour and 30 minutes.

Turn out the dough onto a very lightly floured surface. Punch down, knead briefly, and shape into a rough circle. With a rolling pin, press the dough into a more even circle. Then, using your hands, mold the dough into a tight ball, about 8 inches in diameter, tucking under the sides. Set on a lightly oiled flat baking pan, or place the shaped dough in an oiled 9-inch long by 5-inch wide by 3-inch deep metal or glass loaf pan.

Cover with a lint-free, clean kitchen towel that has been wetted and wrung almost dry. Let rise in a warm place until doubled, about 1 hour.

Preheat the oven to 400°F. With a sharp, serrated knife, horizontally slash the top of the loaf in three places. Place in the oven and bake for 35 minutes, until the bread is browned on top. Transfer from the pan to a metal rack. Let cool completely before slicing.

Thick or Thin

Spreads can either enhance or diminish a sandwich, depending on three factors: the quality and freshness of the spread, its compatibility with the bread and fillings, and how thickly or thinly it is spread. Too thick a spread can overwhelm the flavors of the filling.

In general, less is more. If the bread is fresh, and the filling is flavorful and moist, you can be happy with lettuce or tomatoes—and no spread at all. At the Berghoff Restaurant, our sandwiches were served "clean," and the table was always set with little vats of mustard, mayonnaise, and horseradish to add as desired.

A word of warning: Horseradish is a pungent condiment, some brands more so than others. Don't serve it straight to unsuspecting guests who may not be familiar with its effect on the nose and throat.

Rather than try to dictate our preferences, at family gatherings we usually present spreads in their own separate bowls so guests can satisfy their own tastes. Nothing replaces freshly made aïolis and tapenades. But don't overlook the simple trick of enlivening purchased mayonnaise with a dab of horseradish, a puréed garlic clove, or a teaspoon of finely chopped fresh basil, dill, thyme, or chives.

Some flavor-pairing tips: Pick complementary flavors; for example, pesto turkey breast with olive bread and either basil aïoli or ripe olive tapenade. Or combine contrasting flavors, for example, tuna salad with rye bread and lemon aïoli.

BERGHOFF BEER BREAD

Makes 1 large loaf | *Third-generation Herman cut his baby teeth on Berghoff's rye bread. So by the time he owned the restaurant, he was ready for something different. When visiting the brewery one day he noticed the "spent grain," which is the by-product of the brewing process. He got a bright idea and hired a professional baker to create Berghoff Brewer's Bread. The bread that was served at the Berghoff Restaurant is impossible to duplicate at home—unless you own or have access to a brewery and can get the spent grain. It is a unique loaf indeed. The beer bread we have created using Berghoff beer is excellent and easy to make at home. Use Berghoff Pilsner or Original Lager for a milder flavor; use Berghoff Red Ale or Genuine Dark for a hearty bread.*

3 cups unbleached all-purpose flour, plus extra for kneading

1¹/₂ cups whole wheat flour

1 (¹/₄-ounce) package rapid-rising active dry yeast or bread machine yeast

2 teaspoons salt

¹/₄ cup packed brown sugar

1 (12-ounce) bottle Berghoff beer of choice

2 tablespoons canola oil, plus extra for bowl and pan

In the bowl of a standing mixer fitted with the paddle attachment, place the unbleached flour, whole wheat flour, yeast, salt, and brown sugar. Mix on low speed.

Add the beer and oil, and mix on low to form a cohesive dough. Turn off the mixer, scrape down the paddle, and replace with the dough hook. Knead the dough on low for 10 minutes, adding all-purpose flour as necessary by the tablespoon for desired consistency. The dough should leave the sides of the bowl and cling to the dough hook.

Alternatively: Mix by hand in a 6-quart bowl, using a whisk to combine the dry ingredients and then a large, sturdy spoon to stir the dough. You may knead the dough by hand directly in the bowl, adding all-purpose flour, until it becomes cohesive and leaves the side of the bowl.

Turn out the dough onto a surface lightly dusted with all-purpose flour, and knead to shape into a ball. Lightly oil a large bowl. Put in the dough, turning once so the oiled side is on top. Cover with plastic wrap and let rise in a warm (85°F) place until doubled, 1 hour 15 minutes to 1 hour and 30 minutes.

Turn out dough on a surface lightly dusted with all-purpose flour, and knead to remove any air pockets. Shape into an oblong loaf and place in an oiled 9-inch long by 5-inch wide by 3-inch

Loaves of Berghoff Brewer's Bread that have fully risen and are ready for the oven.

deep loaf pan. Cover with a lint-free, clean kitchen towel that has been wetted and wrung almost dry. Let rise in a warm place until doubled, about 1 hour.

Preheat the oven to 350°F.

Bake for 40 minutes, until the top is browned. Transfer from the pan to a wire rack. Do not slice until completely cool.

CAPRESE SANDWICH

Makes 8 sandwiches | *Tomatoes are not one of Carlyn's favorite fruits, but she loves them in Italy's famous Caprese salad. Here she transforms the alternating layers of ripe tomatoes, fresh mozzarella, and fresh basil into a juicy sandwich. The traditional drizzle of olive oil becomes a flavorful balsamic vinaigrette that is lightly brushed onto the bread, to round out the flavors.*

2 tablespoons extra-virgin olive oil

1 tablespoon balsamic vinegar

16 slices sourdough or olive bread

2 pounds tomatoes, sliced (a variety of colored tomatoes is preferred)

1 pound fresh mozzarella cheese, sliced

24 large fresh basil leaves

Salt and freshly cracked black pepper

In a small mixing bowl, whisk together the olive oil and balsamic vinegar. Using a pastry brush, lightly brush one side of each slice of bread with the vinaigrette. Top eight of the bread slices, vinaigrette side up, with alternating slices of tomatoes, cheese, and basil leaves. Season with salt and pepper. Top each sandwich with the remaining slice of bread, vinaigrette side down. Slice in half and serve.

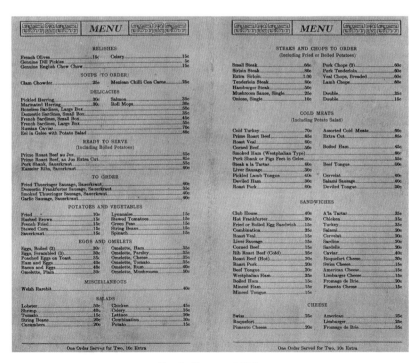

Berghoff menu, 1914.

BRIE and RASPBERRY GRILLED CHEESE SANDWICH

Serves 4 | *Can a grilled cheese sandwich be elegant? Carlyn's grilled Brie and raspberry preserves sandwich fits the description, especially when cut into triangles.*

8 slices whole-grain bread

2 tablespoons salted butter, softened

¹⁄₄ cup raspberry preserves

12 (¹⁄₄-inch-thick) slices Brie cheese

Lightly butter one side of each slice of bread. Lay one slice, butter side down, in a medium-size skillet. Evenly spread 1 tablespoon raspberry preserves over each slice of bread and top with three slices of Brie. Top the sandwich with a second slice of bread, butter side up. Cook over low heat until the bottom side is golden brown, then turn over the sandwich and repeat the process until both sides are golden and the cheese in the center is warm and melted, about 3 minutes per side. Continue until all the sandwiches are toasted. Cut in half or into triangles, and serve immediately.

The Berghoff family crest.

SMOKED TURKEY WRAP

Makes 8 wraps | *Carlyn began to make wraps as the solution to a problem—soggy sandwiches for picnics. Wraps, unlike sandwiches, hold up well without becoming limp. Green spinach tortillas, spiraled around tender smoked turkey, crunchy alfalfa sprouts, and well-seasoned cream cheese, can be sliced for hors d'oeuvres or halved for lunch or dinner.*

1 (8-ounce) package Boursin cheese, softened

1 tablespoon minced shallots or red onion

$\frac{1}{8}$ teaspoon white pepper

8 (12-inch) spinach tortillas

2 pounds smoked turkey breast, sliced thinly, deli style

2 ounces alfalfa sprouts

Using an electric mixer fitted with a paddle attachment mix the cheese, shallots, and pepper together until well combined. Set aside until needed.

Place a tortilla flat on a work surface. Spread evenly with the cheese mixture. (Be sure to spread the cheese all the way to the ends of the tortilla; the cheese will help seal the tortilla closed when it is rolled up.) Divide the turkey into eight equal portions and place one portion in a single layer on half of the tortilla. Place a layer of sprouts on top of the turkey. Roll up the tortilla tightly into a cylinder. Trim off and discard the loose ends. Repeat the process for the remaining wraps. The wraps can be made a few hours in advance and kept tightly wrapped in plastic in the refrigerator. They can be cut into smaller sizes, for cocktail hors d'oeuvres, or in half for lunch- or dinner-size portions. Serve with Sweet Potato Chips (page 38).

Left to right: Smoked Turkey Wrap, Grilled Vegetable Wrap, and Smoked Salmon Wrap with Capers and Dilled Cream Cheese.

GRILLED VEGETABLE WRAP

Makes 8 wraps | *Chopped grilled vegetables and kalamata olives stud feta cream cheese like jewels in this colorful tomato tortilla wrap sandwich. Wraps can be made several hours ahead, tightly wrapped in plastic, and refrigerated.*

1 (8-ounce) package cream cheese, softened

1 tablespoons minced shallots or red onion

1/8 teaspoon white pepper

2 ounces crumbled feta cheese

6 red bell peppers, seeded and quartered

12 small yellow squash, halved lengthwise

12 small eggplants, halved lengthwise

1/4 cup olive oil

Salt and freshly ground black pepper

8 (12-inch) tomato tortillas

1/2 cup chopped kalamata olives

Using an electric mixer fitted with a paddle attachment mix the cream cheese, shallots, white pepper, and feta cheese together until well combined. Set aside until needed.

Heat an outdoor or indoor grill. In a large bowl, toss the vegetables with the oil, and season with salt and pepper. Grill the vegetables in batches on a rack set 5 to 6 inches away from the heat, turning them until cooked, 10 to 15 minutes. Transfer the vegetables to a platter and cool

completely. When completely cool, chop into 1/2-inch chunks. The vegetables may be grilled one day ahead and chilled, covered. Bring the chilled vegetables to room temperature and drain any accumulated juices before making wraps.

Place a tortilla flat on a work surface. Spread evenly with the cheese mixture. (Be sure to spread cheese all the way to the ends of the tortilla, because the cheese will help seal the tortilla closed when it is rolled up.) Place 1/2 cup of grilled vegetables in a single layer on the lower half of the tortilla. Sprinkle with chopped olives. Roll up the tortilla tightly into a cylinder. Trim off and discard the the loose ends. Repeat the process for the remaining wraps. The wraps can be made a few hours in advance and kept tightly wrapped in plastic in the refrigerator. They can be cut into smaller sizes, for cocktail hors d'oeuvres, or in half for lunch- or dinner-size portions. Serve with Sweet Potato Chips (page 38).

SMOKED SALMON WRAP with CAPERS and DILLED CREAM CHEESE

Makes 8 wraps | *Smoked salmon comes in many varieties, and everyone has a favorite. As long as it is boneless and thinly sliced, it will work in this wrap.*

1 (8-ounce) package cream cheese, softened

2 tablespoons chopped fresh dill

1 tablespoon minced shallots or red onion

¹/₈ teaspoon white pepper

8 (12-inch) whole wheat tortillas

Arugula or baby spinach leaves (optional)

2 pounds smoked salmon or lox

1 tablespoon chopped, drained capers

Using an electric mixer fitted with a paddle attachment, mix the cheese, dill, shallots or red onion, and white pepper together in a bowl. Beat until well combined. Set aside until ready to use.

Place a tortilla flat on a work surface. Spread evenly with the cheese mixture. (Be sure to spread the cream cheese all the way to the ends of the tortilla, because the cheese will help seal the tortilla closed when rolled up.) Add a layer of arugula, if using. Place four ounces of smoked salmon in a single layer on the lower half of the tortilla. Sprinkle with chopped capers. Roll up the tortilla tightly into a cylinder. Trim off and discard the loose ends. Repeat the process for the remaining wraps. The wraps can be made a few hours in advance and kept tightly wrapped in plastic in the refrigerator. They can be cut into smaller sizes, for cocktail hors d'oeurvres, or in half for lunch- or dinner-size portions. Serve with Sweet Potato Chips (page 38).

TUNA SALAD

Makes 8 sandwiches | *Tuna salad sandwiches stay popular year after year. Many deli versions, however, are loaded with fat and sodium. This version is light on the mayo, uses water-packed rather than oil-packed tuna, and has no added salt. It's high on flavor thanks to the chopped herbs and vegetables. For optimal development of flavor, make the salad a few hours in advance, cover, and refrigerate. Stir just before serving. Spread on your choice of sandwich bread or roll.*

⅓ cup mayonnaise

1 tablespoon fresh lemon juice

1 tablespoon finely chopped capers

⅔ cup finely chopped celery

⅔ cup finely chopped red onion

3 tablespoons chopped fresh flat-leaf parsley

2 (7-ounce) cans water-packed chunk light tuna, drained and flaked

Salt and freshly ground pepper

Whisk together the mayonnaise, lemon juice, and capers in a medium-size bowl. Stir in the celery, onion, parsley, and tuna. Season with salt and pepper. The salad can be made up to 6 hours in advance and stored, covered, in the refrigerator until needed.

If you like a little zing, add 1 tablespoon of your favorite mustard. And for extra moistness, substitute two (7-ounce) packages of pouch-packed tuna for the canned tuna.

PESTO TURKEY SALAD

Makes 8 sandwiches | *Turkey has a heartier flavor than chicken and is complemented by the basil pesto in the mayonnaise dressing. To save preparation time, substitute prepared purchased pesto for homemade.*

BASIL PESTO

> **1 large clove garlic**
>
> **$1/4$ cup toasted pine nuts**
>
> **$1^1/2$ cups loosely packed fresh basil leaves**
>
> **$1/3$ cup extra-virgin olive oil**
>
> **$1/2$ teaspoon salt**
>
> **$1/4$ teaspoon white pepper**
>
> **$1/4$ cup Parmesan cheese (optional)**

TO ASSEMBLE

> **2 pounds turkey meat, cooked and diced**
>
> **1 cup mayonnaise**
>
> **$1/2$ cup diced celery**
>
> **$1/4$ cup scallions**
>
> **$1/2$ teaspoon salt, or to taste**
>
> **$1/4$ teaspoon white pepper, or to taste**

Make the pesto: In a food processor or blender, chop the garlic finely. Add the nuts and basil leaves, and process until fully chopped. With the motor running slowly, add the oil until it is incorporated and the pesto has a smooth consistency. Season with salt and white pepper. The pesto can be made up to one day in advance and stored in an airtight jar in the refrigerator, or it can be frozen for as long as one month. Makes about 1 cup. If you like cheese, add $1/4$ cup grated Parmesan to the recipe; however, this variation will not freeze well.

To assemble: In a mixing bowl, combine the turkey, mayonnaise, $1/4$ cup of the pesto, and the diced vegetables, and season with salt and pepper. The salad can be made up to 6 hours in advance and stored in the refrigerator until needed. Serve with any of the Berghoff breads—rye, olive, or beer bread.

BLACK OLIVE TAPENADE with WALNUTS

Makes 2 cups | *Tapenade originated in Provence, France, as a thick paste of ripe olives, anchovies, capers, seasonings, and olive oil—all locally abundant. It lends itself to variations, and this combination of black olives and toasted walnuts is a favorite with our family as well as our guests. Serve it as a spread or a relish.*

3 cloves garlic, peeled

1½ cups pitted kalamata olives

¼ cup chopped fresh parsley

¼ cup vegetable oil

1 tablespoon walnut oil (optional)

¼ cup toasted walnuts, chopped

In a food processor, mince the garlic. Add the olives and parsley, and pulse until the olives are chopped. Slowly add the oil and process until incorporated but not pureed. Add the walnut oil for heightened flavor, if desired. The mixture should be chunky. Fold in the chopped nuts. Allow the tapenade to stand for at least 1 hour before serving, so the flavors have time to blend.

Variation: For Green Olive Tapenade with Hazelnuts, substitute 1½ cups pimiento-stuffed green olives for the kalamata, 1 tablespoon hazelnut oil for the walnut oil, and ¼ cup toasted chopped hazelnuts for the walnuts.

BASIC AÏOLI

Makes 1 cup | *Provence, France, is the birthplace of aïoli, an assertive, garlicky mayonnaise. It's easy to make, stores well (up to one week, covered and refrigerated) and lends itself to endless variations mentioned below. Cut the garlic cloves in half lengthwise; if you see a greenish sprout, remove and discard it; otherwise it will give your aïoli a bitter flavor.*

2 cloves garlic

2 large egg yolks

1 tablespoon lemon juice

1 teaspoon Dijon mustard

$^1/_2$ cup extra-virgin olive oil

Salt and white pepper

Chop the garlic to a pastelike consistency, and place in a small mixing bowl. Add the egg yolks, lemon juice, and mustard. In a slow and steady stream, whisk in the oil to form an emulsion, whisking constantly. The consistency should be like mayonnaise. If the aïoli becomes too thick, add a few drops of warm water. Season with salt and white pepper. Refrigerate, covered, until ready to use.

Variations:

Basil Pesto Aïoli: Add $^1/_2$ cup of basil pesto to the basic aïoli recipe.

Red Pepper Aïoli: Add $^1/_2$ cup of prepared puréed roasted red peppers to the basic aïoli recipe.

Double Lemon Aïoli: Increase the amount of fresh lemon juice to 2 tablespoons, and add 1 teaspoon of grated lemon rind to the basic aïoli recipe.

Cranberry Aïoli: Combine $^1/_2$ cup of frozen cranberries with $^1/_2$ cup of orange juice and $^1/_4$ cup of light brown sugar in a small saucepan. Simmer over low heat until the juice is reduced by half. In a food processor or blender, blend the cranberry mixture until smooth, then add to the basic aïoli recipe.

MAIN DISHES

Our Crown Jewels

Berghoff Classics — Meat & Poultry

WIENER SCHNITZEL 130

CHICKEN SCHNITZEL 132

RAHM SCHNITZEL 134

OSSO BUCO 136

VEAL CORDON BLEU 137

VEAL and MUSHROOM RAGOUT 138

VEAL MARSALA 139

BISTRO-STYLE LAMB SHANK 140

CORNED BEEF and CABBAGE 142

SAUERBRATEN 143

POT ROAST 144

SCHLACHT PLATTE 145

PORK JÄGER SCHNITZEL 146

PORK TENDERLOIN 147

Carlyn's Favorites — Meat & Poultry

STUFFED BEEF TENDERLOIN with FONTINA and DRIED TOMATOES 148

CHICKEN VALENCIANO 150

Berghoff Classics — Seafood

WHITEFISH with BASIL RELISH and SAUTÉED SPINACH 152

HALIBUT LIVORNESE with SAUTÉED SPINACH 153

STIR-FRIED CATFISH with ASIAN-STYLE VEGETABLES 154

SESAME-CRUSTED AHI TUNA 156

SALMON with HERBED BREAD CRUMBS 157

BOUILLABAISSE 158

SALMON CAKES with ANCHO CHILE DRESSING 160

HONEY SALMON 162

Carlyn's Favorites — Seafood

CRAB CAKES 163

PAN-SEARED TILAPIA with TABASCO BROTH 164

THE RECIPES IN THIS CHAPTER ARE our family's crown jewels—the dishes that have made us famous for more than a century. And for the first time, you can re-create these Berghoff classics at home. Among them are the hearty, historical German favorites, along with many of the post-1986 classics after Jan took over menu development. Before Jan and Herman ran the restaurant, the menu was mostly German, but after they came on board, almost 70 percent of the menu consisted of more contemporary Continental and American dishes.

The traditional recipes are a challenge in two ways. Although their preparation is very, very simple, they are time consuming. Berghoff's wasn't dubbed the "Scratch House" by Peter Berghoff without reason. So, trust us, you don't want to divide the recipes to make fewer portions of any of these dishes—the effort that goes into them is not worth it. Even if you're cooking for two, don't you want leftovers or extra servings to reheat quickly for another meal? Make the entire recipe and enjoy it until it's gone!

The second challenge is presentation. The Wiener Schnitzel, Osso Buco, Sauerbraten, and even Corned Beef and Cabbage are basically brown. They taste a thousand times more interesting than they look. But the aromas wafting from the kitchen and the mouthwatering flavors that delight your palate prove the adage that beauty is more than skin deep. Besides,

Mahogany clock in the Berghoff bar with 1914-era murals.

people really want something simple such as mashed potatoes and creamed spinach with sauerbraten, and straightforward sides such as green salad, grilled asparagus, steamed green beans, green peas, and glazed carrots with the substantial meat and fish dishes that follow. You'll be amazed to see what a bright yellow lemon wedge can do to a plate of perfectly cooked Wiener schnitzel, or how a sprinkling of parsley will adorn a plate of corned beef and cabbage.

Some of the recipes that follow are more contemporary, such as Sesame-Crusted Ahi Tuna, Whitefish with Basil Relish, and Salmon Cakes with Ancho Chile Dressing. Given a hundred years of cooking, Berghoff's not only re-created the old but created some new classics.

WIENER SCHNITZEL

Serves 4 | *For as long as anyone in our family can remember, Wiener Schnitzel has been our number one best-selling entrée. In 2005, the Berghoff Restaurant cooked and served 41,872 plates of Wiener Schnitzel. Chilling the breaded cutlets before frying is the secret to their perfectly crisp exterior and tender juicy interior. Third-generation Herman says the best way to eat this dish is to squeeze lemon over all, then accompany every bite of cutlet with a thin slice of pickle.*

1 cup all-purpose flour, seasoned with salt and white pepper

2 large eggs, lightly beaten

2 tablespoons milk

1 cup cracker meal or fine bread crumbs

4 (5-ounce) veal cutlets, pounded thin and chilled

Vegetable oil, as needed, for pan-frying

Lemon wedges, for garnish

Kosher dill pickle wedges, for garnish

In a small bowl, place the seasoned flour. In a shallow container, whisk the eggs and milk together. In a medium-size bowl, place the cracker meal. Entirely coat each cutlet with the flour, then the egg mixture, and finally the cracker meal. Pat the cutlets with the meal to ensure they are completely coated. Place one layer of cutlets on a baking sheet, cover, and refrigerate at least 30 minutes before cooking.

Pour the oil to a $^1/4$-inch depth into a large skillet. Heat over medium-high heat. Gently add a few cutlets at a time, and cook until golden brown on both sides, 2 to 3 minutes per side. Transfer to a baking sheet lined with absorbent paper. Keep warm until ready to serve.

Heat eight plates. Place each cutlet on a heated plate with a lemon wedge and a pickle wedge. Accompany with German Fries (page 174), Mashed Potatoes (page 178), or German Potato Salad served warm (page 81). A simple tossed salad completes the meal.

Wiener Schnitzel with dill pickle, German Fries, lemon wedge, and a side of Red Cabbage.

CHICKEN SCHNITZEL

Serves 8 | *Over the decades, variations on the crispy fried schnitzel, both in Germany and America, proliferated—witness Chicken Schnitzel, which made its way onto our menu around 1990. It's a less-expensive schnitzel than veal, and the red sauce complements the chicken both in color and flavor.*

CHICKEN

8 (6-ounce) portions chicken breast, butterflied

1 cup all-purpose flour

2 teaspoons salt

1 teaspoon ground black pepper

1/2 teaspoon dried basil

1/2 teaspoon dried oregano

3 large eggs

3 tablespoons water

1 teaspoon Tabasco sauce

3 1/2 cups cracker meal or dry bread crumbs

SAUCE

2 tablespoons canola oil

1/2 cup white onions, diced finely

1 tablespoon chopped garlic

1 (28-ounce can) crushed tomatoes

1 (10.75-ounce can) tomato purée

1 1/2 cups chicken stock

1 tablespoon chopped fresh basil

2 teaspoons chopped fresh oregano

1 tablespoon sugar

1/4 teaspoon red pepper flakes

Salt and ground black pepper

Oil for pan-frying, as needed

Place plastic wrap on top of each butterflied chicken breast and, with a meat mallet or the back of a small skillet, pound until 1/8 inch thick. In a small bowl, combine the flour, salt, pepper, and dried herbs. In a shallow container, whisk the eggs, water, and Tabasco sauce together. In a medium-size bowl, place the cracker meal. Entirely coat each cutlet with the flour, then the egg mixture, and finally the cracker meal. Lay flat, in one layer, on a baking sheet. Cover and refrigerate until ready to prepare. (This procedure may be done 4 to 6 hours before ready to cook.)

Make the sauce: In a 2-quart saucepan, heat the canola oil until hot; add the onions and sauté for 1 to 2 minutes. Add the garlic and continue to sauté for 1 minute. Add the tomato products, chicken stock, 2 teaspoons of the basil, 1 teaspoon of the oregano, the sugar, and the pepper flakes, and bring to a boil. Decrease the heat to a simmer, and cook for 50 to 60 minutes, stirring occasionally. Adjust the seasonings, and stir in the remaining teaspoon each of both basil and oregano. Remove from the heat. Keep warm.

Waiter with orders of schnitzel and Corned Beef and Cabbage.

Make the chicken: Pour the canola oil to a 1-inch depth in a 12-inch skillet, and heat until medium hot. Gently add a few cutlets at a time to the pan and cook until golden brown on both sides, 2 to 3 minutes per side. Transfer to a baking sheet lined with absorbent paper. Repeat the process with remaining chicken cutlets. Place in a warm oven until ready to serve.

Serve one crispy brown chicken cutlet on a plate and ladle with $1/2$ cup of warm sauce. Steamed broccoli and warm German Potato Salad (page 81) go well with this dish.

RAHM SCHNITZEL

Serves 8 | *Rahm Schnitzel fulfills the definition of schnitzel, literally "little slice," with thinly sliced pork medallions, fried crisply. But as we prepare it, traditional Rahm Schnitzel is served with a sour cream sauce that our customers love. For the sauce, the restaurant uses ham stock, made by first simmering ham bones and trimmings in water with chopped onions and parsley and then straining it. But you may substitute chicken broth (page 66).*

PORK

> 16 (3-ounce) pork medallions, cut from center of pork loin
>
> 1 cup all-purpose flour
>
> 2 teaspoons salt
>
> 1 teaspoon ground black pepper
>
> 3 large eggs
>
> 3 tablespoons water
>
> 1 teaspoon Tabasco sauce
>
> 3 1/2 cups cracker meal or dry bread crumbs
>
> Oil for pan-frying, as needed

SAUCE

> 1 tablespoon canola oil
>
> 1/3 cup white onions, diced finely
>
> 2 cups sliced white button mushrooms
>
> 1 cup white wine
>
> 3 cups chicken broth (page 66), or ham stock (see Note)
>
> 1 cup tomato purée
>
> 1 small bay leaf
>
> 3 tablespoons cornstarch

> 3 tablespoons water
>
> 3/4 cup sour cream
>
> Salt and ground black pepper

Place plastic wrap over each pork medallion and, with a meat mallet or the back of a small skillet, pound until 1/8 inch thick. In a small bowl, combine the flour, salt, and pepper. In a small bowl, place the seasoned flour. In a shallow container, whisk the eggs and milk together. In a medium-size bowl, place the cracker meal. Entirely coat each medallion with the flour, then the egg mixture, and finally the cracker meal. Lay flat, in one layer, on a baking sheet. Cover and refrigerate until ready to cook. (This procedure may be done 4 to 6 hours before ready to cook.)

Make the sauce: In a 2-quart saucepan, heat the canola oil until hot; add the onions and sauté for 1 to 2 minutes. Add the mushrooms and continue to sauté for 3 to 4 minutes. Add the white wine and bring to a boil. Stir in the stock, tomato purée, and bay leaf, bring to a simmer, and cook for 30 to 45 minutes, stirring occasionally. Create a slurry of the cornstarch and water (page 33), whisk into the sauce, and bring to a boil, whisking constantly. Whisk in the sour

Meat delivery to Berghoff's in the early 1930s, before refrigerated trucks were standard.

cream, adjust the seasonings, and remove from the heat. Keep warm.

Make the pork: Pour the canola oil to a 1-inch depth in a 12-inch skillet. Heat until medium hot. Gently add two medallions at a time to the pan and cook until golden brown on both sides, 2 to 3 minutes per side. Remove from the heat and place on a baking sheet lined with absorbent paper. Repeat the process with the remaining pork medallions. Place in a warm oven until ready to serve.

Shingle two crispy brown pork medallions on each plate and ladle with $1/2$ cup of warm sauce. This dish goes well with Sautéed Spinach (page 152), and Mashed Potatoes (page 178).

Note: To make ham stock, in a large saucepan place 2 pounds total of ham bones, trimmings, and skin; one large onion, chopped; two celery stalks, chopped; six parsley sprigs. Add 2 quarts of cold water. Over medium-high heat, bring to a boil. Decrease the heat and simmer, skimming off surface foam, until the stock is reduced by half, about $1^1/2$ hours. Strain through a fine-mesh sieve, and cool to room temperature. Refrigerate, covered, overnight. Skim off the congealed surface fat and discard. Makes about 1 quart.

OSSO BUCO

Serves 8 | *In the late 1990s, when Italian cuisine was so fashionable and the dining public was in love with osso buco, we put it on our menu and it was received with great success. But veal shanks had been a menu standard since 1914. Osso Buco was just a smaller cut—for which we charged a higher price.*

8 pieces veal shank, each approximately 2 inches thick

1/2 cup all-purpose flour, seasoned with salt and pepper

3–6 tablespoons canola oil

2 cups diced celery

2 cups diced onion

2 tablespoons minced garlic

1 1/2 cups dry white wine

4 cups veal broth or chicken broth (page 66)

1 cup tomato purée

1 teaspoon dried marjoram

1/4 teaspoon red pepper flakes

Kosher salt and pepper

1/4 cup chopped fresh parsley

Tie the veal shanks with kitchen twine to hold the meat on its bones. Dredge well in seasoned flour.

In a large, heavy-bottomed pot, heat 3 tablespoons of the oil over high heat; brown the veal shanks for 2 to 3 minutes on each side, until golden brown. Remove the shanks from the pan and degrease the pan.

Place in the pan the remaining 3 tablespoons of oil, and sauté the celery, onion, and garlic for 3 to 4 minutes. Add the white wine to deglaze the pan. Add all the other ingredients except the parsley, and bring to a boil. Return the veal shanks to the pot, cover, and simmer slowly over low heat for 2 hours, or until the meat is tender and offers almost no resistance when pierced with a fork. Remove the meat from the pan and adjust the seasonings in the sauce. Stir the fresh parsley into the sauce.

To serve: Cut and remove the twine from the shanks, and place one shank on each dish or soup plate. Ladle 1/2 cup of sauce over the top of each shank. Serve with crusty bread and salad.

Shank of the Evening

Berghoff's was a pioneer in cooking shanks—an old-fashioned dish that became very newfangled in the 1990s. The popular Osso Buco is just a cut above the long-bone veal shank that was on Berghoff's menu since 1914, served with sauerkraut and boiled potatoes for 55 cents. In 1932, both veal and pork shanks had dropped to 50 cents. By 1990, lamb shanks had joined the lineup at $15.25 for dinner.

VEAL CORDON BLEU

Serves 8 | *In the 1980s, before Berghoff's became their full-time job, Herman and Jan owned Tosi's, an Italian fine-dining restaurant in nearby Stevensville, Michigan. When they moved to Chicago, they brought Veal Cordon Bleu to Berghoff's from Tosi's—but the dish lost its white Italian truffles en route.*

8 (4-ounce) veal cutlets

8 (1-ounce) slices smoked, deli-style ham

³/₄ pound grated Gruyère cheese (3 cups)

1¹/₂ cups all-purpose flour

3 large eggs

1 teaspoon salt

1 teaspoon ground black pepper

4 cups fresh white bread crumbs

1 cup vegetable oil, for pan-frying

Arrange the cutlets on a dry, clean surface. Place one slice of ham and ¹/₃ cup of grated Gruyère on top of each cutlet. Fold the cutlets over and place on a clean baking sheet in a single layer. Refrigerate for at least 1 hour.

In a small bowl, place the flour. In a shallow container, whisk the eggs, salt, and pepper together. In a medium-size bowl, place the bread crumbs. Entirely coat each cutlet with the flour, then the egg mixture, and finally the bread crumbs.

In a heavy skillet, heat the oil over medium-high heat. Pan-fry the cutlets in batches until golden brown on both sides and completely cooked through, 2 to 3 minutes per side. Transfer to a baking sheet lined with absorbent paper. Keep warm until ready to serve.

Serve with German Fries (page 174) and a pickle.

VEAL and MUSHROOM RAGOUT

Serves 8 | *This rich, creamy stew has been popular since the 1950s—more than half a century and two or three generations of customers. Its original German name on the menu was Geschnetzeltes, meaning "meat cut into strips." Sometime in the '80s, we changed the name to this more appetizing description for the menu.*

3 tablespoons vegetable oil

3 pounds veal stew meat

Salt and cracked black pepper

2 cups sliced sweet onions

1 teaspoon chopped garlic

1/2 cup tomato paste

2 bay leaves

4 cups veal broth or chicken broth (page 66)

1 cup white wine

4–6 cups sliced white button mushrooms (1¼ pounds)

1/2 cup roux (page 59)

1/2 cups sour cream

8 cups cooked wide noodles

Minced parsley, for garnish

In a heavy 2-gallon pot, heat the oil until hot. Season the veal with salt and pepper, and cook in batches, stirring gently, for 2 minutes. Return all the cooked meat to the pot, add the onion and garlic, and cook for 5 minutes. Stir in the tomato paste and bay leaves, and continue to cook for 5 minutes. Pour in the broth and wine, decrease the heat, and simmer for 1 to 1½ hours, until the meat is tender, stirring occasionally. Remove the bay leaves.

When the meat is tender, add the mushrooms and cook for another 10 minutes.

Gently whisk in the roux until thoroughly distributed, and bring to a boil. Decrease the heat and simmer for 10 more minutes, stirring constantly, until slightly thickened.

Place the sour cream in a bowl. Remove 1 cup of the ragout cooking liquid and whisk into the sour cream until well blended. Pour the sour cream mixture into the ragout, stirring constantly until well blended. Simmer over very low heat for another 5 minutes. Adjust the seasonings.

Heat eight soup plates. Mound 1 cup of hot noodles on each heated plate. Top with 1½ cups of ragout, and garnish with minced parsley.

VEAL MARSALA

Serves 8 | *When we first announced that we were going to write a Berghoff cookbook, literally thousands of e-mails came in, most of them wanting to make sure we would have their favorite recipes in the book. Our recipe for Veal Marsala was among the top five requested main dishes, along with Wiener Schnitzel, Sauerbraten, Rahm Schnitzel, and Chicken Schnitzel.*

VEAL

> 24 (1¹/₂-ounce) veal medallions
>
> Salt and ground black pepper
>
> 1 cup all-purpose flour
>
> 4–6 tablespoons canola oil, plus more as needed

SAUCE

> 3 tablespoons finely diced shallots or white onions
>
> 3–4 cups sliced white button mushrooms
>
> 1 cup Marsala
>
> 3 cups veal stock
>
> 1 bay leaf
>
> 2 tablespoons cornstarch
>
> 3 tablespoons water

Make the veal: Cover the veal medallions with plastic wrap and, using a meat mallet or the back of a small skillet, pound to less than ¹/₈ inch thick. Season the veal with salt and pepper, if desired. Place the flour in a medium-size bowl. Dredge each medallion in the flour, coating thoroughly. Lay flat, in a single layer, on a baking sheet. Cover and refrigerate until ready to cook. (This process may be done 4 to 6 hours before ready to cook.)

Heat the oil in a 12-inch skillet. Add the coated medallions to the pan and cook until lightly browned on both sides. Make sure to not overcrowd the pan. When fully cooked (approximately 2 minutes per side), transfer the veal to a baking sheet lined with absorbent paper. Repeat the process with the remaining medallions, adding more oil as needed. Place the cooked veal in a warm oven until ready to serve.

Make the sauce: Discard most of the excess oil from skillet. Add the shallots and sauté for 1 minute. Stir in the mushrooms and sauté for 3 to 4 minutes. Add the wine and simmer for 3 to 4 minutes. Add the stock and bay leaf, and bring to a boil. Decrease the heat and simmer for 6 to 8 minutes. Create a slurry of the cornstarch and water (page 33), whisk into the sauce, and bring to a boil, whisking constantly. Keep warm until ready to serve.

Shingle three medallions on each dinner plate. Spoon ¹/₃ cup of sauce over each serving. Accompany with Mashed Potatoes (page 178) and a crisp-cooked green vegetable.

BISTRO-STYLE LAMB SHANK

Serves 8 | *Jan doesn't mince words. She calls this dish "huge, ungainly, and absolutely delicious." It's a recipe originally from her friend Adriana Streicher. Shanks in some form have been on the menu since 1914, and their gawky joints haven't made them any less popular.*

3 tablespoons olive oil

8 (10- to 12-ounce) lamb shanks

Salt and cracked black pepper

$^1\!/_2$ cup diced white onions

$^1\!/_2$ cup diced celery

$^1\!/_2$ cup diced carrots

1 tablespoon chopped garlic

1 cup white wine

4 cups beef broth

1$^1\!/_2$ cups tomato purée

2 bay leaves

1 sprig fresh rosemary, plus extra
 for garnish

$^3\!/_4$ cup dry sherry

3 tablespoons cornstarch slurry
 (page 33)

1 (14-ounce can) cannellini beans,
 rinsed and drained

Salt and ground black pepper

2 diced fresh plum tomatoes (2 cups)

$^1\!/_2$ cup minced parsley

3 chopped scallions ($^3\!/_4$ cup)

Preheat the oven to 350°F.

In a large, heavy roasting pot, heat the oil over high heat until smoking. Season the lamb shanks with salt and pepper. Brown on all sides in the hot oil; remove the lamb and set aside. Do not clean the pot.

In the same pot, place the onions, celery, carrots, and garlic, and sauté for 3 minutes. Add the wine to deglaze the pan, and then reduce wine by two-thirds. Add the broth, tomato puree, bay leaves, and rosemary sprig, and bring to a boil. Return the lamb to the pot and return to a boil. Cover and place in the oven to bake for 1$^1\!/_2$ to 2 hours, or until the meat is cooked through (165°F) and tender.

Remove the lamb from the pan and keep warm until ready to serve. Remove the rosemary sprig and bay leaves. Add the sherry to the sauce and thicken with the cornstarch slurry. Bring to a boil, whisking constantly. Decrease the heat and stir in the cannellini beans, cooking just long enough to heat them through. Adjust the seasonings. Stir in the diced plum tomatoes, parsley, and chopped scallions.

To serve: Place a lamb shank on each individual dinner or soup plate, and top with 1 cup of sauce.

CORNED BEEF and CABBAGE

Serves 8 | *Our perfect, but perfectly simple, corned beef was ordered by 5,459 customers in 2005—and not all of them Irish. Because no fat is added in cooking and the broth is its own sauce, this could be construed as a "light" dish.*

4 pounds corned beef

2 cloves garlic, smashed

1 tablespoon pickling spices, tied in cheesecloth

Cold water, as needed

1 head green cabbage, cored and cut into 8 wedges

16 small whole, unpeeled red potatoes

2 tablespoons cider vinegar

Salt and pepper

$^1/_4$ cup minced fresh parsley, for garnish

In a large, heavy pot, place the corned beef, along with any of its brine, plus the garlic and bag of pickling spices. Cover completely with cold water. (Make sure the pot is large enough that corned beef is covered, with 3 to 4 inches of space remaining below the rim.) Bring to a boil. Decrease the heat and simmer for $2^1/_2$ to 3 hours. The corned beef is done when an inserted fork comes out easily. Remove the meat from the broth and discard the spice bag. Set aside the broth in its pot. Set the meat aside and keep warm.

In same pot with the broth, add the cabbage wedges, potatoes, and vinegar. Simmer over low heat for 30 minutes, or until the cabbage and potatoes are tender. If needed, add salt and pepper.

Thinly slice the corned beef, cutting against the grain of the meat. Serve in soup plates with cabbage wedges and potatoes, and ladled with broth. Sprinkle with parsley and serve.

SAUERBRATEN

Serves 8 to 10 | *This is a German classic, and in 2005 Berghoff's sold 27,382 orders. Because it was on the menu year-round and because of the potent aroma, it was kept in its own walk-in refrigerator. When making this at home, place it in a large zippered bag to marinate, and then place that bag in a second bag.*

BEEF

5-6 pounds eye of the round of beef

MARINADE

1 quart cider vinegar

1 onion, chopped coarsely

2 carrots, chopped coarsely

3 stalks celery, chopped coarsely

$^1/_2$ cup pickling spices

3 bay leaves

SAUCE

2 cups red wine

1 to 1$^1/_2$ cups sugar

2 beef bouillon cubes

2 tablespoons Worcestershire sauce

1 tablespoon Kitchen Bouquet browing sauce

4 tablespoons ($^1/_2$ stick) unsalted butter

$^1/_4$ cup all-purpose flour

Make the marinade: Place the beef in a large zippered plastic bag and pour the marinade ingredients over the beef to cover completely.

Zip up the bag, enclose it in a second zippered plastic bag, and place in the refrigerator for at least 3 days, turning twice daily.

Preheat the oven to 350°F.

Place the meat with its marinade in a lidded braising pan or pot. Cover and braise in the oven for 3 hours, or until the meat is fork-tender. Add water to pan as the meat roasts, to keep it moist and prevent burning. Remove the meat from the pan, cover, and keep warm. Let rest for at least 15 to 20 minutes before slicing to serve.

Make the sauce: Season the remaining pan juices with the red wine, sugar, bouillon cubes, Worcestershire sauce, and Kitchen Bouquet. Simmer for 15 to 20 minutes. Meanwhile, heat the butter in a saucepan over low heat. Add the flour and cook until the resultant roux browns evenly, about 10 minutes. Slowly whisk the browned roux into the hot pan sauce, whisking until smooth. Bring to a boil, decrease the heat, and simmer for 15 to 20 minutes, until thickened and smooth. Strain and keep warm. Add water to thin, if needed.

Slice the meat and serve family style on a warm platter. Pour 1$^1/_2$ cups of hot sauce over top of the meat and serve the remainder on the side.

POT ROAST

Serves 8 | *Pot roast has been on the menu since the 1950s, when second-generation Lewis was running the restaurant and the menu greatly expanded. What makes this pot roast special is the rich brown roux gravy. The brown roux is optional, but we always include it.*

2 tablespoons vegetable oil

4¹/₂ pounds beef ball tip or eye of round

2 cups diced onion

1¹/₂ cups diced celery

1¹/₂ cups diced carrots

2 bay leaves

1 tablespoon minced garlic

1 teaspoon ground marjoram

¹/₂ teaspoon salt

¹/₄ teaspoon ground black pepper

¹/₈ teaspoon red pepper flakes

6 cups beef broth

1¹/₂ cups tomato purée

¹/₂ cup red wine

¹/₄ cup A.1. steak sauce

3-4 tablespoons brown roux (optional) (see Note)

Heat the oil in a large, heavy-bottomed pot. (The pot should be large enough that all the meat and stock should fit with 1 to 2 inches of space remaining below the rim.) Sear the meat on all sides. Add the onion, celery, carrots, and bay leaves, and sauté for 4 to 5 minutes.

Add the garlic and seasonings, and sauté for 3 to 4 minutes. Add the broth and tomato purée to the pot, and bring to a boil. Decrease the heat and simmer, covered, stirring occasionally, for approximately 2 hours, or until the meat offers little or no resistance when pierced with a fork.

Remove the meat from the sauce and set aside. Add the red wine and A.1. to the cooking liquid, and simmer for 5 to 7 minutes. If the sauce needs thickening, whisk in a brown roux (see Note) and cook several minutes, until the sauce has thickened to the desired consistency.

Slice the meat ¹/₄ inch thick and serve family style on a warm platter. Ladle the sauce on top. (The vegetables may be left in the sauce or strained out.) Accompany with steamed seasonal vegetables.

Note: To make brown roux, place 3 to 4 tablespoons each of flour and butter in a saucepan over medium heat. Cook for approximately 10 minutes, stirring constantly. Roux darkens as it cooks. Remove from the heat when the roux reaches medium-brown stage and has pleasant toasty smell. Be careful not to burn it.

SCHLACHT PLATTE

Serves 8 | *A real meat-lover's delight for which we became famous is the Schlacht Platte: a thick smoked pork chop, knockwurst, and bratwurst atop a bed of sauerkraut. A pot of Düsseldorf mustard and a basket of Berghoff Rye bread make the meal complete. In 2005, Berghoff's served 7,885 Schlacht Plattes.*

1 tablespoon olive oil

2 teaspoons chopped garlic

8 cups sauerkraut (page 181)

3 cups chicken broth (page 66)

¹/₂ teaspoon ground white pepper

5 bratwursts (3:1 size), cut ³/₄ inch thick

5 knockwursts (3:1 size), cut ³/₄ inch thick

8 smoked pork chops (kasseler rippchen)

1 tablespoon chopped fresh parsley, for garnish

Heat the oil in a large pot until hot. Add the garlic and sauté until golden brown. Add the sauerkraut, chicken broth, and pepper. Bring to a simmer and cook for 30 minutes. Add the bratwurst, knockwurst, and pork chops. Simmer for 30 more minutes.

Remove the meat and sausages, and keep warm. Slice the sausages. Using a slotted spoon, transfer the sauerkraut to a large, heated serving platter. Top the sauerkraut with the pork chops and sliced sausages. Garnish with chopped fresh parsley and serve family style.

PORK JÄGER SCHNITZEL

Serves 8 | *Jägermeister makes a unique and delicious sauce for this dish, which has been on the menu—usually during the fall-winter season—since 1960. This is Herman's favorite schnitzel, and in 2006, on the special fall-winter menu, we sold 1,835 every day.*

PORK

> 24 (3-ounce) pork scaloppine cutlets (4$^1/_2$ pounds)
>
> 1$^1/_2$ cups all-purpose flour, seasoned with salt and white pepper
>
> $^1/_4$ cup vegetable oil, as needed for sautéing

SAUCE

> 1 cup chopped applewood-smoked bacon (5 ounces)
>
> 3 tablespoons chopped shallots
>
> 1 cup sliced shiitake mushroom caps (3 ounces)
>
> 1 cup sliced white button mushrooms (3 ounces)
>
> 1 tablespoon all-purpose flour
>
> 3 tablespoons Jägermeister (see Note)
>
> 2 cups pork or beef broth
>
> Salt and ground black pepper
>
> $^1/_2$ cup minced chives and parsley

Make the pork: Dredge the cutlets in the seasoned flour. Heat 1 tablespoon of the oil in a skillet and sauté one cutlet for about 1 minute each side, and remove from pan. Drain on absorbent toweling. Place on baking sheet, in single layer, uncovered, and keep warm in very low oven until ready to serve. Repeat the process, adding oil as necessary, until all the cutlets are browned.

Make the sauce: Place the bacon into the skillet and sauté until almost browned. Drain off most of the fat from skillet. Stir the shallots into the bacon and cook for several minutes, stirring often, until they become translucent. Add the mushrooms and continue sautéing for 2 minutes. Sprinkle the flour over the bacon mixture and cook for 1 minute, stirring often. Stir in the Jägermeister to deglaze the pan. Add the broth, bring to a simmer, and cook for 15 minutes. Adjust the seasonings.

Heat eight dinner places. For each serving, place three hot, crisp cutlets on each plate. Ladle 3 tablespoons of sauce over each plate of cutlets, and garnish with 1 tablespoon of minced herbs. Accompany with Mashed Potatoes (page 178) and steamed peas.

Note: Jägermeister is a potent (70-proof) German liqueur intensely flavored with fifty-six bitter herbs, fruits, spices, barks, resins, and seeds. The liqueur is actually sweet, with a chocolatey aftertaste. It adds a very special flavor note in this recipe.

PORK TENDERLOIN

Serves 8 | *How many ways can you cook a pork tenderloin? Since 1914, Berghoff's must have tried them all as a way to bring variety to this popular cut of meat. This is our latest version. It goes very well with Creamed Spinach (page 170) and Potato Galette (page 184).*

MARINADE

 $^1/_4$ **cup vegetable oil**

 2 tablespoons fresh lemon juice

 2 tablespoons chopped garlic

 2 tablespoons chopped fresh rosemary

 1$^1/_2$ teaspoons salt

 1 teaspoon ground black pepper

PORK

 3 tablespoons vegetable oil

 8 (7-ounce) pork tenderloin pieces, silverskin removed

SAUCE

 2 tablespoons chopped garlic

 2 tablespoons diced white onions

 2$^1/_2$ cups pork, veal, or chicken broth

 2 tablespoons fresh lemon juice

 1 tablespoon chopped fresh rosemary

 2 teaspoons lemon zest

 1–2 teaspoons caramel color

 Salt and ground black pepper

 1 tablespoon cornstarch slurry (page 33)

Make the marinade: In a large bowl, whisk the oil, lemon juice, garlic, rosemary, salt, and pepper together. Place the pork into the marinade and toss to coat. Cover and marinate for 4 hours in the refrigerator, turning occasionally, until ready to cook.

Preheat the oven to 375°F. Grease a baking sheet.

Make the pork: In a large, heavy skillet, heat the oil over high heat. Place the tenderloins in the skillet and sear on all sides. Remove from the skillet and place on the prepared baking sheet. Bake in the oven for 10 to 15 minutes, or until cooked to the desired degree of doneness (approximately 160°F). Remove from the heat, cover, and let stand for 10 minutes before slicing to serve. Do not clean the skillet.

Make the sauce: Using the same skillet as was used for the pork, lightly sauté the garlic and onions for 2 minutes. Add the broth, lemon juice, rosemary, lemon zest, and caramel color, and simmer for 30 minutes. Season with salt and pepper, and thicken slightly with the cornstarch slurry to achieve desired consistency. Keep warm.

Slice the pork into $^1/_4$-inch-thick slices and fan out on a plate. Ladle the pork jus over the top. Serve with your favorite starch and vegetable.

STUFFED BEEF TENDERLOIN with FONTINA and DRIED TOMATOES

Serves 8 | *Carlyn likes beef tenderloin because, with it, you can make a dish like this one that looks as if you really fussed with it—but you didn't. The tenderloin can be stuffed ahead of time and baked at the last minute, sauced, and served.*

BEEF

1 (3-pound) beef tenderloin

¹/₄ cup olive oil

1¹/₂ teaspoons salt

1¹/₂ teaspoons ground black pepper

SAUCE

¹/₂ cup shallots

¹/₂ cup brandy

1 cup beef broth

1 cup heavy cream

2 tablespoons julienned sage leaves

Salt and ground black pepper

STUFFING

1 pound fontina cheese, diced (4 cups)

8 oil-cured dried tomatoes, diced

8 fresh sage leaves, slivered

Make the beef: Rub the beef with 2 tablespoons of the oil; season with salt and pepper. In a large skillet, heat the remaining 2 tablespoons of olive oil until hot. Sear the beef on all sides until browned. Remove from the skillet and cool completely.

Make the sauce: In the skillet where the beef was browned, add shallots and sauté for 2 minutes. Deglaze with brandy and add broth. Bring to a boil, decrease the heat, and simmer for 12 minutes, or until reduced by two-thirds. Whisk in the cream and boil for 5 minutes. Stir in the sage and adjust the seasonings. Keep warm until ready to serve.

Make the stuffing: In a separate bowl, combine the cheese, tomatoes, and sage, and toss to mix.

Preheat the oven to 375°F. Insert a long boning knife near the center of each end of the beef so that the knife cuts through to the middle from both ends. Cut carefully horizontally to form a 1-inch-wide pocket for the stuffing. Pack the stuffing into the pocket, working from end to end, and packing it full. Place the beef on a baking pan and bake for 1 hour for rare, 1 hour and 15 minutes for well done. Test for doneness by making a small cut in the middle with the boning knife. Remove from the oven and serve immediately.

Preheat eight dinner plates. Slice the stuffed beef crosswise into eight slices that have the stuffing up the center. Arrange one stuffed slice on each plate on a bed of Mashed Potatoes (page 178), with roasted asparagus and sautéed red bell pepper strips. Ladle 3 tablespoons of sauce over and around the beef just before serving.

CHICKEN VALENCIANO

Serves 6 | *Chicken Valenciano is the most popular entrée at Artistic Events–catered weddings. Now you can make this gorgeous orange and salsa–topped chicken at home, and serve it family style. It can be made with boneless chicken breasts, or with airline chicken breasts (see Note).*

SALSA

> 3 navel or Valencia oranges, peeled and segmented
>
> 1/2 red onion, minced and soaked in 1 cup water, then drained
>
> 2 scallions, sliced
>
> 1/4 cup chopped fresh cilantro
>
> 1/4 cup olive oil
>
> 1 clove garlic, minced

CHICKEN

> 6 boneless chicken breasts, lightly pounded, or 6 (7-ounce) airline chicken breasts
>
> 1/4 cup olive oil
>
> 1 tablespoon kosher salt
>
> 1 teaspoon cracked pepper
>
> 1 tablespoon ground cumin
>
> 12 small red potatoes

Make the salsa: In a medium-size bowl, toss together the orange segments, onion, scallion, cilantro, oil, and garlic. Allow to marinate for 20 to 30 minutes before serving.

Make the chicken: Preheat the oven to 400°F.

Brush the chicken breasts with 2 tablespoons of the oil and season with salt, pepper, and cumin. Place in batches in a large, heavy ovenproof skillet over medium heat. Cook until well browned on both sides. Place in the oven and roast until the chicken is cooked through, about 15 minutes for boneless breasts, about 20 minutes for airline breasts. Remove the chicken from the pan and set aside, keeping warm.

Place the red potatoes and the remaining 2 tablespoons of oil in the same skillet, and roast in the oven for 30 to 35 minutes, or until golden and tender.

Slice the boneless chicken breasts and arrange on a serving platter, family style; serve the airline chicken breasts on individual serving plates. Either way, top with the salsa, and garnish with roasted red potatoes.

Note: An airline breast is a boneless chicken breast with the first wing bone attached.

WHITEFISH with BASIL RELISH and SAUTÉED SPINACH

Serves 8 | *Whitefish are native to the Great Lakes and are prized for their tender white flesh and delicate flavor. They're a Chicago favorite. Add the flavors and colors of the green spinach and basil-tomato relish, for one of Jan's favorite dishes.*

BASIL RELISH

3 cups diced fresh Roma tomatoes

1/4 cup diced sweet onions

1/4 cup chiffonade-cut fresh basil (a fine julienne)

2 tablespoons balsamic vinegar

2 tablespoons olive oil

Salt and ground black pepper

WHITEFISH

8 (8-ounce) fresh whitefish fillets (see Note)

2 tablespoons olive oil

2 teaspoons paprika

Salt and ground black pepper

SAUTÉED SPINACH

2 tablespoons olive oil

1 cup diced sweet onion

2 pounds fresh spinach, washed well and trimmed

Salt and ground black pepper

Make the relish: In a lidded container, mix the tomatoes, onions, basil, balsamic vinegar, and oil together. Season with salt and pepper. Cover and refrigerate at least 2 hours to allow the flavors to develop before serving. To serve, bring to room temperature.

Make the fish: Preheat the oven to 375°F. Place the fillets on a lightly oiled baking sheet. Lightly brush the fish with 2 tablespoons of olive oil, and season with paprika, salt, and pepper. Bake for 8 to 10 minutes, depending on the thickness of the fillets, or until completely cooked through.

Make the spinach: While the fish is cooking, heat the olive oil in a 12-inch skillet. Add the onions and sauté until transparent, approximately 2 minutes. Add the spinach, in batches, and sauté for 2 to 3 minutes, or until tender and just cooked. Remove from the heat, and season with salt and pepper before serving as directed.

Place 1/4 cup of the spinach mixture in the center of each plate to form a mound. Place one cooked whitefish fillet on top of the spinach and ladle 1/3 cup of the relish on top of and around the fish. Serve with French bread, if desired.

Note: Whitefish is a delicate, bright-skinned fish and should be handled minimally. The fillet should be firm to the touch.

HALIBUT LIVORNESE with SAUTÉED SPINACH

Serves 8 | *Livorno is a port city in Tuscany, and there are almost as many versions of Livornese sauce as there are fish in the sea. Many are intended for fish, and this Berghoff version is a rich and sumptuous one that complements the biggest flatfish in the ocean. Just be careful not to overcook the fish.*

SAUCE

> 1 cup white wine
>
> 1 cup heavy cream
>
> 1 tablespoon roux (see Note)
>
> 1/2 pound (2 sticks) cold unsalted butter, cut into cubes
>
> 1/4 cup chopped scallions
>
> 1/4 cup finely diced pimientos
>
> 3 tablespoons capers with their brine

HALIBUT

> 2 tablespoons olive oil
>
> 8 (8-ounce) fresh skinless Alaskan halibut fillets
>
> 1/2 teaspoon paprika
>
> Salt and ground black pepper
>
> 1 recipe Sautéed Spinach (page 152)
>
> Crisp bread croutons, for garnish

Make the sauce: In a 2-quart saucepan, mix the wine and cream together. Bring to a simmer and allow the mixture to reduce by half. After the reduction, slowly add 1 tablespoon roux, whisking continuously. Continue to simmer until thickened, whisking occasionally. Add the butter, one cube at a time, whisking constantly until incorporated. The sauce should be thickened and smooth. Stir in the scallions, pimientos, and

capers with their brine. Season with salt and pepper, and keep warm, not hot, until ready to use as directed. This recipe makes 2 cups of sauce. Make the spinach if it has not been made in advance.

Make the fish: Preheat the broiler. On an oiled baking sheet, place the halibut fillets in one layer. Brush both sides of each fillet with oil and sprinkle both sides evenly with paprika, salt, and pepper. Place the baking sheet 1 to 2 inches from the heat and broil the fish for 1 to 2 minutes (do not brown) on each side. Remove the fish from the broiler, and decrease the oven temperature to 375°F. Place the fish in the oven for 4 to 5 minutes (depending on the thickness of the fish). The halibut is cooked thoroughly when it is slightly springy to the touch.

To serve: Place a 1/4-cup mound of the spinach mixture in the center of each dinner plate and place a prepared fillet to one side of the spinach. Ladle 1/4 cup of the Livornese sauce over and around the halibut, and serve with crisp bread croutons.

Note: To make 1/4 cup of roux, in a small saucepan, over low heat, stir together 1/3 cup of melted butter and 1/3 cup of all-purpose flour until incorporated. The consistency should be similar to that of wet sand. Cook for 1 minute, then remove from the heat. Use as directed.

STIR-FRIED CATFISH with ASIAN-STYLE VEGETABLES

Serves 8 | *We created this recipe for the restaurant because we were looking for a non-Southern way to cook the very popular catfish.*

SAUCE

- 3 tablespoons prepared seasoned rice vinegar
- 3 tablespoons soy sauce
- 3 tablespoons mirin (Japanese cooking wine)
- 2 tablespoons sesame oil
- 1 tablespoon packed light brown sugar
- 2 teaspoons finely grated fresh ginger
- 2 teaspoons finely chopped garlic
- 3 tablespoons cornstarch slurry (page 33)

FISH

- 3 pounds catfish strips or pieces
- Salt and ground black pepper
- Peanut or any type of vegetable oil, as needed, for frying
- 1 cup cornstarch, plus water as needed to make slurry (page 33)

VEGETABLES

- 2 tablespoons peanut or vegetable oil
- 1 tablespoon sliced scallions, white part only (reserve green part for garnish)
- 1 teaspoon minced garlic
- 1 teaspoon finely grated fresh ginger
- 1/2 cup broccoli florets
- 1/2 cup sliced carrots
- 1/2 cup sliced yellow squash
- 1/2 cup seeded red bell pepper strips
- 1/2 cup seeded green bell pepper strips
- 1/2 cup drained canned Asian baby corn (sold in Asian or gourmet markets)
- 1/2 cup straw mushrooms
- 1/2 cup snow peas
- 8 cups cooked white rice

Make the sauce: In a 2-quart saucepan, whisk the vinegar, soy sauce, mirin, sesame oil, sugar, ginger, and garlic together, and bring to a boil over medium heat. Decrease the heat and simmer for 2 to 3 minutes. Thicken with as much as necessary of the cornstarch slurry to a sauce consistency. Keep the sauce warm until the vegetables are ready.

The kitchen staff, 1930s.

Make the fish: Place the catfish on a baking sheet and season with salt and pepper. Cover and refrigerate until ready to use.

Preheat the frying oil to 350°F in a deep-fryer or heavy, deep saucepan. Place the cornstarch slurry in a bowl. When ready to fry the fish, dip the seasoned catfish into the cornstarch batter, removing from the batter with a fork. In batches, gently place the battered catfish into the hot oil, being sure not to overcrowd the pot, and fry until crisp outside and just opaque in the center, 3 to 4 minutes per batch. Transfer to paper towels to drain, and keep warm until ready to serve.

In a wok or medium-size skillet, heat the oil until hot. Add chopped white scallions, garlic, and ginger, and sauté briefly (do not brown) for 30 seconds. Add the remaining vegetables, sturdiest first, and stir-fry until they are crisp-tender (approximately 2 minutes). Add the sauce to the vegetables and heat thoroughly. Remove from the heat.

For each serving, place a 1-cup ring of cooked rice on a plate, fill with $1/2$ cup of the stir-fried vegetable mixture, and top with 6 ounces of fried catfish. Drizzle with extra stir-fry sauce, if desired. Garnish with sliced green scallion.

SESAME-CRUSTED AHI TUNA

Serves 8 | *The Berghoff, despite all its classic traditional German specialties, always kept pace with the times. In the year 2000, a visiting food writer from the* New York Times *expressed amazement to find this dish on our menu. As Jan said, "But we're not just a German restaurant."*

¹/₄ **cup white sesame seeds**

¹/₄ **cup black sesame seeds**

¹/₄ **cup all-purpose flour**

¹/₂ **teaspoon salt**

¹/₂ **teaspoon ground black pepper**

8 (6-ounce) portions fresh tuna loin

¹/₃ **cup vegetable oil**

Teriyaki Sauce (page 32)

Cooked white rice, as needed

In a medium-size bowl, mix the two kinds of sesame seeds, and the flour, salt, and pepper together.

Place 3 tablespoons of the oil in a small bowl. Dip the tuna into the oil, and then into the sesame coating. Place on a baking sheet, cover, and refrigerate until ready to cook.

Using a large griddle or skillet, heat the remaining oil until hot. Sear the tuna to medium doneness on both sides, about 2 minutes per side, depending upon the thickness of the tuna. Remove from the heat.

Serve the tuna on individual plates and accompany with Teriyaki Sauce, stir-fried seasonal vegetables, and cooked rice.

SALMON with HERBED BREAD CRUMBS

Serves 8 | *Many times we thought we should have written a cookbook titled 1,001 Ways to Serve Salmon, because we have had so many versions on our menu. The combination of mustard and crisp golden herb bread crumbs made this version a customer favorite. The Dill Beurre Blanc is the icing on the cake; however, these salmon fillets are good even without the sauce.*

SALMON

8 (6-ounce) salmon fillets

Salt and ground black pepper

2 tablespoons olive oil

1 cup fresh bread crumbs

2 tablespoons olive oil

1 tablespoon chopped fresh chives

1 tablespoon chopped fresh thyme

3 tablespoons whole-grain Dijon mustard

Steamed snow peas, as needed

Sautéed cherry tomatoes, as needed

DILL BEURRE BLANC

1 cup white wine

2 tablespoons minced shallots

$1/2$ cup heavy cream

Pinch of salt

Pinch of freshly ground white pepper

$1/2$ pound (2 sticks) cold unsalted butter, cut into small pieces

1 tablespoon chopped fresh dill, plus extra for garnish

Make the salmon: Preheat the oven to 400°F.

Season the salmon fillets with salt and pepper. In a 10-inch skillet, heat the oil until hot. Sear the fillets until golden brown, approximately 3 minutes on each side. Remove from the skillet, and place in a large, lightly greased, ovenproof baking dish.

In a small bowl, combine the bread crumbs, olive oil, chives, and thyme, and toss to mix. Spread each salmon fillet with approximately 1 teaspoon of Dijon mustard and sprinkle evenly with the bread crumb mixture. Bake for 10 to 12 minutes, or until the crumbs are golden and the salmon is cooked through.

Make the Dill Beurre Blanc: In a heavy 3-quart saucepan, over medium heat, bring the wine and shallots to a boil and reduce to a syrup consistency, about 5 minutes. Add the cream, salt, and white pepper, and boil for 3 more minutes. Decrease the heat to low and add the butter pieces, a few pieces at a time, whisking constantly until incorporated and thickened. Adjust the seasonings with salt and pepper. Strain the sauce and stir in the dill. Keep warm until ready to serve.

Place the salmon on individual dinner plates and ladle 3 tablespoons of Dill Beurre Blanc on top of each fillet. You may garnish the entire dish with additional chopped fresh dill, for color.

BOUILLABAISSE

Serves 8 | *For at least sixty years, and long before this stew became trendy, Berghoff's served bouillabaisse on the Thursday, Friday, and Saturday lunch and dinner menus. In Chicago, payday was on Friday, and people would cash their checks and treat themselves to lunch or dinner. (And for Catholics, bouillabaisse was a Friday luxury.) Thursday? Perhaps customers were anticipating the prosperity ahead. Saturday? They were still flush. Like all Berghoff classics, this is easy to make. Today's bounty of available fresh seafood makes it great.*

2 quarts fish broth (page 67)

2 cups canned, diced tomatoes

1 cup julienned celery

1 cup julienned leeks

2 bay leaves

¹/₈ teaspoon red pepper flakes

Pinch of saffron threads

48 mussels, debearded and scrubbed (3 pounds) (see Note)

32 littleneck clams, scrubbed (3 pounds) (see Note)

1 pound fresh salmon fillet, cut into 16 pieces

1 pound fresh halibut fillet, cut into 16 pieces

4 (4-ounce) lobster tails, shelled and halved

32 raw shrimps, peeled and deveined (1 pound)

Salt and ground black pepper

In a heavy 2-gallon stockpot, combine the fish broth, tomatoes, celery, leeks, bay leaves, red pepper flakes, and saffron. Bring to a simmer and cook for 15 minutes. Keep warm.

When ready to serve, add all the seafood. Cover and cook over medium heat for 5 to 7 minutes to allow the flavors to develop, the shellfish to open, and the other seafood to cook through. Season with salt and pepper.

Ladle into eight large soup plates or bowls, and serve with a simple tossed green salad and crisp, warm garlic bread.

Note: Discard any raw mussels or clams that do not close tightly when you touch them.

SALMON CAKES with ANCHO CHILE DRESSING

Makes 16 patties/Serves 8 | *This was a recent addition to our menu, in response to the fish cake trend and to find yet another way to serve the wildly popular salmon. You can mix and shape the cakes up to six hours ahead of time, and refrigerate them until you are ready to sauté them. The Ancho Chile Dressing can be mixed a day ahead.*

SALMON CAKES

2 pounds fresh salmon fillets, chopped (4-plus cups)

2 cups mayonnaise

2 large eggs

1/2 cup finely chopped sweet onion, drained of its liquid

1/2 cup finely chopped celery

1/3 cup finely chopped dill pickles

2 tablespoons fresh lemon juice

1 tablespoon chopped fresh dill

1 teaspoon Old Bay seasoning

1/2 teaspoon salt

1/2 teaspoon ground black pepper

1/8 teaspoon Tabasco sauce

3 cups fresh sourdough bread crumbs, or 4 cups French bread crumbs

1/4 cup vegetable oil

8 cups mixed greens (8 ounces)

DRESSING

1 cup mayonnaise

2 tablespoons prepared chile sauce

2 tablespoons minced shallot

2 tablespoons finely diced celery

2 tablespoons dill pickle relish

1 tablespoon chopped fresh parsley

1 tablespoon fresh lemon juice

1 tablespoon Worcestershire sauce

1 1/2 teaspoons dried ground ancho chile

1/8 teaspoon red pepper flakes

1/8 teaspoon Tabasco sauce

Salt and ground black pepper

Make the salmon: In a large bowl, combine the salmon, mayonnaise, eggs, onion, celery, pickles, lemon juice, dill, Old Bay, salt, pepper, and Tabasco, and mix well. Stir in the bread crumbs and mix to incorporate. Cover and let stand for 1 hour. Mix again and then form into sixteen 4-ounce patties (approximately 1/2 cup mixture per patty). The patties should be 3 to 4 inches wide and no more than 1/2 inch thick. Place in one layer on a baking sheet, cover, and refrigerate until ready to use as directed. The patties may be made 4 to 6 hours ahead and kept refrigerated.

Make the dressing: In a medium-size bowl, combine the mayonnaise, chile sauce, shallot, celery, pickle relish, parsley, lemon juice, Worcestershire sauce, ancho chile, red pepper flakes, Tabasco, salt, and pepper, and whisk together until blended. Cover and refrigerate until ready to use as directed. The dressing may be prepared one day in advance and stored, covered, in the refrigerator. This recipe makes 1¹/₂ cups of dressing.

Preheat the oven to 325°F. When ready to cook, in a 14-inch skillet, heat the oil. Add the salmon patties and sear 4 minutes on both sides, until slightly browned and crispy on the outside. Place the patties back on their baking sheet and bake for 6 to 8 minutes, to heat through.

Place a 1-cup mound of mixed greens on each plate and top with two crisp, hot salmon patties. Drizzle each serving with 3 tablespoons of dressing.

Keeping Food Hot

Fortunately many of the Berghoff classics keep well, and for a buffet, the only challenge is keeping them somewhat hot. For soups and stews, we recommend the tried-and-true chafing dish that sits over a hot water bath and keeps a steady temperature by means of the alcohol burner beneath. The dish is also easy to replenish from the kitchen. Sauces keep nicely warm in fondue pots. And for sliced meats in gravy, there are oven-safe dishes that can sit on electric warming trays that have a range of settings from low to high.

It also helps to boil a kettle of water and pour it into serving dishes, deep platters, and tureens before dinner. Then just pour out the water when ready to fill the nicely warmed serving dish. This is especially good when serving family style. Some contemporary dishwashers have plate-warmers built in. And if you plan well, you can wash your serving dishes in the dishwasher, where they will be still warm from the drying cycle when you're ready to fill them.

HONEY SALMON

Serves 6 | *Simple as it can possibly be to prepare, this was one of our most popular salmon entrées, and it was on the menu until the day that Jan and Herman put on their coats and stepped out the front door and into retirement. The salmon cooks in an orange-honey sauce that is then reduced to be drizzled on top of the sweet, juicy fillet.*

SAUCE

$3/4$ **cup fish broth (page 67)**

$1/2$ **cup orange juice**

$1/4$ **cup cider vinegar**

3 tablespoons honey

Zest of $1/4$ orange, julienned

SALMON

2 tablespoons vegetable or olive oil

6 (7-ounce) fresh salmon fillets, skinned and boned

Salt and ground black pepper

1 recipe Sautéed Spinach (page 152)

Make the sauce: In a small bowl, whisk together the fish broth, orange juice, vinegar, honey, and orange zest. Cover and set aside until ready to use as directed. If not using within 1 hour, refrigerate until ready to use. This recipe makes 1 cup of sauce.

Make the salmon: In a 12-inch skillet, over high heat, heat the oil until hot. Season the salmon with salt and pepper, place in the skillet, and sear for 30 seconds on each side. Add the sauce, decrease the heat, cover, and simmer for 8 to 10

minutes, depending on the thickness of the salmon. When the salmon is done, remove it from the skillet. Continue to reduce the sauce slightly until thickened. Strain the sauce and reserve the zest for garnish, if desired.

Mound $1/2$ cup of the spinach mixture in the center of each plate. Place a salmon fillet in the middle of the spinach and drizzle the sauce on top. Garnish with the reserved orange zest. This dish goes well with Mashed Potatoes (page 178).

CRAB CAKES

Serves 6 as an entrée or 12 as an appetizer | *Everybody needs a good crab cake in their reper-toire, and this is a good one. There's a lot of crab and very little bread crumbs, but the cakes don't fall apart. They can be mixed, shaped, and refrigerated until ready to coat and cook. The coating fries up crispy and the crab cakes can double as an entrée or an appetizer. Serve hot, or at room temperature.*

1 pound lump crabmeat, picked over and broken into small pieces

¹/₂ cup minced red onion

¹/₂ cup minced red bell pepper

¹/₂ cup frozen corn kernels, thawed

2 tablespoons chopped fresh parsley

1 tablespoon capers, drained and chopped coarsely

1 tablespoon fresh lemon juice

¹/₂ cup cream cheese, softened

¹/₂ cup dry bread crumbs

Salt and pepper

¹/₂ cup all-purpose flour seasoned with salt and ground black pepper

3 large eggs

2 cups dry bread crumbs

Vegetable oil, as needed, for frying

In a medium-size bowl, combine the crabmeat, red onion, red pepper, corn, parsley, capers, and lemon juice. Mix well and set aside.

Using an electric mixer fitted with paddle attachment, beat the cream cheese until very soft. (If you do not have a mixer, beat the cream cheese by hand in a bowl. Presoftening the cream cheese makes it easier to incorporate it into the crabmeat mixture.) Gently stir the crab mixture into the cream cheese along with the bread crumbs, until the cakes are firm enough to hold a shape. Adjust the seasonings. Form into twelve 3-inch round patties for entrée-size portions or twenty-four 1-inch mini patties for hors d'oeuvres. Cover and refrigerate until ready to coat and cook.

Place the seasoned flour in one bowl. In a separate bowl, beat the eggs; and in a third bowl, place the cornflake crumbs. Coat each crab cake in the flour, then in the eggs, and finally in the bread crumbs. Shake off any excess coating. Place the cakes in single layer on a baking sheet and let rest up to 30 minutes before frying. (At this point, the crab cakes may be covered and frozen for up to one week or until ready to cook.)

In a large, heavy skillet (or use a deep-fryer if you have one), heat the oil to 360°F. Fry the crab cakes in batches until slightly golden brown on both sides. Transfer to a large plate lined with paper towels to drain.

Serve the crab cakes as an entrée atop mixed baby greens or couscous. If serving as an hors d'oeuvre, line a platter with baby spinach leaves, then watch the crab cakes disappear.

PAN-SEARED TILAPIA with TABASCO BROTH

Serves 8 | *Carlyn created this pretty fish dish for catered events, and she makes it at home for parties—for all the same reasons. Tilapia is mild in flavor and superb in texture, neither too flaky nor too firm. It is inexpensive to buy, and the small fillets are the perfect portion size. The cornflake-crusted sautéed fillets are crispy, and can be kept warm for a while before serving with a ladle of spicy red broth.*

TILAPIA

    8 (6-ounce) skinless tilapia fillets

    Salt and ground white pepper

    1 cup all-purpose flour, seasoned with salt and white pepper

    4 large eggs

    2 cups cornflake crumbs

    1 cup vegetable oil

    1 cup minced parsley or chives, for garnish

TABASCO BROTH

    2 cups tomato juice

    1/2 teaspoon minced garlic

    2 tablespoons unsalted butter

    1 teaspoon Tabasco sauce, or to taste

Make the tilapia: Season the fillets with salt and pepper. Place the seasoned flour in one bowl. In a separate bowl, beat the eggs; and in a third bowl, place the cornflake crumbs. Coat each fillet in the flour, then in the eggs, and finally in the cornflake crumbs. Shake off any excess coating. Place on a baking sheet and let rest for 20 to 30 minutes before cooking.

In a 12-inch nonstick skillet, heat the oil over high heat to 360°F. Add the breaded fillets and pan-fry, until golden brown on both sides (turn only once) and cooked through, approximately 3 minutes per side. Remove from the pan and keep warm.

Make the broth: In a 2-quart saucepan, bring the tomato juice and garlic to a boil; decrease the heat and whisk in the butter. Simmer for 5 minutes, or until the butter is incorporated into the sauce. Stir in the Tabasco.

Ladle 1/4 cup of hot broth into each soup plate. Place a crisp tilapia fillet in the center of each bowl on top of the broth, and garnish with a sprinkling of minced parsley, chives, or green herbs.

SIDES

Vegetables and Grains That Matter

Berghoff Classics

CREAMED SPINACH 170

BEETS with ORANGES and CANDIED ALMONDS 172

GERMAN FRIES 174

BERGHOFF CHIPS 175

POTATO PANCAKES 176

MASHED POTATOES 178

EGGPLANT RATATOUILLE 179

RED CABBAGE 180

SAUERKRAUT 181

Carlyn's Favorites

SZECHUAN GREEN BEANS 182

POTATO GALETTE 184

PEAS with MINT 185

ROASTED VEGETABLES 186

CAULIFLOWER FRITTERS with LEMON-PEPPER MAYONNAISE ... 187

CRIMSON RED LENTIL and FAVA BEAN RELISH 188

WHEAT BERRY and WILD RICE SALAD 189

AT BERGHOFF'S AND AT HOME, we've never considered side dishes to be afterthoughts. Sides make the meal complete. Our philosophy has always been to start with an entrée, then pick the appetizer and salad—and after all that, we select the sides. Working in that order, it's easier to avoid repeating ingredients or picking side dishes that clash with the entrée.

Interesting side dishes are the antidote to the monotony of carrots, potatoes, and peas, which, while they do add color to a plate, tend to breed boredom. And if a side dish is truly delicious, it can steal the show. We should know. Our Creamed Spinach was one of the side dishes that made us famous, and for the first time we share our official recipe for it here. A side dish can also be the main attraction; for example, mashed potato bars (see page 264).

A word about quantity: If you are serving a sit-down dinner for family or friends, one or two side dishes—a starch and a vegetable—are perfectly sufficient, especially if you are serving salad. But when you set out a buffet, a strange thing happens: One or two side dishes seems both skimpy and boring. You need at least three side dishes and, what's more, you need to double the quantities. Not convinced? Consider this: a buffet for eight with roast chicken or beef tenderloin as the main dish, accompanied by one medium-size bowl of Eggplant Ratatouille and one casserole of Potato Gratin. Now add a dish of Szechuan Green Beans and a platter of Roasted Vegetables. That takes you from bare minimum to *abbondanza*.

The Mashed Potato Lady

Herman remembers her. She first called in the year 2000. "Your potatoes are not made from scratch," she said. Herman assured her that Berghoff's mashed potatoes started with peeled, steamed Idaho potatoes, and that the restaurant had a special machine for peeling the tons of potatoes the restaurant used. Next she wrote Herman a letter, saying she knew her potatoes, and Berghoff's were not made from scratch, but from dried potatoes. "A letter from the Mashed Potato Lady," he told Jan. Other letters followed. "Another letter from the Mashed Potato Lady." Everybody has their limits. Another letter from the Mashed Potato Lady arrived during the hectic holiday season. Herman decided to send his bill for Idaho potatoes to her return address. During that month the restaurant had used five thousand pounds of potatoes. The Mashed Potato Lady wrote back, and she was indignant as ever, but this time because she was proven foolish.

Some of the following side dishes may be made two or three days in advance and refrigerated, such as Potato Galette, Mashed Potatoes, German Potato Salad, and Red Cabbage. Others are à la minute. There are lots of recipes to choose from. Just remember to vary the texture and color on the plate and on the table.

Top: A Berghoff-size supply of potatoes.
Bottom: The Berghoff potato peeler.

CREAMED SPINACH

Makes 5 cups/Serves 8 | *One of the dishes that made Berghoff's famous, Creamed Spinach was put on the menu around 1945 by our Swiss then-executive chef Karl Hertenstein, and has been there ever since. Up until now, the recipe, although simple, has been our secret. We made everything "from scratch" in Berghoff's kitchen—except the Creamed Spinach. Because spinach is so bulky when fresh and shrinks to almost nothing when cooked, we have always made our enormous daily quantity from frozen spinach. Frozen spinach is minimally processed: quickly blanched, drained of excess water, then flash frozen. If you want to try making our recipe from fresh spinach, we have included a recipe. But we bet that, side by side, you can't taste the difference.*

2 cups half-and-half

1 cup milk

$1^1/_2$ teaspoons chicken base, or 1 cube chicken bouillon

$1/_2$ teaspoon Tabasco sauce

$1/_2$ teaspoon ground nutmeg

$1/_4$ teaspoon granulated garlic (see Note)

$1/_8$ teaspoon celery salt

4 tablespoons ($1/_2$ stick) unsalted butter

$1/_4$ cup all-purpose flour

3 (10-ounce) packages frozen chopped spinach, thawed and squeezed dry ($2^1/_2$ cups)

Salt and ground white pepper, if desired

Ground nutmeg, for garnish

Crisp, cooked, crumbled bacon, for garnish

In a medium-size saucepan, heat the half-and-half, milk, chicken base, Tabasco, and seasonings to a simmer. Remove from the heat and keep warm.

In another medium-size saucepan, heat the butter over medium heat. Add the flour and whisk well to combine. Cook this mixture for 2 to 3 minutes, stirring often. Slowly whisk the heated milk mixture into the butter mixture, a little at a time, whisking constantly until smooth. Bring the mixture to a simmer and cook for 5 minutes, stirring constantly, until it thickens. The sauce will be very thick.

Stir in the spinach and simmer for 5 minutes. Adjust seasonings. Serve while hot.

To serve: Place the hot creamed spinach in a bowl, sprinkled with an extra touch of ground nutmeg on top. Top each serving with 1 tablespoon of crisp, cooked, crumbled bacon, if desired.

Note: Granulated garlic is dried granular garlic, not the same as dried minced, dried chopped, or garlic powder. It has the best flavor of all the dried garlic products, in our opinion. Some supermarkets carry it in the gourmet spice section, and it's available from spice shops.

Variation: To make the recipe with fresh spinach, you will need 4 (10-ounce) bags trimmed, washed spinach (not baby spinach).

Working in four batches, wash one bagful of spinach at a time in a basin of cold water. Drain in a colander. Place the batch in a 6-quart pot over high heat, cover, and steam. While the spinach is steaming, repeat the process for the other three bags, putting each on top of the spinach in the pot (it will shrink down considerably). Cover and steam until the spinach is wilted and cooked. Drain in a large colander. Press down on the spinach with a spatula to extract as much water as possible. Transfer the spinach to a cutting board and chop finely.

Line the colander with a lint-free, clean kitchen towel. Put in the chopped spinach, bring up the ends of the towel, and, as soon as it's cool enough to handle, twist the towel to form a sack and squeeze dry. You should have 2^1/$_2$ cups of cooked, chopped, squeezed spinach.

Stir the spinach into the cream mixture and simmer for 5 minutes, stirring to mix. Adjust the seasonings. Serve hot.

A Cauldron of Creamed Spinach

Creamed spinach has been the single most popular side dish on the menu since its introduction around 1945. Berghoff's made it in a Jacuzzi-size cauldron, every day. The secret-but-simple recipe has been the subject of much speculation and frequent "recipes" for it have been published in newspapers over the years—none of them authentic. The recipe in this chapter is authentic. You got it from us.

BEETS with ORANGES and CANDIED ALMONDS

Serves 8 | *This is the creation of Berghoff executive chef Matt Reichel—who absolutely loves beets.*

4 large oranges, plus extra for garnish

6 tablespoons (³/₄ stick) unsalted butter

1 tablespoon red wine vinegar

¹/₂ teaspoon salt

¹/₄ teaspoon ground black pepper

2 pounds boiled or roasted fresh baby beets, peeled

1 cup Candied Sliced Almonds (follow Candied Pecan recipe page 80, substituting sliced almonds for pecans), for garnish

2 tablespoons chopped chives, for garnish

Zest one orange and reserve the zest. Into a small bowl, juice all four oranges.

Place the orange juice and zest, butter, vinegar, salt, and pepper in a shallow saucepan. Bring to a boil. Decrease the heat to medium and reduce the mixture for 3 minutes.

Add the reserved beets to the saucepan and continue to cook for 10 minutes, stirring occasionally. Raise the heat to high and continue cooking, to reduce the sauce mixture to a thickened glaze consistency (the beets should be coated). Add more salt and pepper, if necessary.

Serve at room temperature in a bowl or on a platter; sprinkle with Candied Almonds and chives. You may also garnish the dish with sliced oranges or slivered orange peel.

Variation: You may use larger beets and cut them into ³/₄-inch cubes.

GERMAN FRIES

Makes 8 (5-ounce) servings | *These round, crispy fries can accompany Wiener Schnitzel and many other classic Berghoff dishes. The secret to their texture and flavor and the way they brown, lies in precooking and prechilling.*

4 large Idaho potatoes (about 3 pounds), peeled and left whole

¹/₂ cup melted butter

Salt and pepper

Place the potatoes in a 1-gallon pot with enough salted water to cover. Bring to a boil. Decrease the heat and simmer for 20 to 25 minutes, depending on the size of the potatoes. To test for doneness, insert a fork into the middle of a potato. You should encounter only slight resistance when removing the fork.

Transfer to a platter and let cool to room temperature for 2 hours. Refrigerate overnight, uncovered.

When ready to cook, slice the potatoes horizontally about ¹/₈ inch thick. Heat the butter in a 12-inch nonstick skillet over medium-high heat and add a layer of sliced potatoes. Cook until golden brown on one side, and then flip over and brown on the other side. Season with salt and pepper.

Serve with Wiener Schnitzel and other hearty Berghoff main dishes, as well as with many Berghoff sandwiches.

BERGHOFF CHIPS

Serves 8 to 10 | *Third-generation Herman Berghoff deserves credit for this—indirectly. He used to steal the German Fries intended for the Weiner Schnitzel plates, but only the ones that were well done and crisp. So eventually chef Matt Reichel came up with these Berghoff Chips. They were an immediate hit with customers, and Herman kept his fingers off the German Fries.*

Salted water

3 pounds Idaho potatoes, peeled and left whole (5 large)

Vegetable oil, as needed, for deep-fat frying

Salt and ground black pepper

In a large pot of boiling, salted water, cook the potatoes for approximately 20 minutes, or until al dente. Remove from the heat, drain, and refrigerate, uncovered, at least 12 hours in advance of slicing and frying.

Slice the chilled potatoes into $^1/_8$-inch-thick slices. Fill a deep-fryer or heavy, deep saucepan with oil at least $1^1/_2$ inches deep; heat to 350°F. Fry the potato slices in batches, turning them with tongs or a slotted spoon until they are golden brown. Remove from oil with slotted spoon and transfer the chips to paper toweling to drain. Sprinkle with salt and pepper. Serve while still warm.

POTATO PANCAKES

Makes 8 pancakes/Serves 8 | *Potato pancakes are a staple of German cookery and everyone has their version. We think ours is especially tasty and our customers agreed, making it a menu favorite year after year. Chef Matt Reichel says to make the quick and easy batter just before you plan to cook the pancakes. If you let the batter sit, it will turn brown.*

2 pounds Idaho potatoes, peeled (3 large)

1 cup all-purpose flour

2 large eggs

$^1/_3$ cup thinly sliced scallions, plus extra for garnish

2 teaspoons minced garlic

1 teaspoon salt

$^1/_2$ teaspoon ground white pepper

Vegetable oil, as needed, for pan-frying

Sour cream, for garnish

Applesauce, for garnish

Into a large bowl, grate the potatoes, using the medium-size hole on grater. Mix with all other ingredients except the garnish. Mix well and cover completely with plastic wrap (place right onto the surface of the mixture so the potatoes will not oxidize). The pancake mixture should be used within 10 (at the most 15) minutes after preparing. *Do not* let sit, or the mixture will turn brown by oxidation.

To pan-fry, turn on an electric griddle or heat a skillet on high heat and fill with at least $^1/_{16}$ inch of oil. Scoop $^1/_2$ cup of batter onto the hot griddle, spreading the mixture out so the pancake is $^1/_4$ inch thick. Decrease the heat to medium and cook until one side is crispy and brown. Flip the pancake over, and brown the other side. Transfer to paper toweling to absorb the excess fat. Keep warm and crisp.

Serve these delicious potato pancakes with a dollop of sour cream and/or applesauce. Garnish top with more sliced scallions.

Fully cooked pancakes can be placed in a single layer on a cookie sheet in the freezer until frozen, then stored in zippered plastic bags in the freezer. When ready to use, heat on cookie sheet in oven until crisp.

MASHED POTATOES

Serves 8 | *Serve these, as we did at the restaurant, with any of Berghoff's traditional main dishes, serve them at home for a side dish, and by all means serve them as Carlyn does—on a mashed potato bar (see page 264).*

3 pounds Yukon Gold or russet potatoes, peeled and quartered

³/₄ cup heavy cream

¹/₂ cup sour cream

12 tablespoons (1¹/₂ sticks) unsalted butter, cut into cubes

Salt and ground white pepper

In a large, heavy-bottomed pot, place the potatoes and just enough water to cover them. Over high heat, bring to a boil and simmer until tender, approximately 25 minutes. Using a colander, drain the potatoes. Return to the empty, dry pot and heat over high heat for 1 minute. Remove from the heat and place in a large bowl.

In a small saucepan, melt the butter and add the cream; heat for 2 minutes. Using an electric mixer (it is okay to mix by hand, just more labor intensive), whip the potatoes until blended. Add the butter mixture and whip until well combined. Whip in the sour cream, salt, and white pepper. Continue to mix until all the ingredients are incorporated. Adjust the seasonings, and keep covered and warm until ready to serve.

Place the hot mashed potatoes in a serving bowl and top with a pat of butter to serve.

EGGPLANT RATATOUILLE

Makes 2 quarts/Serves 8 | *Chef Matt Reichel asked if he could make ratatouille for the menu, because he really liked it. But because the restaurant works at a faster pace than the home kitchen, he created this recipe that is far less time consuming than a traditional recipe. In the summer when tomatoes were ripe and plentiful, he used fresh tomatoes. But the dish was so popular that he made it year round, substituting canned tomatoes in winter.*

1 large eggplant, cut into ¹/₂-inch cubes

1 large zucchini, cut into ¹/₂-inch cubes

Salt and cracked black pepper

¹/₃ cup olive oil

2 white onions, cut into ¹/₂-inch cubes

1 red bell pepper, cut into ¹/₂-inch cubes

1 green bell pepper, cut into ¹/₂-inch cubes

1 (28-ounce) can diced tomatoes, or 1 pound Roma tomatoes, peeled, seeded, and cut into ¹/₂-inch cubes

1 tablespoon minced garlic

3 tablespoons chopped fresh flat-leaf parsley

3 tablespoons chopped fresh basil

Romaine or spinach leaves, for garnish

Place the eggplant and zucchini in a large bowl. Season with salt and pepper, and let stand for 10 minutes.

In a large, straight-sided skillet, heat 3 tablespoons of the oil until hot. Sauté the eggplant and zucchini until lightly browned. Using a slotted spoon, remove the vegetables from the skillet and set aside.

Add the remaining oil to the skillet. Stir in the onions and peppers, and sauté until lightly browned. Add the tomatoes and garlic, and bring to a boil. Return the eggplant and zucchini to the skillet, and reduce to a simmer. Cook for 15 to 20 minutes more, or until most of the juice from the tomatoes has thickened. Stir in the parsley, basil, salt, and pepper. Gently toss all the vegetables together and cook for 3 minutes longer, to heat through.

The ratatouille may be served hot or at room temperature, but not chilled. Place in a serving bowl lined with romaine or spinach leaves, for a nice presentation.

RED CABBAGE

Serves 8 | *Red Cabbage has been on Berghoff's menu since day one. It's a simple recipe, but not everyone knows how to make it. For example, until Jan Berghoff ate red cabbage at Berghoff's, she never appreciated it. Now she makes it at home. The secret is in the slow cooking and the sweet-and-sour seasoning.*

1½ **cups red wine vinegar**

1½ **cups sugar**

¼ **pound (1 stick) unsalted butter**

12 **cups shredded red cabbage
(1 large head)**

In a 6-quart pot, bring the vinegar, sugar, and butter to a simmer over medium heat. Add the cabbage and toss to coat. Simmer, uncovered, over low heat for 1 hour. If you prefer a softer cooked cabbage, you may simmer for a longer period of time; cook less time if you prefer it al dente.

Variations: You may also add 2 cups of sliced onion and/or 2 cups of chopped, seeded, and peeled Granny Smith apples or 1 cup of chopped cooked bacon to the cabbage at the beginning of the simmering period.

SAUERKRAUT

Serves 8 | *Sauerkraut has been a staple since the first printed Berghoff's menu. This is a variation of the original recipe that founder Herman Joseph Berghoff brought from Dortmund. Our bet is that even he didn't think of putting Berghoff beer in the kraut, much less applewood-smoked bacon.*

1¹/₂ **cups applewood-smoked bacon, chopped (1 pound)**

1 cup Berghoff Lager beer

6 cups bagged or canned sauerkraut, rinsed and drained

¹/₄ **pound (1 stick) unsalted butter**

1 tablespoon toasted caraway seeds

In a 12-inch skillet, cook the bacon until crisp; drain off the fat. Add the beer to the pan to deglaze it. Stir in the sauerkraut, butter, and caraway seeds. Simmer over low heat for 45 minutes, stirring occasionally. Keep warm.

Enjoy this traditional German side dish with any of the Berghoff family recipes.

Made fresh daily, *left to right:* Sauerkraut, Cabbage, and Red Cabbage in Berghoff's kitchen.

SZECHUAN GREEN BEANS

Makes 1 quart/Serves 8 | *This makes a great side dish for a buffet, says Carlyn, who serves it often at catered events as well as at home. It can be made ahead and served chilled.*

SAUCE

2 tablespoons soy sauce

1 tablespoon minced ginger

1 tablespoon minced fresh garlic

2 teaspoons light brown sugar

2 teaspoons dark sesame oil

2 teaspoons rice wine vinegar

2 teaspoons dry sherry

1–2 fresh hot red peppers, seeded and minced, or Asian dried red chiles (Be careful not to touch with your bare hands while preparing.)

Pinch of ground white pepper

BEANS

6 quarts salted water

1¹⁄₂ pounds fresh green beans, cleaned and trimmed

¹⁄₂ medium-size red onion, sliced (1 cup)

¹⁄₂ cup whole toasted cashews, chopped, for garnish

2 tablespoons toasted white sesame seeds, for garnish

Canned crisp chow mein noodles, for garnish

Make the sauce: In a large bowl, whisk together the soy sauce, ginger, garlic, sugar, sesame oil, vinegar, sherry, hot peppers, and white pepper. Adjust the seasonings and refrigerate, covered, until ready to use.

In a medium-size pot, bring 6 quarts of salted water to a boil. Add the beans and blanch for 3 to 4 minutes. Remove from the heat and immediately plunge into ice-cold water; drain in a colander.

In a medium-size bowl, toss the green beans, onions, and sauce until coated. Cover and refrigerate until chilled.

The beans should be served chilled. Spoon the bean mixture into a serving bowl and garnish with the cashews, sesame seeds, and crisp chow mein noodles, if desired. Serve as a side dish with grilled smoked fowl, pork, or fish.

POTATO GALETTE

Serves 8 to 10 | *This potato gratin is the choice above all other potato dishes at Carlyn's catered wedding events. It's pretty, it holds well, it's creamy and satisfying, it's easy to make, and it looks elegant.*

3 cups heavy cream

3 cloves garlic, chopped

2 1/2 pounds Idaho potatoes, peeled (4 large)

2 cups shredded Parmesan cheese

2 cups dry bread crumbs

Preheat the oven to 350°F. Grease a 9 by 13-inch casserole dish well.

In a medium-size saucepan, mix the cream and garlic together and bring to a boil. Remove from the heat and set aside. Using a sharp knife, a mandoline, or a tabletop slicer, slice the potatoes 1/8 inch thick. In a separate bowl, combine the cheese and bread crumbs.

Cover the bottom of the prepared casserole with a thin layer of potatoes. Lightly sprinkle with the cheese mixture and ladle about 1/2 cup of the cream mixture over the crumbs. Press down firmly, and repeat the process until the casserole is full, leaving about a 1/2-inch space at the top. Cover with aluminum foil and bake for 40 minutes. Remove the foil and bake for an additional 20 minutes, or until the top of the gratin is golden brown. Remove from the oven and let cool 15 minutes before cutting.

Cut the gratin into squares or triangles, and serve as a side dish for roasted meat, poultry, or fish.

PEAS with MINT

Makes 8 cups/Serves 8 | *Carlyn says that every household needs an "emergency pantry" dish that can be made quickly from ingredients you are likely to have on had but that looks as if you planned it. Frozen green peas come to the rescue. If you don't have any fresh mint, use chopped fresh basil, or finely sliced green onions.*

2 pounds frozen peas, thawed and drained

6 tablespoons (³/₄ stick) unsalted butter

¹/₄ cup heavy cream

3 tablespoons chopped fresh mint leaves, plus extra for garnish

2 teaspoons sugar

Salt and ground white pepper

In a medium-size skillet, mix the peas, butter, cream, mint, and sugar. Heat over medium heat to a simmer, and cook until the butter coats the peas. Season with salt and pepper.

Transfer to a bowl and garnish with extra chopped mint, if desired. Serve with any meat or fish, roasted, grilled, or sautéed.

ROASTED VEGETABLES

Serves 8 | *This is a great way to clean out the vegetable bin of perfectly good vegetables that you may have in quantities too small for a single vegetable dish. Use the recipe as a guideline, substituting whatever vegetables you have on hand.*

1 medium-size eggplant, quartered and cut into ¹/₂-inch-thick slices

2 yellow squash, cut into ¹/₂-inch-thick slices

2 zucchini, cut into ¹/₂-inch-thick slices

1 large red onion, cut into eighths

6—8 baby purple onions or shallots, halved

Olive oil, for coating vegetables

Salt and ground black pepper

3 large portobello mushroom caps, sliced thickly

1 pound asparagus, trimmed and halved

2 green bell peppers, seeded and cut into chunks

2 red bell peppers, seeded and cut into chunks

Preheat the oven to 425°F.

In a large bowl, place the eggplant, squash, zucchini, onions, and shallots. Toss with olive oil until fully coated, stirring in salt and pepper (reserve the bowl for later use). Place the vegetables on a baking sheet in the middle of the oven and roast, shaking the pan occasionally, until tender and golden, 20 to 25 minutes. Remove the vegetables from the oven and allow to cool to room temperature.

In the same bowl as was used earlier, toss the mushrooms, asparagus, and peppers with olive oil to coat well, and season with salt and pepper. Place on another baking sheet and roast, shaking the pan occasionally, until slightly golden and softened, 15 to 18 minutes. Remove the vegetables from the oven and allow to cool to room temperature.

Arrange the roasted vegetables by color and shape on a decorative platter. These delicious vegetables can also be served with crumbled feta cheese. Or serve sprinkled with Balsamic Vinaigrette (page 92).

CAULIFLOWER FRITTERS with LEMON-PEPPER MAYONNAISE

Serves 8 to 10 | *Carlyn first made these for hors d'oeuvres at catered parties. But they were so popular that they became an all-purpose vegetable, served as a side dish and as an appetizer.*

LEMON-PEPPER MAYONNAISE

 $^1/_2$ **cup mayonnaise**

 $^1/_2$ **cup sour cream**

 1 tablespoon grated lemon zest

 1 teaspoon fresh lemon juice

 1 teaspoon cracked black pepper

 $^1/_2$ **teaspoon Tabasco sauce**

 Kosher salt

CAULIFLOWER

 3 quarts water

 1 tablespoon salt (optional)

 1 head cauliflower, broken into florets

 Vegetable oil, as needed, for frying

FRITTER BATTER

 1 cup all-purpose flour

 $^3/_4$ **cup lukewarm water**

 1 tablespoon vegetable oil

 $^1/_4$ **teaspoon kosher salt**

 $^1/_8$ **teaspoon ground red pepper**

 2 large egg whites

Make the Lemon-Pepper Mayonnaise: In a bowl, whisk together all the ingredients; cover and refrigerate at least 2 hours before serving as directed.

Make the cauliflower: Preheat the oven to 200°F. In a 6-quart pot, bring 3 quarts of water (salt if you desire) to a boil. Add the cauliflower florets and boil, uncovered, for 3 to 4 minutes. Transfer to a colander, drain, and immediately plunge into an ice-water bath. When chilled, drain very well and coarsely chop the florets into $^1/_2$ -inch pieces. Wrap in paper toweling and set aside until ready to fry.

Make the fritter batter: In a medium-size bowl, beat the flour, water, oil, salt, and red pepper together until smooth. Cover the batter and let it stand for at least 30 minutes. Just before frying, beat the egg whites until stiff peaks form, and fold into batter until the mixture is smooth.

Make the fritters: In a large, heavy, deep pot or deep-fryer, pour oil to a depth of at least 4 inches. Heat to 350°F. When the oil is hot, gently fold the cauliflower florets into the fritter batter. Drop by teaspoonfuls into the hot oil and fry in batches until golden brown, 4 to 5 minutes. Remove the browned fritters with a slotted spoon and transfer to a baking pan lined with paper towels; drain well. Place on additional paper toweling on another baking sheet, and keep warm in the oven until all the fritters are fried and ready to be served in a napkin-lined basket or bowl. Accompany with a small bowl of Lemon-Pepper Mayonnaise as a dip.

CRIMSON RED LENTIL and FAVA BEAN RELISH

Makes 1¹/₂ quarts/Serves 6 | *When Carlyn got bored with the popular and ubiquitous three-bean salad, this colorful, flavorful two-legume salad was the result. You can make it ahead and refrigerate it for two or three days before serving, which enhances the flavor.*

Salted water, as needed

2 cups fresh fava beans (see Note)

3 cups chicken broth (page 66)

1¹/₂ cups baby red lentils

1 cup finely diced plum tomatoes

³/₄ cup olive oil

¹/₂ cup finely chopped onion

¹/₂ cup finely chopped celery

¹/₄ cup balsamic vinegar

2 tablespoons chiffonade-cut fresh basil (a fine julienne)

2 tablespoons sugar

1 tablespoon fresh garlic

Salt and freshly ground black pepper

Fill a large pot with lightly salted water. Bring to a boil and cook the fava beans until crisp-tender, about 3 minutes. Drain the beans and transfer to a large bowl to chill quickly. Set aside.

Meanwhile, in a heavy stockpot, bring the chicken broth to a boil. Add the lentils and cook, stirring occasionally, for 5 to 7 minutes. Remove from the heat and cool completely. The lentils should absorb all of the extra cooking liquid.

In a large bowl, combine the remaining ingredients. Stir in the cold lentils and fava beans, and refrigerate.

Serve with cold roasted chicken or salmon, along with a green salad and a loaf of French bread.

Note: Fava beans may be found in the frozen section of your grocery store, preshelled and blanched. Notify guests that you are serving favas, because the beans should be avoided by people taking monoamine oxidase (MAO) inhibitors and by a few individuals who carry a rare but serious allergy to favas.

WHEAT BERRY and WILD RICE SALAD

Serves 6 | *In the 1990s, Carlyn was searching for a more exciting alternative to both plain white potatoes and plain white rice as side dishes, and created a grain bar for catered events. This recipe was so popular that it became part of her permanent repertoire.*

10 cups salted water

$^1/_2$ **pound raw wild rice, rinsed (about 1$^1/_2$ cups)**

$^1/_2$ **pound wheat berries, rinsed (see Note)**

3 scallions, sliced

$^1/_2$ **cup shelled pistachio nuts, toasted and chopped**

$^1/_4$ **cup dried apricots, chopped**

6 tablespoons red wine vinegar

3 tablespoons vegetable oil

1 tablespoon honey

1 teaspoon minced shallots

Salt and pepper

In a large saucepan, bring 5 cups of salted water to a boil. Add the wild rice and cook, uncovered, stirring occasionally, until tender, about 40 minutes. Drain and transfer to a bowl. Chill, covered, until cold, approximately 2 hours.

Meanwhile, repeat the process for the wheat berries. They are cooked when they begin to split slightly, and may take longer to cook than the wild rice.

Place the chilled wild rice and wheat berries in a large bowl. Add the scallions, pistachios, and apricots.

In a small bowl, whisk together the vinegar, oil, honey, shallots, salt, and pepper until well mixed. Pour the dressing over the wild rice salad and toss well. This salad may be made two days ahead; however, in that case do not add the pistachios until ready to serve, or else they will become soft. Keep chilled and covered in the refrigerator.

Serve as a side dish to accompany hearty meats and poultry such as lamb, pork and duck. This also works well as a vegetarian main dish.

Note: Wheat berries are whole, unpolished wheat kernels that have a crunchy texture and nutty flavor. Presoaking for 8 hours speeds up the cooking. Soft white wheat berries cook faster than hard red wheat berries.

GRILLING

From Barbecue to Oktoberfest

Family Favorites

BARBECUED PESTO TURKEY BREAST 195

BERGHOFF BOURBON SHORT RIBS 196

ZESTY GARLIC SHRIMP 197

SESAME SEED TUNA 198

BANANA-COCONUT CHICKEN 200

MARINATED BEEF TENDERLOIN 201

ITALIAN SAUSAGE 202

GRILLED VEGETABLES with RED PEPPER AÏOLI 203

RED POTATOES VINAIGRETTE 204

S'MORES on the GRILL 205

This chapter belongs to Carlyn. Of the entire Berghoff clan, she is the one who most loves to grill. "I could live without a stove, but not without a grill," she says. "Weather permitting, my family grills four nights a week." Most of the time Carlyn's husband, Jim McClure, the acknowledged grillmeister of the family, wears the apron and wields the tongs.

Grilling is also her favorite way to entertain for the extended family and friends. She believes it doesn't matter how basic or how elaborate your grilling equipment—from a simple kettle grill to a hooded gas grill with all the bells and whistles. Nor does the size of your real estate count when it comes to having a good time. You can grill on a postage-stamp patio and serve indoors, or do it in the garden—and still have a first-rate feast.

What she loves about grilling is the informality, the participation that allows the hosts to enjoy their own party and spend time with guests, and, of course, the memories.

Her favorite kind of grill party is the kabob bar (see page 263). Premarinated ingredients are assembled for skewering, and guests make their own skewers and take them to the grill. She always appoints one or two men or women skilled at cooking on the grill to be grillmeister for the evening or a part thereof.

When it comes to outdoor barbecues, Carlyn learned from the biggest and the best. Every year, since 1984, the Berghoff Restaurant threw a mammoth Oktoberfest featuring grilled food plus Berghoff Oktoberfest beer brewed specially for the season. By comparison to that annual party for upward of fifty thousand guests, a backyard barbecue for friends and family seems like a walk in the park. (To throw your own Oktoberfest, see page 263.)

September Oktoberfest

The world's largest outdoor festival, Oktoberfest, held annually in Munich, Germany, began on October 12, 1810, when Crown Prince Ludwig (later King Ludwig I of Bavaria) married Princess Therese of Saxony-Hildburghausen. The royal couple invited the citizens of Munich to celebrate with a festival held on the fields in front of the city gates. The fields have been called Thereienwiese (Theresa's fields) ever since. Today 6 million visitors from all over the world celebrate what locals affectionately call "The Wies'n."

Berghoff's Oktoberfest started in September 1984 and was so well attended that it moved outdoors in 1985. It has been held every year except for 2001—in the demoralizing aftermath of 9/11.

Why was Berghoff's Oktoberfest always held in September? "Have you ever tried to spend time outdoors in Chicago in October?" asks Jan. "It's too cold!"

Berghoff's Oktoberfest featured Berghoff Oktoberfest beer, bratwurst and sauerkraut on buns, barbecued chicken thighs, corn on the cob, huge pretzels, root beer, beer, and wine. Every year, special disposable cups were used for the beer. In 1998, after the 100th-anniversary Oktoberfest, they counted the used cups—one hundred thousand of them.

Marinating

What to use:

- Original marinades such as Balsamic Vinaigrette (page 92), or your own favorite recipe

- Purchased oil-and-vinegar-based salad dressings in a world of flavors

- Dry seasoning mixes to which you add oil and vinegar

- Fruit juices: pineapple for ribs, orange for fish, and a squeeze of lemon or lime juice for poultry

- Dry spices and herb rubs

How long to marinate:

- Proteins such as meat and poultry: 2 hours

- Fish: 15 minutes if the marinade includes acid (citrus, vinegar, wine); 1 hour or longer if the marinade contains no acid (pesto, soy sauce, garlic, pepper)

- Vegetables: 1 to 2 hours

- Always cover and refrigerate.

If you are using dry rubs, you may marinate the ingredients overnight, refrigerated. Brush off the herbs and spices before grilling. You may also marinate ingredients overnight in nonacidic marinades, such as pesto.

Do not reuse marinades cold, especially those used for fish or other protein foods. Either bring the marinade to a boil and boil for 10 minutes, or make a fresh batch for basting or saucing. Shortcut: Double the recipe and use half for marinating; save half for saucing.

Marinate vegetables in separate zippered plastic bags in the refrigerator to prevent the transfer of flavors. Before marinating, it helps to blanch dense vegetables such as baby carrots, broccoli, cauliflower, and whole onions: Drop into boiling, lightly salted water for 2 to 3 minutes, then shock in ice water and drain. Small, whole potatoes or 2-inch potato chunks and large carrot chunks should be parboiled briefly, about 8 minutes.

Food Safety

When using knives, spoons, cutting boards, and bowls to cut, marinate, mix, or otherwise prepare protein foods—uncooked meat, fish, or poultry—for the grill, always immediately consign used preparation implements to the dishwasher, and wash with hot, soapy water. To prevent cross-contamination, use only fresh, clean implements and containers for the cooked food to be served. Be especially vigilant against serving with the same unwashed tongs, spatulas, or forks that have been used to transfer or pierce uncooked or semicooked protein foods during the grilling process.

Because the temperature of the grill changes with outdoor weather conditions, such as wind, the surest way to test foods, especially protein, for doneness is to use an instant-read thermometer. Barbecue forks with thermometers in the handles are widely available.

And remember that, once removed from the source of heat, meat continues to cook for several minutes. The internal temperature may rise by 10 to 20 degrees. The safest, surest way

to check the temperature accurately is to measure the final temperature with a meat thermometer. Covering meat accelerates and extends this residual cooking, so Carlyn recommends letting meats and poultry stand briefly, uncovered, before carving or serving.

Internal Temperature Ranges*

Ground meat and meat mixtures
(beef, pork, veal, lamb)—160°F

Fresh beef, veal, and lamb
medium rare—145°F
medium—160°F
well done—170°F

Poultry (chicken and turkey)
whole—165°F
breast—165°F

Duck and goose—165°F

Fresh pork
medium—160°F
well done—170°F

Ham
raw—160°F
precooked—140°F

Egg dishes—160°F

*Recommended by the USDA

BARBECUED PESTO TURKEY BREAST

Serves 8 | *Carlyn loves turkey, and not just on holidays. And she loves pesto. One day she had a turkey epiphany and combined the two. This is now a classic at her catering company and a favorite at home. The turkey breast can marinate for two days, refrigerated. And, she only uses fresh turkey, which she orders from her neighborhood butcher.*

1 (6–8 pound) boneless turkey breast

1 cup pesto, without cheese (page 123)

¹/₂ cup olive oil

1 cup prepared barbecue sauce

Rinse the turkey in cold water, pat dry. Place in a large bowl. Combine the pesto and olive oil, and pour over the turkey, coating evenly. Cover and refrigerate overnight.

Heat the grill. Brush the turkey with the barbecue sauce and place on the grill. Turn the turkey as it cooks, brushing with sauce. Grill for 30 to 40 minutes, or until golden brown.

Preheat the oven to 300°F. Transfer the turkey to a roasting pan and roast in the oven until it reaches an internal temperature of 160°F, about 45 minutes. Remove immediately. The turkey will continue to cook by residual heat, and its internal temperature will rise.

Serve with Grilled Vegetables (page 203) and Red Potatoes Vinaigrette (page 204).

Note: For a shortcut, use prepared pesto.

BERGHOFF BOURBON SHORT RIBS

Serves 8 | *Carlyn created this, as she calls it, "one-pan wonder." She was inspired by the Berghoff bourbon dishes and created something new. The ribs cook in their own juices, and the bourbon seals in the flavor.*

6 pounds boneless beef short ribs (or 9 pounds of bone-in)

Salt and ground black pepper

6 cups beef stock, or enough to cover ribs in pan

2 ¹/₂ cups Berghoff bourbon

2 cubes beef bouillon

1¹/₂ cups prepared barbecue sauce

Nonstick cooking spray

Preheat the oven to 350°F.

Rinse the ribs in cold water, pat dry. Place in a large (18 by 12-inch or larger) roasting pan. Season with salt and pepper. Add enough beef stock to completely cover the ribs. Stir in 2 cups of the bourbon and the bouillon cubes. Cover the pan tightly with foil and place on the middle rack of the oven. Roast for 3 hours, or until very tender. Remove from the oven. Remove the ribs from the braising liquid and keep warm.

Skim off and discard the fat from the top of the braising liquid and over high heat reduce the liquid to 1 to 1¹/₂ cups, 35 to 40 minutes. Stir in the barbecue sauce and ¹/₂ cup of reserved bourbon and mix well. Heat to a boil, remove from the heat, and set aside.

Heat the grill. Spray each rib with cooking spray, and grill to heat completely through and brown slightly. Brush with the barbecue sauce mixture and grill over low heat until well caramelized, brushing with extra barbecue sauce as needed. Don't allow to char or burn.

Serve the ribs stacked on a platter with potato salad, roasted corn on the cob, and steamed green beans.

ZESTY GARLIC SHRIMP

Serves 8 | *Carlyn created this recipe for her family one day when she needed something fast to make for dinner. On the way home from work, she stopped by the market and purchased peeled and deveined shrimp. When she reached home, she mixed the simple marinade from pantry ingredients, and marinated the shrimp. By the time the table was set and the grill was ready, it took no more than six minutes to grill the shrimp. With a salad and a loaf of bread, this makes a meal. It can also be one dish in a barbecue.*

¼ cup finely chopped fresh cilantro

3 tablespoons olive oil

2 tablespoons fresh lemon juice

2 cloves garlic, minced

2 teaspoons lemon zest

½ teaspoon red pepper flakes

16 jumbo shrimp, peeled and deveined

Preheat the grill. In a medium-size bowl, whisk cilantro, oil, lemon juice, garlic, lemon zest, and pepper flakes together to make a marinade.

Add the shrimp, toss to coat, cover, and refrigerate to marinate about 20 minutes before grilling. Drain the shrimp before grilling and, in a small saucepan, heat the marinade to boiling; keep warm until ready to use with grilled shrimp.

Grill the shrimp for 2 to 3 minutes per side over medium heat, and toss in the heated marinade before serving with other barbecue fare.

SESAME SEED TUNA

Serves 8 | *"Interesting ingredients make for interesting eating," says Jan, who wanted to grill seafood other than shrimp or salmon for a family dinner. Tuna marinated in a fragrant Asian marinade, then rolled in black and white sesame seeds and grilled on skewers, was an inspiration that is now a family favorite and a menu item when she's entertaining. For a spicier dish, roll the tuna in cracked black pepper.*

3 tablespoons soy sauce

2 tablespoons rice wine or sherry vinegar

1 tablespoon brown sugar

1 tablespoon peeled, minced fresh ginger

1 tablespoon minced fresh garlic

2 pounds fresh tuna, cut into 1-inch cubes

¹/₄ cup mixed black and white sesame seeds

Pickled ginger, if desired

8 soaked bamboo or metal skewers

Preheat the grill.

In a medium-size bowl, mix the soy sauce, wine, brown sugar, ginger, and garlic together to make a marinade. Add the tuna, toss well, cover, and refrigerate for about 30 minutes before grilling. Remove from the marinade and roll in the mixed sesame seeds before grilling. Discard the leftover marinade.

Thread the cubes of tuna onto the presoaked skewers and grill for 2 minutes per side over medium heat. Serve with coleslaw and fresh fruit. Accompany with pickled ginger, if desired.

Variation: Instead of using sesame seeds, roll the tuna cubes in coarsely ground black peppercorns before grilling. Alternate sweet red peppers and mushroom caps with tuna on skewers if desired before grilling.

BANANA-COCONUT CHICKEN

Serves 8 | *Carlyn usually matches the drink to the menu, but in this case, she created a menu in the summer of 2004 to celebrate the sixtieth anniversary of the Mai Tai. This rum-based cocktail was created in 1944 by Victor Bergeron, proprietor of Trader Vic's restaurants. Banana-coconut chicken is the entrée, served with grilled vegetables and a bean salad and, of course, Mai Tais.*

MARINADE

2 tablespoons unsalted butter

3 large shallots, minced (1 cup)

2 large very ripe bananas, mashed (1 cup)

³/₄ cup chicken broth

³/₄ cup orange juice

2 tablespoons brown sugar

1¹/₂ teaspoons salt

1 teaspoon ground black pepper

¹/₄ cup coconut-flavored rum

CHICKEN

2¹/₂ pounds skinless, boneless chicken breasts and/or thighs, cut into large chunks

Nonstick cooking spray

Make the marinade: In a medium-size saucepan, melt the butter. Add the shallots and sauté over low heat for 2 minutes, stirring, without adding color to shallots. Add the banana, chicken broth, orange juice, brown sugar, salt, and pepper, and simmer over low heat 5 minutes. Remove from the heat and cool to room temperature. Stir in the rum. Transfer the ingredients to a blender or food processor and process until smooth. Chill completely.

Make the chicken: Place the blended marinade in a large bowl; add the chicken and toss well to coat. Cover and refrigerate to marinate for at least 1 hour before grilling.

Preheat the grill. Remove the chicken from the marinade and discard the marinade. Spray the chicken with cooking spray and grill over medium heat on all sides, 2 to 3 minutes per side, until browned and cooked through.

Serve the chicken on a platter or in a large bowl, and accompany with grilled vegetables and a bean salad.

MARINATED BEEF TENDERLOIN

Serves 8 | *Carlyn calls this another one of her "one-pot wonders." Beef tenderloin is a classic cut, and this makes a great entrée for a dinner party when you don't want a lot of mess. It's simply marinated, then grilled—or broiled if you like—and served with your choice of grilled vegetables, roasted potatoes, and a green salad.*

3–4 tablespoons vegetable oil

3 tablespoons minced fresh parsley

2 tablespoons fresh lemon juice

2 tablespoons Worcestershire sauce

2 tablespoons A.1. sauce

1 tablespoon mustard powder

1¹⁄₂ teaspoons ground black pepper

2¹⁄₂ pounds beef tenderloin, cut into 8 steaks or mignons

In a medium-size bowl, whisk together the oil, parsley, lemon juice, Worcestershire, A.1., mustard, and pepper. Add the beef, toss to coat, cover, and refrigerate to marinate for at least 2 hours before grilling.

Preheat the grill. Remove the beef from the marinade and discard the marinade. Grill the steaks for 3 to 4 minutes per side, or to the desired degree of doneness.

Serve with roasted potatoes, grilled vegetables, and a green salad.

ITALIAN SAUSAGE

Serves 8 | *Our family friend Linda Coronato, who created this recipe, once remarked that there is more than one way to serve Italian sausage. Splitting and marinating the sausages creates a new flavor profile.*

3–4 tablespoons olive oil

3 tablespoons chopped fresh oregano

3 cloves garlic, minced

2 teaspoons crushed fennel seeds

1½ teaspoons salt

1½ teaspoons ground black pepper

2½ pounds fresh sweet Italian sausage links, split

In a medium-size bowl, whisk together the oil, oregano, garlic, fennel seeds, and salt and pepper to make a marinade. Add the sausage, toss to coat, cover, and refrigerate to marinate at least 2 hours before grilling.

Preheat the grill. Remove the sausages from the marinade and discard the marinade. Grill the sausages for 4 minutes per side, or until cooked completely through.

Serve with German Potato Salad (page 81), and Grilled Vegetables (page 203).

GRILLED VEGETABLES with RED PEPPER AÏOLI

Serves 8 | *According to Carlyn, grilled vegetables are a must-have for every barbecue party, especially when farmers' markets are in full swing.*

2 eggplants, sliced ½ inch thick lengthwise

2 yellow squash, sliced ½ inch thick lengthwise

2 zucchini, sliced ½ inch thick lengthwise

2 jumbo peeled carrots, sliced ½ inch thick lengthwise

2 bell peppers (your choice of colors), halved and seeded

3 medium-size red onions, quartered and skewered

3 portobello mushroom caps, cleaned

12 spears thick asparagus

Salt and ground black pepper

Olive oil

Red Pepper Aïoli as needed (page 125)

When serving, the grilled vegetables may be cut into strips or cubes, and the asparagus left whole or cut into thirds. Serve as a side dish at your barbecue, or tuck into pita pockets to make a delicious sandwich. Garnish with Red Pepper Aïoli.

Preheat the grill.

Place the vegetables in a large bowl and toss with olive oil until fully coated. Season with salt and pepper. Place the vegetables directly on the hot grill to get good markings. Grill just to the desired degree of doneness. (Remember that the hot vegetables will continue to cook after they are removed from the grill.) Transfer in a single layer to a baking sheet, and allow to cool to room temperature before using. (After cooling, these vegetables may be refrigerated until ready to use.)

RED POTATOES VINAIGRETTE

Serves 8 | *This is such a relief from mashed potatoes and mayonnaise-based potato salad, says Carlyn. It's tasty, easy to make, and much safer than potato salad for picnics and outdoor eating because of the oil-and-vinegar dressing.*

3–4 quarts water

1¹/₂ pounds small unpeeled red-skinned potatoes (1–1¹/₂ inches in diameter), scrubbed and halved

3–4 tablespoons olive oil

3 tablespoons Dijon mustard

2 tablespoons white wine vinegar

2 tablespoons minced fresh rosemary

1 clove garlic, minced

1 teaspoon kosher salt

¹/₂ teaspoon cracked black pepper

In a 6-quart pot, heat the water over high heat until boiling. Add the potatoes and parboil, 8 to 10 minutes. Remove from the heat and drain well. Allow the potatoes to cool completely before marinating.

In a large bowl, whisk together the remaining ingredients to make a marinade. Add the well-drained potato halves and toss gently to coat; cover and let marinate for at least 2 hours before serving. The potatoes may be refrigerated overnight but should be brought to room temperature before serving.

Place in a serving bowl and use to accompany grilled or roasted meat, poultry, or fish, and a dressed green salad.

S'MORES on the GRILL

Makes 12 S'mores/Serves 6-8 | *Carlyn and Jan enjoyed this recipe together during their mother-daughter days at a Girl Scouts sleepover camp. Over the years they have prepared it for the children and their friends. "Go ahead," says Carlyn, "give your kids a thrill."*

24 honey-graham crackers, separated into squares

12 (2-inch) squares crispy rice or plain bar chocolate

12 large marshmallows

Preheat the grill.

On a serving platter, preassemble the S'more bases: each graham cracker square topped with one chocolate square. Place the marshmallows on a cleaned tree twig or long wooden skewer, and toast over the grill until golden brown. Place one heated marshmallow on top of each chocolate square. Top with a second graham cracker square to make a sandwich. Serve immediately.

Option: S'mores may be made ahead and individually wrapped in foil. When ready to serve, place the packets on the grill briefly, to melt the chocolate and the marshmallow. Serve hot.

DESSERTS

Happy Endings

Berghoff Classics

FLOURLESS CHOCOLATE CAKE 209

APPLE STRUDEL 210

OLD WORLD APPLE CAKE 212

ROOT BEER FLOAT 213

BLACK FOREST CAKE 214

RICE PUDDING 217

BLUEBERRY PIE 218

WHITE CHOCOLATE MOUSSE 220

YULE LOG 222

Carlyn's Favorites

SEASONAL BERRY SHORTCAKE with LEMON-CHANTILLY CREAM 224

ALMOND-PEAR TARTLETS 226

CRÈME BRÛLÉE 228

PECAN DIAMONDS 229

PISTACHIO CHEESECAKE SQUARES 230

SACHER TORTE CAKES 232

PEOPLE WHO DINED AT BERGHOFF'S for the past hundred years always enjoyed desserts. During the holiday season, they enjoyed them twice as much, because the dessert orders always doubled. In this chapter we celebrate dessert, the happy ending to every dinner—and often lunch—with the top traditional Berghoff's favorites, plus six of Carlyn's most popular Artistic Events desserts.

During the 1960s, Berghoff's was the destination for shoppers, museum visitors, and people attending theater and concert matinees. They would come in for afternoon dessert and coffee, and, in summer, for chilled May wine with a strawberry in the glass.

The world seems to be spinning so much faster now. But rather than relinquish the sweet things of life, we adjust. For example, several of the desserts in this chapter can be made in advance and refrigerated, and a few even frozen. When you refrigerate desserts, be sure to wrap them airtight and, if possible, place them in a large covered plastic container to prevent flavor transfer. The refrigerator, with all its aromas from pickles, cold cuts, olives, cheeses, and leftovers, is the enemy of delicate desserts.

Dessert is the last and some say the most important course in any meal, leaving a good taste in everyone's mouth. But desserts can be their own event. We often host a dessert buffet after a movie, concert, or play. Sometimes we invite friends over just for dessert—and then surprise them with a sweet table (see page 265). And a dessert buffet is always a showstopper at a big holiday party.

FLOURLESS CHOCOLATE CAKE

Makes two 9-inch round cakes/Serves 16 to 24 | *Herman points out that flourless chocolate cake—which became so trendy in the 1980s—isn't new at all, but an old German recipe that was on the menu long before he and Jan took over the restaurant in 1986. However, the sudden trendiness didn't hurt the sales of this dessert.*

1³/₄ pounds (7 sticks) unsalted butter, plus extra for pans

¹/₂ cup dried plain bread crumbs

1¹/₂ pounds bittersweet chocolate, cut into small pieces

2¹/₄ cups granulated sugar (1 pound)

1¹/₄ cups brewed coffee (strongly brewed from a very dark roast)

13 large eggs, beaten slightly

Unsweetened whipped cream, for garnish

Fresh berries, for garnish

Preheat the oven to 325°F. Line two 9-inch round cake pans with heavy-duty aluminum foil, with a ¹/₂-inch overhang. Grease the bottom and sides well with butter. Dust the bottoms of each pan with crumbs to coat lightly.

In a large saucepan over medium heat, heat the butter, chocolate, sugar, and coffee, stirring occasionally, until the chocolate is completely melted. Remove from the heat and pour the chocolate mixture into a mixing bowl. Mix for 5 minutes with an electric mixer fitted with the paddle attachment; slowly add the eggs, one at a time, until incorporated. Continue mixing for another 3 minutes on low speed. Pour 4¹/₂ cups of batter into each prepared cake pan and place on a sheet pan filled with ¹/₂ inch of hot water. Bake for 55 to 60 minutes, until a food pick comes out almost clean when tested in the center of the cake. Remove from the oven and place the pans on a wire rack to cool completely to room temperature. Cover and refrigerate overnight before removing the cake from the pans and peeling off the aluminum foil. (If the cakes crack slightly, push back together gently.)

Slice each cake into at least 8 to 12 slices, and serve with unsweetened whipped cream and fresh berries.

APPLE STRUDEL

Serves 6 to 8 | *This number one all-time most popular Berghoff dessert has a history longer than the restaurant. It takes its name from the flaky pastry used to wrap around the filling like a Strudel, the old German word for "whirlpool," or "vortex." In Germany, it was a traditional harvest-time dessert and still is today during Munich's annual Oktoberfest. The thin pastry itself originated with the Turks. Strudel is best served the same day it is baked, and warming it for ten minutes in a 350°F oven (never in a microwave) enhances it, especially if you serve it with a scoop of vanilla ice cream.*

1¼ cups apple juice

2 tablespoons cornstarch

1½ pounds Granny Smith Apples, peeled, cored, and sliced ¼ inch thick (5 cups)

½ cup dark seedless raisins

3 tablespoons granulated sugar

1 teaspoon ground cinnamon

⅓ cup chopped pecans

4 sheets phyllo dough

⅓ cup (5⅓ tablespoons) melted butter

3 tablespoons fine dry bread crumbs (see Note)

Confectioners sugar, for garnish

Vanilla ice cream, for garnish

In a small bowl, create a slurry by combining ¼ cup of the apple juice with 2 tablespoons of cornstarch; mix until smooth and set aside.

In a large saucepan over medium heat, cook the apples with the remaining apple juice, and the raisins, sugar, and cinnamon until the apples are tender, 8 to 10 minutes. Stir the cornstarch slurry (it may have settled) and add to the apple mixture, stirring constantly until smooth and lump free. Simmer 1 more minute, stirring constantly. Remove from the heat and cool. Stir in the pecans, cover, and chill.

Preheat the oven to 450°F. Line a baking sheet with parchment paper.

Lay out one phyllo sheet on a clean, flat, lightly floured surface. Brush with melted butter and sprinkle with 1 tablespoon of dry bread crumbs. Repeat this procedure with two more layers of phyllo, butter, and crumbs. Top with the fourth sheet of phyllo. Spread the apple filling evenly onto phyllo surface, leaving a ½-inch clean edge on all sides. Roll into a log, folding edges at each end beneath the log, and brush with melted

butter. Carefully place the strudel on the pre-pared baking sheet, seam side down. Bake the strudel for 15 to 18 minutes, or until golden brown. Remove from the oven and cool for 15 minutes before cutting into 2-inch slices and sprinkling with confectioners' sugar just before serving. Serve plain or with ice cream.

Note: We substitute dried cake crumbs for bread crumbs, using what is saved after leveling the tops of baked cakes before frosting (see page 216).

Strudel Secret

People always tell us our Apple Strudel tasted so much better than others they have tried. We do have one little secret. Before frosting our cakes, Berghoff's pastry chef leveled the tops of the baked layers by slicing them off evenly with a large knife. He then dried these extra pieces and made cake crumbs in a food processor. He used cake crumbs instead of dried bread crumbs in the strudel recipe.

OLD WORLD APPLE CAKE

Makes one 8-inch square cake/Serves 8 | *This recipe was a gift to Berghoff's in 1986 from Jan's good friend Alma Lach, a cookbook editor and former food editor for the* Chicago Sun-Times. *The cake is good on its own, but with caramel sauce spooned over it, it becomes spectacular.*

SAUCE

- **¹/₂ pound (2 sticks) unsalted butter**
- **1¹/₄ cups granulated sugar**
- **³/₄ cup heavy cream**
- **3 tablespoons Berghoff bourbon**
- **1 teaspoon vanilla extract**

CAKE

- **¹/₄ pound (1 stick) unsalted butter, softened, plus 1 tablespoon for pan**
- **1 cup all-purpose flour, plus 2 tablespoons for pan**
- **³/₄ cup toasted chopped pecans**
- **¹/₂ cup brown sugar**
- **¹/₂ teaspoon baking soda**
- **¹/₂ teaspoon baking powder**
- **¹/₂ teaspoon ground cinnamon**
- **¹/₈ teaspoon freshly grated nutmeg**
- **¹/₄ teaspoon salt**
- **1 cup granulated sugar**
- **1 large egg**
- **1 teaspoon vanilla extract**
- **2 cups peeled, cored, and minced Granny Smith apples**

Make the sauce: In a small saucepan, melt the butter over medium heat. Add the sugar and cream, and bring to a boil. Decrease the heat and simmer, stirring constantly, until the mixture thickens, about 10 minutes. Remove from the heat and stir in the bourbon and vanilla. Set aside until ready to use as directed.

Preheat the oven to 350°F. Butter and flour the bottom and sides of an 8-inch square cake pan. Tap out any excess flour and set the pan aside.

In a small bowl, combine the pecans and brown sugar; set aside. In another bowl, combine the flour, baking soda, baking powder, cinnamon, nutmeg, and salt; mix well and set aside.

With an electric mixer fitted with a paddle attachment, cream the butter and sugar together until light and fluffy. Add the egg and vanilla, and continue to beat until very light. Stir into the flour mixture and add the apples. Spoon the batter into the prepared pan. Sprinkle the pecan mixture over the top of the batter. Bake for 30 to 35 minutes, or until firm. Remove from the oven and place the pan on a wire rack.

Spoon half of the sauce over the hot cake and allow to cool completely before serving.

Cut the cake into eight pieces and serve with the remaining, warmed sauce on the side.

ROOT BEER FLOAT

Serves 8 | *Jan remembers this from her girlhood, and from when her children enjoyed root beer floats at A&W drive-in restaurants. "The kids would sit in the back of the car and squabble, and Herman and I would pray for the order to be delivered fast!" she recalls.*

2 quarts Berghoff root beer, chilled

8 scoops vanilla ice cream

Line up eight 10-ounce serving or float glasses. Place one scoop of ice cream in each glass, and top with 8 ounces (1 cup) of root beer. Serve immediately with a drinking straw and a long-handled spoon.

Sign advertising Berghoff's soft drinks, circa 1920.

BLACK FOREST CAKE

Makes one 10-inch round cake/Serves 8 to 10 | *The second-most-popular dessert at Berghoff's for decades, this updated version was added to the menu when Herman and Jan established the bakery in its main location on the third floor above the restaurant. Head baker Enrique Sta. Maria created this cake, and the recipe is as easy as any layer cake. You simply bake two cake layers, split them, spread them with jam, and fill them with whipped cream and cherry filling. Then you frost the cake with the remaining whipped cream and cover it with chocolate shavings. When you level the baked cakes, reserve and dry the crumbs, and freeze them for use in Apple Strudel.*

CHOCOLATE CAKE

2 cups cake flour

³/₄ cup cocoa powder

1 teaspoon baking soda

¹/₂ teaspoon baking powder

¹/₂ teaspoon salt

1¹/₂ cups granulated sugar

1 cup milk

¹/₂ cup canola oil

2 large eggs, lightly beaten

YELLOW CAKE

2 cups cake flour

2 teaspoons baking powder

¹/₄ teaspoon salt

1¹/₄ cups granulated sugar

³/₄ cup milk

¹/₂ cup canola oil

2 large eggs, lightly beaten

1 teaspoon vanilla extract

PRESERVES FILLING

1¹/₄ cup cherry or raspberry preserves, for filling

CHERRY FILLING

¹/₃ cup brown sugar

¹/₃ cup granulated sugar

¹/₄ cup cornstarch

2 (16-ounce) cans cherries in water, drained, juice reserved

¹/₂ teaspoon ground cinnamon

1 tablespoon unsalted butter

WHIPPED CREAM FILLINGS AND FROSTING

1¹/₂ quarts heavy cream

¹/₂ cup confectioners' sugar

¹/₄ cup cocoa powder

TO ASSEMBLE

1 (4-ounce) rectangular block semi-sweet baking chocolate, for garnish

Maraschino cherries, for garnish

Make the chocolate cake: Preheat the oven to 350°F. Grease and flour one 10-inch round cake pan.

In a large bowl, sift together the flour, cocoa powder, baking soda, baking powder, and salt. Stir in the sugar and set aside.

In another bowl, combine the milk, oil, and eggs, and whisk together. Pour the egg mixture into the flour mixture and incorporate. Pour the batter (it will be thin) into the prepared pan.

Bake for 25 to 30 minutes, or until firm to the touch. Remove from the oven and cool the pan on a wire rack. When cool, remove the cake from the pan and level the top carefully with a smooth or serrated 12-inch knife. Save the crumbs (see Note). Split the cake into two equal layers and set aside.

Make the yellow cake: Preheat the oven to 350°F. Grease and flour one 10-inch round cake pan.

In a large bowl, sift together the flour, baking powder, and salt. Stir in the sugar and set aside.

In another bowl, combine milk, oil, eggs, and vanilla and whisk together. Pour the egg mixture into the flour mixture and incorporate. Pour the batter (it will be thin) into the prepared pan.

Bake for 25 to 30 minutes, or until firm to the touch. Remove the pan from the oven and cool on a wire rack. When cool, remove the cake from the pan and level the top with a smooth or serrated 12-inch knife. Save the crumbs (see Note). Split the cake into two equal layers, and set aside.

Make the cherry filling: In a saucepan, mix together the sugars and cornstarch. Stir in 1 cup of the reserved cherry juice and cinnamon, and mix well. Bring to a boil, decrease the heat, and simmer over low heat, stirring constantly, until the mixture thickens. Add the butter and cherries, and stir until the butter is melted. Remove from the heat. Cool completely, stirring occasionally, before using as directed.

Make the whipped cream and chocolate whipped cream: Chill your beaters. Place the cream in a chilled bowl, and whip until stiff peaks form. You will have 16 cups of whipped cream.

Transfer 3 cups of the whipped cream to a separate bowl. Sift together the confectioners' sugar with the cocoa, and whisk into these 3 cups of whipped cream. Set aside both bowls of whipped cream.

Make the chocolate shavings: Using the coarse side of a grater, grate the chocolate along the long side of the block to create long, thin curls. Set aside.

To assemble: Place one layer of the chocolate cake on a cake round or cake plate, split side up. Spread with half of the chocolate whipped cream. Spread the chocolate whipped cream with half of the cherry filling.

Gently place the bottom layer of the yellow cake, split side up, on top of the cherry filling, and press down gently. Spread with a thin layer of raspberry preserves, followed by 1 cup of plain whipped cream.

Place the second layer of chocolate cake, split side up, on top of the whipped cream, and press down gently. Spread with the remaining chocolate whipped cream and cherry filling.

Top with the second layer of yellow cake, split side down, and press down gently. Frost the entire cake with the remaining plain whipped cream. Pat the chocolate shavings onto the sides of the cake. Pipe any remaining whipped cream into rosettes on top of the cake, and garnish with maraschino cherries.

Note: To dry cake crumbs, break the scraps saved from leveling into small pieces. Bake on a parchment-lined cookie sheet in a 200°F oven until pieces are dry but not browned, about 45 to 50 minutes. Remove from the oven and let cool.

Place the dried cake pieces in a food processor and pulse to make crumbs. Freeze the crumbs in zippered plastic bags for up to one month, for later use.

RICE PUDDING

Makes eight 1-cup servings/Serves 8 | *Rice pudding is a nostalgic old-fashioned dessert, the most comforting comfort food we can imagine. It is time-consuming to make, but worth the trouble. We like this rich, creamy pudding served cold.*

4 cups milk

1 cup heavy cream

²/₃ cup granulated sugar

1 vanilla bean, split

1 cinnamon stick

1 teaspoon salt

³/₄ cup uncooked white rice

Peel of 1 lemon

2 egg yolks

2 tablespoons cornstarch

1 cup dark seedless raisins, plumped

Cinnamon sugar, for garnish

In a 4-quart saucepan over medium heat, heat 2 cups of the milk, and the heavy cream, sugar, vanilla bean, cinnamon stick, and salt. Bring to a slow boil. Stir in the rice and lemon peel. Decrease the heat to low and simmer, uncovered, for 35 to 45 minutes, or until the rice is completely cooked, stirring occasionally. Remove and discard the lemon peel, cinnamon stick, and vanilla bean.

In a medium-size bowl, using a wire whisk, combine the remaining 2 cups of milk, egg yolks, and cornstarch until smooth. Gradually whisk ¹/₂ cup of the rice mixture into the cornstarch mixture,

until completely incorporated. Whisk in another ¹/₂ cup of the rice mixture into the cornstarch mixture. Continue to temper the cornstarch mixture until 2 cups of the rice mixture have been whisked in. While stirring constantly, slowly add the tempered mixture into the pan with the remaining rice mixture. Bring to a boil, stirring constantly. Remove from the heat.

Divide the plumped raisins among the bottoms of eight individual custard cups, and pour the pudding mixture over the raisins, about ³/₄ cup per custard cup.

Garnish each cup with cinnamon sugar. Serve at room temperature, or cover and refrigerate, and serve cold.

Variation: Other plumped, dried fruit, such as dried cherries, dried currants, dried plums or dried apricots, chopped into smaller pieces, may be substituted for the raisins. Plumped dried fruit can also be stirred directly into the pudding.

BLUEBERRY PIE

Makes one 9-inch covered pie/Serves 8 to 10 | *Blueberry pie has been on Berghoff's menu seemingly forever. In 1932, a slice cost ten cents. It's strictly seasonal, and Jan and Herman used to bring fresh blueberries to work from their home in Michigan for this pie. For an out-of-season treat, you may use frozen blueberries.*

DOUBLE PIE CRUST

2¹/₄ **cups all-purpose flour**

³/₄ **teaspoon salt**

³/₄ **cup shortening or butter-flavored shortening**

1 **large egg, beaten**

1 **tablespoon white vinegar**

3–5 **tablespoons cold water**

PIE FILLING

2 **pints fresh or frozen (thawed) blueberries (4–5 cups)**

²/₃ **cup sugar**

¹/₄ **cup all-purpose flour**

1 **teaspoon grated lemon peel**

¹/₂ **teaspoon ground cinnamon**

¹/₂ **teaspoon ground nutmeg**

2 **tablespoons butter, cut into pieces**

EGG WASH

1 **large egg mixed with 2 tablespoons water**

Make the double crust: In a large bowl, using a fork, mix 2 cups of the flour with the salt. Using a food processor, cut the shortening into the flour mixture until the texture resembles coarse crumbs. In a small bowl, stir together the egg, vinegar, and 3 tablespoons of the cold water. Add the egg mixture to the flour mixture, mixing lightly with the fork until the dough holds together, adding more water if necessary. With your hands, shape the dough into two balls, one slightly larger than the other. On a lightly floured surface and using a floured rolling pin, roll out the larger ball of dough into a 10¹/₂-inch circle. Ease the dough into a 9-inch pie tin, to line evenly. Roll out the smaller ball into a 9¹/₂-inch top crust and set aside.

Prepare the egg wash: Mix the egg and water together in a small bowl.

Preheat the oven to 400°F.

Make the filling: If using frozen berries, drain them well. In a large bowl, using a rubber spatula, gently toss together the blueberries, sugar, flour, lemon peel, cinnamon, and nutmeg. Spoon the blueberry mixture into the prepared

Berghoff's middle dining room in the 1920s.

pie crust bottom. Dot the filling with pieces of the butter. Moisten the edge of the bottom crust with water; place the top crust over the filling. Trim the dough edge, leaving a 1½-inch over-hang. Fold the overhang under, and crimp. Brush the top crust with the egg wash. Cut slits in the top of pie for ventilation. Bake the pie for 40 minutes, or until the crust is golden. (If the crust browns too quickly, cover the edge loosely with foil.) Cool the pie on a wire rack before serving.

Bygones

Some of the once-popular desserts on bygone menus include Raisin Pie and Hot Mince Pie, each 10 cents a slice in 1932. The 1944 menu offered Stewed Prunes, 15 cents; and Figs in Syrup, 15 cents.

WHITE CHOCOLATE MOUSSE

Makes 10 cups mousse/Serves 8 to 10 | *A comfort food dessert that is also elegant—that describes White Chocolate Mousse, the third-most-popular dessert among Berghoff's customers in 2005. This version, which came from our dear friend Alma Lach in 1986, is incredibly simple to make and is wonderful served on its own or garnished with chocolate shavings, fresh raspberries, and raspberry sauce. It makes a fabulous sauce for other cakes, pies, and even chocolate ice cream. And it may be made in advance and keeps well, covered, in the refrigerator for three days. Serve in champagne glasses.*

5 cups heavy cream

¹/₂ pound white chocolate, broken into small pieces

Raspberry purée, for garnish

Fresh raspberries, for garnish

Dark chocolate shavings, for garnish (page 215)

In a heavy saucepan over medium heat, bring 1 cup of the heavy cream to a boil; stir in the white chocolate and continue to stir until the chocolate is melted. Remove from the heat and cool to room temperature. Cover and refrigerate at least 4 hours.

In a large mixing bowl, using an electric mixer at high speed, beat the remaining 4 cups of heavy cream until soft peaks form. Add the white chocolate mixture to the whipped cream and continue to beat until stiff. Cover and refrigerate until ready to serve.

Using a pastry bag with an open star tip, pipe 1-plus cup of mousse into each champagne glass. (Any style dessert bowl may be used for serving, including a large bowl for a buffet table.) Drizzle with raspberry purée, and garnish with fresh raspberries. Or, sprinkle with dark chocolate shavings. This mixture may also be used to accompany other desserts, including slices of chocolate cake, pie, puddings, etc.

Sweet Tooth

Berghoff's customers never hesitated to order dessert. Berghoff Apple Strudel was always the number one best-selling dessert, and was listed on the first printed menu. In 1932, a slice sold for fifteen cents. In 2005, the restaurant sold 4,148 orders of strudel alone, and 11,637 orders of strudel with ice cream. Next came Black Forest Cake: customers ate 5,345 slices in 2005. That same year, they spooned down 3,557 dishes of White Chocolate Mousse.

White Chocolate Mousse ready to be sauced and garnished with raspberries and chocolate.

YULE LOG

Makes one 10-inch long log/Serves 12 | *Jan introduced the traditional Yule Log in 1986 and, every year after that, customers enjoyed it from the day after Thanksgiving until January 1. It's easier to make than it looks because the thin cake is rolled while still warm, and it holds its shape from then on.*

ROULADE

5 large eggs, separated

1 cup sifted confectioners' sugar, plus additional for sprinkling towel

²/₃ cup all-purpose flour

³/₄ teaspoon baking powder

1 teaspoon vanilla extract

¹/₄ teaspoon salt

GANACHE

¹/₂ pound (8 [1-ounce] squares) bittersweet or semisweet baking chocolate, chopped

1 cup heavy cream

TO ASSEMBLE

1 cup seedless raspberry preserves

2 cups heavy cream

¹/₃ cup sifted confectioners' sugar

1 teaspoon vanilla extract

Maraschino cherries, as needed

Green sanding sugar (finely granulated), as needed

Hot cinnamon candies ("red hots"), as needed, for garnish

Make the roulade: Preheat the oven to 375°F. Grease a 15¹/₂ by 10¹/₂-inch jelly roll pan or baking sheet, and line the pan with parchment paper.

In a bowl, using an electric mixer on high speed, beat the egg whites until soft peaks form; gradually add ¹/₂ cup of the confectioners' sugar, beating until the sugar completely dissolves and the whites stand in stiff peaks. In a large bowl, beat the egg yolks and remaining ¹/₂ cup of confectioners' sugar at high speed until the mixture is very thick and lemon-colored. Decrease the speed to low and add the flour, baking powder, vanilla extract and salt. Beat the mixture until well mixed, constantly scraping the bowl with a rubber spatula. Using the spatula, gently fold the beaten egg whites into the egg yolk mixture, one-third at a time.

Spoon the batter into the prepared pan, leveling out the top with the spatula. Bake for 12 to 15 minutes, until the cake springs back when lightly touched. Sprinkle confectioners' sugar lightly on a cloth towel. When the cake is done, immediately invert it onto the towel. Carefully peel the parchment paper from the bottom of the cake. Starting at one narrow end, roll up the cake, using the towel to hold it (but do not roll the towel *into* the cake). Place the cake roll, seam side down, on a wire rack; cool completely, approximately 30 minutes. While the roulade is cooling, prepare the filling. (The cake may be made in advance and covered loosely with plastic wrap to prevent drying.)

Make the ganache: In the top of a double boiler, heat the chocolate and cream together over boiling water, stirring frequently, until melted, smooth, and slightly thickened. Keep warm until ready to ice the cake as directed.

To assemble: Unroll the roulade onto a flat, clean surface; spread evenly with the raspberry preserves.

In a bowl, at medium speed, beat the heavy cream, confectioners' sugar, and vanilla extract until stiff peaks form. Spread half of the whipped cream on top of the preserves. Starting at the narrow end, roll up the cake (without using the towel). Place the cake on a wire rack set over a baking pan and refrigerate until chilled. Cover and refrigerate the remaining whipped cream until ready to decorate.

Using a metal spatula, pour and spread the ganache over the chilled roulade, spreading the glaze evenly and completely covering the top and sides. When the ganache has set, lightly score the top and sides of the cake with a fork to resemble bark. Refrigerate until chilled.

Remove the cake from the rack and place on a serving platter decorated with greenery and seasonal decor. Pipe scrolls of the remaining whipped cream over the top and around the base of the cake, and decorate with cherries and green sanding sugar.

Variation: Omit the green sanding sugar and piped whipped cream swirls. Instead, cut a diagonal slice from one end of the unfrosted log, to resemble a short stump or branch.

Then frost the longer section of the log with ganache, reserving enough ganache for the branch. Fasten the branch to the side of the log about 2 inches from one end of the log, using a little ganache to hold it in place. Then frost the branch. Continue as directed, scoring the top and sides of the cake to resemble bark. Serve the cake on a platter decorated with hot cinnamon candies.

SEASONAL BERRY SHORTCAKE with LEMON-CHANTILLY CREAM

Serves 12 | *Strawberry shortcake is a summer classic that Carlyn has given her own spin. Instead of using just strawberries, she combines ripe seasonal berries, macerates them in mint, lime juice, and liqueur, and serves them over buttermilk shortcake topped with lemon-kissed whipped cream.*

BERRY FILLING

2 pints fresh strawberries, hulled and halved

1 pint fresh blackberries

1 pint fresh blueberries

1 pint fresh raspberries

¹/₃ cup granulated sugar

1 tablespoon chopped fresh mint

1 tablespoon fresh lime juice

1 tablespoon Cointreau (or other liqueur of choice)

SHORTCAKE

2¹/₃ cups all-purpose flour

2 tablespoons granulated sugar

1 teaspoon baking powder

¹/₂ teaspoon baking soda

¹/₂ teaspoon salt

12 tablespoons (1¹/₂ sticks) unsalted butter, cut into small pieces

1 cup buttermilk

Crystallized sugar, as needed, for sprinkling

LEMON CHANTILLY CREAM

1 cup heavy cream

3 tablespoons granulated sugar

2 teaspoons lemon zest

¹/₈ teaspoon vanilla extract

Lemon zest, for garnish (see Note)

Make the berry filling: In a large bowl, combine the berries. Add the sugar, mint, lime juice, and liqueur, and gently toss to mix. Cover and refrigerate the macerated berries until ready to use.

Make the shortcake: Preheat the oven to 400°F. Line a baking sheet with parchment paper, or coat with nonstick cooking spray.

In the bowl of a food processor, combine the flour, sugar, baking powder, baking soda, and salt, and pulse until well mixed. Pulse the butter pieces, a little at a time, into the flour mixture until its texture resembles coarse crumbs. Transfer to a medium-size bowl and, with a rubber spatula, stir in the buttermilk just until the flour mixture is moistened and a dough begins to form. Transfer to a floured work surface and gently knead the dough three or four times, until it holds together. Roll out the dough, using a rolling pin, until it is ¹/₂ inch thick. With a

floured $2^1/_2$-inch biscuit cutter, cut out twelve circles from the dough (recombine the dough scraps, if necessary) and transfer to the prepared baking sheet. Sprinkle the tops lightly with crystallized sugar. Bake the shortcakes until risen, 10 minutes. Flip and continue baking until lightly golden, another 6 to 8 minutes. Remove from the oven and cool on a rack.

Make the Lemon Chantilly Cream: In a small bowl, whip the cream, sugar, lemon zest, and vanilla together until firm. Cover and chill for at least 1 hour. Serve as directed.

To assemble: Slice or split each warm shortcake in half. Place the bottom half in a bowl or soup plate, and top with $^3/_4$ cup of the mascerated berries. Spoon the Lemon Chantilly Cream over top of the berries. Cover with the top halves of the shortcake. Garnish with lemon zest. Serve immediately.

Note: Place finely julienned lemon zest in a bowl of ice water, where it will curl.

ALMOND-PEAR TARTLETS

Makes 8 tartlets/Serves 8 | *This is the most-requested dessert for fall parties at Artistic Events. It was created by Artistic Events pastry chef Chon Reynozo. The combination of frangipane-stuffed poached pears encased in flaky pastry and served warm with whipped cream or a scoop of cinnamon ice cream is unforgettable. The tartlets can be made a couple of days in advance and reheated for serving.*

FRANGIPANE

    7 ounces almond paste

    ¼ cup sugar

    ¼ cup all-purpose flour

    3 large eggs

    2 tablespoons unsalted butter

POACHED PEARS

    3 cups water

    1½ cups sugar

    1 cup white wine

    Peels and juice of 1 lemon

    1 vanilla bean

    Pinch of salt

    4 Bartlett pears, peeled and cored

TO ASSEMBLE

    1 box (2 sheets) frozen puff pastry, thawed (see Note)

    Lightly sweetened whipped cream, for garnish

    Ice cream, for garnish

Make the frangipane: Place the almond paste, sugar, flour, eggs, and butter in the bowl of a food processor. Mix until a paste forms. Set aside until ready to use as directed.

Make the poached pears: In a large saucepan, combine the water, sugar, wine, lemon peel and juice, vanilla bean, and salt. Bring to a simmer and cook until the sugar is completely dissolved. Decrease the heat. Place the pears in the poaching liquid, cover, and simmer on medium-low heat until the pears are tender, approximately 30 minutes. Turn the pears while cooking to cook evenly. Check for doneness by inserting a fork or wooden skewer into a pear. If it slides in easily, the pears are done. Remove from the heat, cover, and refrigerate until ready to use as directed, then cut each pear in half.

Preheat the oven to 400°F. Line a baking pan with parchment paper.

To assemble: Unroll the puff pastry dough onto a clean, flat surface. Using a pear half as a guide and paring knife, or with a large pear-shaped cookie cutter, cut the puff pastry dough into eight pear shapes to fit beneath each pear half, leaving an extra ¼-inch border of dough around outside of each pear shape.

Dollop 1 tablespoon of frangipane in the center of each pear-shaped piece of pastry dough, spreading the mixture out but not spreading it all the way to the sides. Place half of a poached pear, cut side down, on top of each puff pastry piece, over the frangipane. Place tarts on the prepared baking pan. Push the edges of the pastry up around sides of each pear, to cup the fruit. Bake for 20 minutes, rotate the pan in the oven, and continue to bake for 5 to 10 more minutes, or until the tarts are golden brown and the pastry puffs up. Remove from the oven, and cool the pan at room temperature on a wire rack until ready to serve.

Reheat for a few minutes in a 300°F oven, and serve with a scoop of cinnamon ice cream, or serve at room temperature with whipped cream.

Note: Puff pastry is widely available frozen in 1.1-pound packages, each containing 2 sheets. Each sheet measures $8^1/_2$ by 10 inches.

Weep-No-More Whipped Cream

There are ways to prevent whipped cream from "weeping," or separating into foam and water. The easiest is to purchase an envelope of a widely available commercial whipped cream stabilizer and follow the directions. Another option is to sprinkle 1 teaspoon of unflavored gelatin into 1 tablespoon of cold water in a medium-size bowl until it softens. Then suspend the bowl over boiling water in a makeshift double boiler, until the gelatin melts. Remove the bowl from the heat. Slowly whisk in 1 pint of heavy whipping cream, mixing well. Cover and chill the bowl for at least 1 hour. Then beat with an electric mixer to stiff peaks, adding $1/4$ cup of confectioners' sugar and 1 teaspoon of vanilla extract, if desired. Refrigerate, covered, until ready to use.

CRÈME BRÛLÉE

Serves 8 | *Before the days of the small handheld butane home-kitchen torch, crème brûlée was the signature of restaurants. And restaurants caramelized the sugar topping with much larger torches. Carlyn put it on the menu once for a sit-down dinner for one thousand guests. "We miscalculated how many torches we had," she said. "So dessert was served a little late that night. But it was good." Today, using the small, inexpensive torch available at kitchenware stores, crème brûlée is easy to make at home.*

2 whole vanilla beans, split lengthwise, seeds removed

1 quart heavy cream

8 large egg yolks

1¼ cups granulated sugar

½ cup brown sugar

Preheat the oven to 275°F.

Into a large saucepot, scrape the the centers of the vanilla beans. Add the scraped bean pods as well. Pour in the heavy cream and bring to almost a simmer over medium heat (do not boil). Remove from the heat and set aside until ready to use as directed.

In a separate bowl, whisk the yolks and granulated sugar together. Remove the vanilla bean pods from the cream and pour it into the egg yolk mixture, whisking until combined. Pour the mixture through a fine-mesh sieve into a deep bowl. Using a ladle or spoon, pop any bubbles that have formed. Ladle ³/4 cup of the mixture into each of eight 8-ounce ceramic ramekins. Set the ramekins into a baking pan that you carefully fill with hot water halfway up the sides of the ramekins. Bake for 25 minutes. Shake a

ramekin to check for firmness. If the custard is still liquefied, bake for an additional 10 minutes. Remove the ramekins from the water bath and allow to cool at room temperature for 10 minutes. Place in the refrigerator and chill until ready to serve. Remove from the refrigerator and let come to room temperature before serving.

Top each ramekin with a thin layer of sifted brown sugar, enough to cover the custard. Using a small butane torch, caramelize the sugar until it forms a crispy shell. You may also place under the broiler for no more than 30 seconds to achieve the same effect. Serve immediately.

Variation: Espresso Crème Brûlée: Follow the above recipe, adding 1 tablespoon good-quality instant espresso powder to the custard before baking.

PECAN DIAMONDS

Makes 96 pieces | *This is not your usual pecan pie, says Carlyn, who regards it not only as party fare for catered events, but pantry fare for home. She makes a batch and freezes them, then reheats them as needed.*

BASE

> 4 sticks (1 pound) unsalted butter, softened
>
> 2 cups confectioners' sugar
>
> 4 cups all-purpose flour

FILLING

> 1 pound (4 sticks) unsalted butter
>
> 2 1/4 cups light brown sugar (1 pound)
>
> 2/3 cup granulated sugar
>
> 1 3/4 cups honey
>
> 1/2 cup heavy cream
>
> 5 cups chopped pecans (1 1/4 pounds)

Preheat the oven to 350°F.

Make the base: Using an electric mixer fitted with the paddle attachment, beat the butter in a mixing bowl. Gradually add the sugar and flour alternately, beating until creamy. Spread the mixture evenly in an ungreased 17 1/2 by 13-inch baking pan. Place the tray in the freezer for 5 minutes. Remove from the freezer and bake for 8 minutes. Remove from the oven and cool the pan to room temperature on a wire rack until ready to use.

To prepare the filling: In a large, heavy saucepan, beat the butter, brown and granulated sugars, and honey over medium heat. Stir constantly with a wooden spatula until very hot. Stop stirring and bring to a boil, and boil for 4 to 5 minutes. Remove the pan from the heat and allow the mixture to cool until it stops bubbling. Stir in the heavy cream and pecans, and mix well. While still hot, spread the mixture evenly on the baked base. Bake for 15 minutes, or until the mixture solidifies and browns slightly. Remove from the oven and place the pan on a wire rack to cool to room temperature. When cool, cut into 2-inch diamonds, or any shape you wish. Cover and refrigerate up to two weeks.

PISTACHIO CHEESECAKE SQUARES

Makes 35 pieces | *Every Christmas season customers wanted green desserts, and Carlyn wasn't big on mint. So she created this, and the lovely light green cheesecake squares made it into Redbook magazine. But never mind Christmas. They're good any time of the year.*

CRUST

> 4 cups graham cracker crumbs
>
> ¼ pound (1 stick) unsalted butter, melted

FILLING

> 2 pounds cream cheese, softened
>
> 1¼ cups granulated sugar
>
> 3 tablespoons all-purpose flour
>
> 5 large eggs
>
> 2 tablespoons vanilla extract
>
> ¼ cup heavy cream
>
> 2 tablespoons fresh lemon juice
>
> 1 cup toasted pistachios, roughly chopped
>
> Finely chopped pistachios, for garnish
>
> Cinnamon sugar, for garnish

Preheat the oven to 300°F. Spray a 15½ by 10½-inch baking pan with nonstick cooking spray.

Make the crust: Mix the graham cracker crumbs and butter in a large bowl until well-combined. Spread the graham cracker crust mixture in an even layer in the prepared pan, and press down evenly. Bake the crust for 8 minutes. Remove from the oven and cool on a wire rack until ready to use.

Make the filling: Using an electric mixer fitted with the paddle attachment, beat the cream cheese for approximately 3 minutes. Gradually add the sugar and flour, and mix until creamy. Add the eggs and vanilla, and continue to mix until incorporated. Stir in the cream, lemon juice, and pistachios. Mix until all the ingredients are incorporated. Using a rubber spatula, gently spread the cheese mixture in an even layer on top of the baked crust. Bake 6 minutes; rotate the pan and bake for another 6 to 8 minutes, checking doneness by placing your finger on top of the cake (the cake should be springy to the touch but not sticky). If the cake is still slightly runny, continue baking for an additional 3 to 5 minutes, until done. Remove from the oven and place the pan on a wire rack to cool to room temperature. Cover and refrigerate until ready to cut.

When fully cooled, cut into 2-inch squares (using a metal ruler to measure for marking) and serve. Or cut into twenty-five 2 by 3-inch rectangles, and serve. Garnish tops with chopped pistachios and cinnamon sugar.

SACHER TORTE CAKES

Makes eight 2¹/₂-inch round cakes/Serves 8 | *This is Carlyn's version of Death by Chocolate, and she stands by it. The original Sachertorte, which is trademarked by the Sacher Hotel in Vienna, was created there in 1832 by Franz Sacher. But when Carlyn ate Sachertorte at the hotel, she decided that her version, created by pastry chef Chon Reynozo, was much better.*

GANACHE

1 pound bittersweet chocolate, chopped coarsely

2 cups heavy cream

RASPBERRY SAUCE

2¹/₄ cups frozen raspberries, thawed

2 tablespoons confectioners' sugar

CAKES

³/₄ cup canola oil

1¹/₂ cups granulated sugar

1 large egg

2 cups all-purpose flour

¹/₂ cup cocoa powder

1 tablespoon baking soda

¹/₂ teaspoon salt

1 cup brewed black coffee

1 cup buttermilk

1 cup seedless raspberry preserves

6 fresh mint sprigs, for garnish

Make the ganache: In a double boiler, combine the chocolate and heavy cream; heat gently, stirring occasionally, until the chocolate is melted and the ingredients are well combined and smooth. Cool slightly.

Make the raspberry sauce: In an electric blender, combine the raspberries and confectioners' sugar, and blend until smooth. Strain the sauce through a fine sieve or cheesecloth to remove the seeds. Refrigerate until serving.

Preheat the oven to 300°F. Spray a 15¹/₂ by 10¹/₂-inch baking pan with nonstick cooking spray and line with parchment paper.

Make the cakes: Using an electric mixer, beat the oil and sugar until well blended. Add the egg, and continue to mix. Set aside.

In a second medium-size mixing bowl, sift all the dry ingredients together. Mix the coffee and buttermilk together in separate small bowl. Slowly add the coffee mixture to egg mixture, alternating with the dry ingredients, ending with the dry ingredients. Continue mixing at low speed for 4 to 5 minutes, scraping the bowl occasionally, until the batter is smooth. The cake batter should have a shiny appearance and will be thin.

A glass of traditional May wine with a strawberry.

Pour the batter into the prepared pan and bake for 12 to 15 minutes, or until a food pick comes out clean from the center of the cake. Remove from the oven and allow the cake pan to cool to room temperature. Remove the cake from the pan and, using a bread knife, cut in half through the middle to make two $7^3/4$ by $10^1/2$-inch pieces. Spread the raspberry preserves on one half of the cake. Invert the other half of the cake, bottom side up, and place on top of the raspberry preserves. Press gently to hold firmly. Place the raspberry-filled layer cake in the freezer for 1 hour. Remove from the freezer when firm and, using a biscuit cutter, cut into 8 by $2^1/2$-inch rounds.

Place the cakes on a wire rack with a tray underneath to catch the chocolate. With a ladle, pour the warm ganache over the top and sides of the cakes, allowing the chocolate to drip down and coat all sides evenly. Refrigerate the cakes for 30 minutes before serving.

For each cake, drizzle 3 tablespoons of the raspberry sauce over the bottom of a dessert plate. Gently place the cake in the center of the sauce and garnish with a fresh mint sprig.

BREAKFAST & BRUNCH

Bright Beginnings

Berghoff Classics

TOMATO, BASIL, and FRESH MOZZARELLA QUICHE 238

BAVARIAN APPLE PANCAKES 240

BERGHOFF EGGS BENEDICT 242

CORNED BEEF HASH 244

BERGHOFF BREAKFAST SANDWICH 246

Carlyn's Favorites

BLUEBERRY MINI-MUFFINS 247

CARLYN'S BREAKFAST GRATIN with LEEKS and SWISS CHEESE 248

FRITTATA with PROSCIUTTO and FRESH MOZZARELLA 249

CARLYN'S KIDS' PANCAKES 250

FRENCH TOAST STICKS 251

ALL OF US TODAY—especially the Berghoff grandchildren—take the weekend for granted. But before the nineteenth century, there was no weekend as such, and the working class (that would be us) worked seven days a week. Certainly in the late 1800s, our founder Herman Berghoff took time off only to go to mass on Sunday. The rest of his week was spent managing his Fort Wayne, Indiana, brewery and running the Berghoff Café in Chicago. When Prohibition inspired him to expand the bar into a full-service restaurant with a bona fide menu, he started serving breakfast. Berghoff's remained a popular weekend brunch destination "Open every day—9 A.M. to Midnight" (according to the menu), where daily breakfast was served until 1932, and Sunday brunch until 1942.

Being a restaurant family gave us renewed appreciation for any precious leisure time. We saw the weekend as a gift that we celebrated at Jan and Herman's house with a brunch for family and friends (see page 265). "We looked forward to Sunday because that was the only day during the week when we were together as a family all day," says Jan.

It seems to us that, for any host, brunch is the most forgiving of meals. It can be served buffet style, and everything is prepared in advance. Your only duty is to refill glasses and replenish the serving dishes, so you can enjoy visiting with your guests.

We invite guests at eleven A.M. And Jan serves everything in glass—bowls, platters, plates—to show off the food and provide a uniform background that almost disappears. One of the dishes that everyone loves is the huge bowl of freshly cut fruit. She uses whatever is perfectly ripe and in season, and it's a real treat to eat as much fruit as you want without having to peel, seed, or slice it.

Another dish people never seem to tire of is quiche. As third-generation Herman says, "Who doesn't like quiche? It works just as well at home as it works in the restaurant. You bake it in advance, you can serve it warm or at room temperature, even cold, and it's easy on the cooks." And those same quiches make a great lunch or dinner main dish.

But if you're not having a party, and simply making breakfast, why not make it special? Try one of Berghoff's traditional breakfast recipes, such as Bavarian Apple Pancakes, and something fun for the kids—Carlyn's Kids' Pancakes.

Breakfast at Berghoff's

"Open every day—9 A.M. to Midnight," the Berghoff Restaurant served breakfast on weekdays from 1914 until 1932. Following are some of the breakfast items from that original 1914 menu, which specified "One Order Served for Two, 10 cents Extra."

Eggs, Boiled (3) . . . . 30 cents
Eggs, Scrambled (3) . . . . . . 30 cents
Poached Eggs on Toast. . . . 35 cents
Ham and Eggs . . . . 40 cents
Bacon and Eggs . . . . 40 cents
Omelette, Plain . . . . 30 cents
Omelette, Ham . . . . 35 cents
Omelette, Parsley . . . . 35 cents
Omelette, Cheese. . . . . . . 35 cents
Omelette Tomato . . . . 35 cents
Omelette, Rum. . . . . 40 cents
Omelette, Mushroom. . . . . 50 cents

In addition, side orders of Fried Potatoes cost 10 cents; Hashed Brown, 15 cents; and Lyonnaise, 15 cents.

By 1934, the prices on the breakfast menu had risen in 5- and 10-cent increments. But the enigmatic Rum Omelette had vanished from the menu. Our best guess is that it was a version of the Omelette Alsterblick, a traditional German three-egg dish that was filled with fried bananas (and sometimes honey, orange juice, and grated chocolate), folded, topped with vanilla sugar, and then sauced with flambéed rum from the pan.

TOMATO, BASIL, and FRESH MOZZARELLA QUICHE

Serves 8 | *This is one of Jan's signature recipes, one of her husband Herman's favorites, and a fixture on her Sunday brunch. The fresh mozzarella—packed in whey or water—has a different taste and texture from factory-made mozzarella. It is softer, sweeter, and more delicate. In this quiche, it showcases the fresh basil and ripe tomatoes.*

QUICHE SHELL

2 cups all-purpose flour

1 teaspoon salt

$^3/_4$ cup shortening or unsalted butter

6 tablespoons cold water

FILLING

1 tablespoon canola oil

$1^1/_2$ cups diced white onions

1 freshly prepared quiche shell
(see Note)

$1^1/_2$ cups fresh mozzarella cheese,
sliced $^1/_8$ inch thick

4 vine ripened plum tomatoes,
sliced $^1/_8$ inch thick

3 large eggs

$^3/_4$ cup milk

$^3/_4$ cup heavy cream

$^1/_2$ teaspoon salt

$^1/_2$ teaspoon ground black pepper

$^1/_8$ teaspoon nutmeg

1 tablespoon chiffonade-cut fresh
basil (a fine julienne)

Make the quiche shell: Combine the flour and salt in the bowl of a food processor and blend. Add the shortening and process in pulses, until the texture resembles coarse meal. Add $^1/_4$ cup of water and pulse until blended in. Add enough additional water by tablespoonfuls to form moist clumps. Gather the dough into a ball and flatten into a disk. Wrap in plastic and chill until cold, at least 1 hour or up to one day.

With a floured rolling pin, on a lightly floured surface, roll out the dough into a 12-inch round. Fit into a 9-inch pie plate or 10-inch quiche pan. Trim the excess dough, leaving a $^1/_2$-inch overhang, then fold the overhang under the pastry. Crimp the edge and and lightly prick the bottom and sides of the shell with a fork. Chill until firm, about 30 minutes.

Adjust the rack in the middle of the oven. Preheat the oven to 375°F.

Line the shell with foil and fill with pie weights. (Or use rice or dried beans, to about 1 inch deep.) Bake until the rim of the pastry is pale golden, about 20 minutes. Carefully remove the foil and weights, and bake the shell until the bottom and sides are pale golden, about 10 more minutes. Place the pan on a cooling rack and cool completely, about 20 minutes or more, before using as directed. Turn off the oven during this cooling period.

Make the filling: Preheat the oven again to 350°F. In a 10-inch skillet, heat the oil and sauté the onions until transparent, about 5 minutes. Allow the onions to cool and then spread on the base of the prebaked quiche shell. Layer the sliced mozzarella and tomatoes over the onions.

In a bowl, whisk together the eggs, milk, cream, salt, pepper, and nutmeg. Gently pour into the shell on top of the mozzarella and tomatoes. Sprinkle with basil, and bake until set, 45 to 60 minutes. Remove from the oven when firm and golden. Allow to cool for 10 minutes before slicing. Slice into eight wedges to serve. Accompany with fresh fruit compote.

Note: For a shortcut, you may use a frozen or refrigerated pie crust from the grocery store.

Coffee and Beverage Station

Make sure you buy good-quality, freshly ground coffee and make both regular and decaf, but avoid flavored coffees. Allow your guests to add flavors with syrups (three flavors is quite enough), sugars, nonsugar sweeteners, or other add-ins. If your brunch will be for more guests than your standard home coffeemaker can handle, borrow, buy, or rent a bigger coffee urn just for entertaining. Keep in mind, however, that coffeemakers of this sort use a lot of power and tend to blow fuses, so don't plug them in if other heating or cooking appliances are being used. Also, they take 40 to 60 minutes to brew, so allow the necessary time.

Label the regular and decaf coffees with a small place card or picture frame. Mugs are best for buffet parties—just make sure the mug isn't so big that it won't fit under the spout of the coffeemaker. Place a small plate directly under the spout to prevent drips. Next to the coffeepots or -makers, set your coffee condiments in small bowls and pitchers, but not so small that you will have to constantly refill them. Whipped cream and chocolate shavings are nice additions to a coffee bar. Don't forget a bowl or other container for the used stirring spoons.

A great beverage for a brunch is a glass of sparkling wine with a berry dropped in, or sliced and placed on the rim of the glass. Mimosas (sparkling wine and orange juice) are also a favorite. Always buy top-quality sparkling wine, because it makes a difference even when mixed with something else. Regular white wine is a nice addition to a brunch. A juice bar can also be fun. Place chilled pitchers of fresh juice on a tray along with small glasses.

Other options are Bloody Marys or Virgin Marys. Garnish for the tomato-based drinks are celery stalks, olives, or a piece of bell pepper. You can also add stuffed olives, for variety.

BAVARIAN APPLE PANCAKES

Makes sixteen 8-inch pancakes | *This Old World treat, brought to America by German immigrants, has flourished in the New World and stood the taste test of time. It was a favorite on Berghoff's menu until 1944, and it became a Berghoff family favorite. The pancakes are easy to prepare, and the batter can be made one day ahead and refrigerated. We often mix the batter the night before so that when we get up in the morning all we need is a hot skillet. Topped with confectioners' sugar, fresh berries, bananas, or yogurt and fruit, they make an extraordinary breakfast. You can even top the warm pancakes with ice cream and berries for a simple but excellent dessert.*

2 cups all-purpose flour

³/₄ cup granulated sugar

1 teaspoon baking powder

1 teaspoon ground cinnamon

Pinch of salt

4 large eggs

1–1¹/₄ cups milk

2 teaspoons canola oil

2 teaspoons vanilla extract

2 teaspoons grated orange or
  lemon zest

4 cups peeled, cored, and diced
  Jonathan, Granny Smith, or
  Fuji apples

Nonstick cooking spray

Optional toppings: confectioners'
  sugar, fresh fruit, yogurt, or
  ice cream

In one bowl, combine the flour, sugar, baking powder, cinnamon, and salt. In a separate bowl, combine the eggs, 1 cup of the milk, and the oil, vanilla, and zest, and mix well. Make a well in the center of the dry ingredients and slowly incorporate the wet ingredients, blending thoroughly. Add the diced apples. If the batter is too thick to spread out easily when spooned into a hot skillet, add more milk little by little. If you choose to make the batter one day ahead, cover and refrigerate without adding the apples until ready to use.

Heat a nonstick 10-inch skillet over medium heat and lightly coat with nonstick cooking spray. Add a thin layer of batter (about ¹/₂ cup) and let brown on one side. With a spatula, gently flip and brown the other side. The pancake should be about twice as thick as a crepe (¹/₁₆ to ¹/₈ inch). Respray the pan with nonstick cooking spray before cooking each pancake.

Fold the cooked pancakes in half, and serve two per serving. Top with confectioners' sugar, fresh fruit, ice cream, or yogurt. You may also serve with fruit or maple syrup.

BERGHOFF EGGS BENEDICT

Serves 8 | *Our special version of Eggs Benedict was not on Berghoff's menu until 1944, even though the original Eggs Benedict dates from the 1920s in New York City. There are at least two stories of its origins. One says the dish was named after Harry Benedict, a regular at the Waldorf-Astoria. Mr. Benedict was a heavy drinker and always ordered poached eggs as a cure for his hangover, so the chef at the Waldorf came up with this upscale recipe. The second version claims it was named after Mrs. LeGrand Benedict, a regular at Delmonico's, who asked the chef to create a new and exciting egg dish. Whatever the truth, chefs and restaurants have been coming up with their own versions ever since. This Berghoff rendition includes bright green baby spinach and savory portobello mushrooms.*

8 (4-inch) portobello mushrooms

1/2 cup Balsamic Vinaigrette (page 92)

CHEESE SAUCE

3/4 to 1 cup milk

1/2 cup cubed Velveeta (2 ounces)

1/4 cup cubed Swiss cheese (1 ounce)

1/4 cup cubed Brie cheese (1 ounce)

1/4 cup cubed Gouda cheese (1 ounce)

1 cube chicken bouillon

1/2 teaspoon Worcestershire Sauce

1/4 teaspoon Tabasco sauce

2 teaspoons each cornstarch and water, stirred to make a slurry (page 33)

SPINACH

1/2 tablespoon canola oil

1 cup diced white onions

8 ounces baby spinach (6 cups)

Salt and pepper

SOFT POACHED EGGS

4 cups hot water

1 1/2 teaspoons distilled white vinegar

8 large eggs

TO ASSEMBLE

4 English muffins, split and lightly toasted

8 slices Canadian bacon, heated slightly (1/2 pound) (see Note)

In a large zippered plastic bag, toss the mushrooms and balsamic vinaigrette to coat. Zip the bag closed and refrigerate at least 1 hour before grilling. Heat a grill. Remove the mushrooms from the bag and shake off any excess marinade. Discard the used marinade. Grill the mushrooms for 2 1/2 to 3 minutes on each side. Remove the mushrooms from the grill and cool slightly before slicing. Keep warm and set aside.

Make the cheese sauce: In a metal bowl, toss together the milk, cheeses, bouillon,

Worcestershire sauce, and Tabasco sauce. Place the bowl over a pan of barely simmering water, to form a makeshift double boiler. Heat the sauce, whisking constantly, until is the cheeses are melted. Whisk in the cornstarch slurry and continue to cook, whisking often, over the boiling water until the sauce is slightly thickened and registers 165°F on an instant-read thermometer, 6 to 8 minutes. Remove the bowl from the pan and keep sauce warm.

Make the spinach: In a 10-inch skillet, heat the oil; add the onions and sauté until transparent, about 5 minutes. Add the spinach and cook for approximately 1¹⁄₂ minutes, or until heated through but firm, keeping the spinach somewhat al dente. Remove from the heat, and season with salt and pepper. The spinach will continue to cook in its pan. Keep warm and set aside.

Poach the eggs: Butter the bottom of a heavy 3-quart saucepan, and add the water and vinegar. Bring the water to a simmer. Break one egg into a measuring cup with a handle, and gently slide it from the cup into the water. Poach at a low simmer until the white is firm but the yolk is still runny, 2 to 3 minutes. Using a slotted spoon, remove the egg from its poaching liquid, drain well, and use immediately as directed. Repeat with the remaining eggs.

For each serving: Place half a toasted muffin on a plate. Top with a slice of Canadian bacon, ¹⁄₄ cup of the sliced portobellos, 1 tablespoon of sautéed spinach, 1 poached egg, and 3 tablespoons of cheese sauce. Serve immediately while warm. Repeat for each serving.

Note: Canadian bacon is precooked. Do not substitute other bacon without cooking it first.

Making Bacon

We Berghoffs like our bacon thick and crispy, not thin and limp. So we favor a ¹⁄₈-inch-thick sliced bacon that is applewood smoked for a full, sweet flavor that seems to complement, not overpower, other foods. You can buy this at a butcher's shop where they will slice it for you from the slab. And even some supermarkets now carry thick-sliced bacon. To make bacon without the stovetop splatter, we bake ours at 350°F to 400°F. Place the bacon strips in a single layer in a large baking pan with at least one-inch-deep sides, and bake to the desired degree of crispness. This can take up to 25 or 30 minutes, depending on your taste. Remove from the oven. Using tongs, transfer the bacon strips to paper toweling to drain excess fat.

CORNED BEEF HASH

Serves 8 | *Corned Beef Hash has been a Berghoff's favorite since Prohibition days. It became so popular that it moved from the breakfast to the lunch menu and remained there until the restaurant closed in 2006. Some say the dish originated in New England as a way to use the leftovers from a traditional New England boiled dinner. Our version is exceptionally tasty because of the generous amount of corned beef, and it's exceptionally easy to make because it is oven-baked. Top each portion with a fried or poached egg.*

1 tablespoon canola oil

1 cup diced white onions

1/2 cup thinly sliced scallions

8 cups finely diced cooked corned beef (80% corned beef, 20% fat)

4 cups cooked diced potatoes

Salt and ground black pepper

Preheat the oven to 325°F.

In a 12-inch skillet, heat the oil until hot. Over medium heat, sauté the onions until transparent, 3 to 4 minutes. Remove from the heat and add the scallions.

In a large bowl, stir together the corned beef and potatoes. Add the onion mixture and toss to mix. Season with salt and pepper, and toss again. Transfer to a deep 3-quart baking dish and bake for 30 to 40 minutes, or until heated through.

Serve with your favorite style eggs.

BERGHOFF BREAKFAST SANDWICH

Serves 6 | *This great sandwich was invented for the Berghoff Café at O'Hare airport by Berghoff's chef Matt Reichel, because we needed something to feed the early morning traveler. O'Hare customers kept asking for a breakfast sandwich, and chef Matt knew we could come up with something extraordinary. Because the bacon is prebaked in the oven, these hearty breakfast sandwiches can be made and assembled all at once as soon as the eggs are scrambled. Serve them on a large platter, family style. They're also good for a brunch buffet.*

12 pieces applewood-smoked bacon (or any other bacon)

6 large croissants, split in half and warmed

6 large eggs, gently scrambled to soft-medium doneness

Salt and ground black pepper

6 slices American or Swiss cheese

Preheat the oven to 350°F. Arrange the bacon on a rimmed baking sheet pan and bake for 15 minutes, or until it has reached desired crispiness. Transfer with tongs to paper towels, to drain.

Make the sandwiches: Arrange the bottom halves of the split croissants on a clean, dry surface. Evenly distribute the scrambled eggs over the croissant bottoms. Sprinkle with salt and pepper. Top each with a slice of cheese and two pieces of bacon. Replace the croissant tops and cut in half to serve. These go well with fresh fruit and juice.

Variation: Sliced tomatoes and onions may also be added to the sandwich.

BLUEBERRY MINI-MUFFINS

Makes 44 mini-muffins or 16 large muffins | *Although these muffins were invented for Carlyn's kids, they wound up on her catering menu, where they have captivated grown-ups for years. Bake the whole batch and pile them into a napkin-lined basket for breakfast or brunch. Or bake and freeze them, defrosting only as many as you need. These little gems make a nice accompaniment to a cup of afternoon tea, and can be packed into a school lunch box.*

¹/₂ pound (2 sticks) unsalted butter, softened

1 cup plus 2 tablespoons sugar

2 large eggs

1 teaspoon vanilla extract

2 cups all-purpose flour

1 teaspoon baking powder

1 teaspoon baking soda

1 teaspoon salt

1 cup sour cream

1 pint fresh blueberries

Preheat the oven to 325°F. Grease or line mini-muffin tins.

Using an electric mixer fitted with the paddle attachment, cream together the butter and sugar until lemon-colored. On low speed, add one egg at a time until each egg is incorporated. Add the vanilla and continue to mix until smooth in texture.

Combine the dry ingredients in a separate bowl, then slowly mix into the butter mixture. When the dry ingredients are incorporated, gently mix in the sour cream. Fold in the blueberries by hand. Scoop the batter into the prepared muffin cups

and bake in the oven until golden brown. Mini-muffins will take 18 to 20 minutes; large muffins will take 26 to 28 minutes. The muffins can be frozen for 1 month: Let cool completely and place in zippered plastic freezer bags to freeze.

Fixing Fresh Fruit

Fruit is a great addition to any party and plays a large role at Berghoff family breakfasts and brunches. Buy fruit in season, when it will taste best, and allow time for such fruit as pears and bananas to ripen properly at home. Fruit bowls are always beautiful, especially glass bowls. But salads, platters, or skewers are additional ways to serve fresh, ripe fruit. For example, cut a melon in half and place, cut side down, on a platter. Then spear uniform, bite-size pieces of fruit on skewers and stick the skewers into the melon for display.

You may rinse, drain, and cut most fruit hours or a day in advance. Store all cut fruits separately in the refrigerator in zippered plastic bags lined with paper towels.

CARLYN'S BREAKFAST GRATIN with LEEKS and SWISS CHEESE

Serves 8 | *A gratin has everything going for it that a quiche does—without the hassle of mixing, forming, and prebaking a crust. This crustless, savory breakfast gratin uses either homemade or convenient prepared hash brown potatoes, is mixed in a few minutes, and bakes into a rich, golden brown casserole that can be cut into squares and served as a side dish for a family breakfast or a brunch buffet.*

HASH BROWNS

> 3 pounds all-purpose potatoes, boiled, chilled, peeled, and diced (see Note)
>
> ½ teaspoon salt
>
> ½ teaspoon pepper
>
> ½ cup clarified butter (see Note)

GRATIN

> 1½ cups sour cream
>
> 2½ cups packed grated Gruyère or Swiss cheese (about 10 ounces)
>
> 2 large leeks, trimmed, cleaned, and sliced
>
> 3 tablespoons chopped fresh chives
>
> ½ teaspoon salt
>
> ¼ teaspoon ground black pepper
>
> 2 tablespoons unsalted butter, plus extra for baking dish

Make the hash browns: Heat the butter in a nonstick 12-inch skillet over medium heat. Add the potatoes, sprinkling with salt and pepper. Cook, turning occasionally with a spatula, until a golden crust forms on most of the potatoes, 10 to 12 minutes. Remove from the heat and let cool for 10 minutes.

Make the gratin: Preheat the oven to 400°F. Generously grease a 13 by 9 by 2-inch glass baking dish with butter.

In a large mixing bowl, combine the cooked potatoes, 2 cups of the cheese, and all the remaining ingredients. Season with salt and pepper. Place the mixture in the prepared baking dish. Sprinkle the remaining ½ cup of cheese on top. Bake uncovered for 30 minutes. Decrease the oven temperature to 350°F; continue to bake until the potatoes are tender and the top is golden brown, about 45 minutes. Remove from the oven. Let stand for 10 minutes and cut the gratin into squares to serve.

Note: Prepared hash brown potatoes (loose-packed, not preformed patties), located in the grocery freezer section, may be substituted for fresh sautéed potatoes.

To clarify butter, melt in a saucepan over medium heat. When hot, remove pan from heat. The milk solids will settle to the bottom of the pan. Carefully pour off the clear (clarified) butter into another container, leaving the solids in the pan.

FRITTATA with PROSCIUTTO and FRESH MOZZARELLA

Serves 6 | *This Italian-inspired omelet is a true brunch dish that can double for a light luncheon or a very simple supper at the end of a long, hard day when you feel like dialing for dinner. Just make sure your skillet has an ovenproof handle, and, if you're pressed for time, slit open a bag of ready-to-use salad greens. Voilà! Brunch, lunch, or dinner in about fifteen minutes. And if you're among the people who like leftover pizza from the fridge, you will love cold frittata.*

10 large eggs

¼ cup heavy whipping cream

6 ounces fresh mozzarella cheese, cubed

¼ pound sliced prosciutto, diced

10 oil-packed sun-dried tomatoes, drained and chopped finely

¾ cup chopped scallions

⅓ cup chopped fresh basil

½ teaspoon salt

¼ teaspoon ground black pepper

3 tablespoons unsalted butter

Preheat the broiler. Whisk the eggs and cream in a large mixing bowl, to blend. Stir in the mozzarella, prosciutto, tomatoes, scallions, basil, salt, and pepper. Melt the butter in a large, ovenproof, nonstick skillet over medium heat. Add the egg mixture to the pan, but do not stir. Cook until the eggs start to firm up, and the sides and bottom begin to brown, lifting the sides occasionally to let uncooked egg run underneath, about 5 minutes. Transfer the skillet to the broiler, and cook until the eggs start to puff and brown, about 2 minutes. Using a rubber spatula, loosen the edges and bottom of the frittata. Allow to cool slightly. Slide the frittata out of the pan onto a serving plate.

Slice the frittata into pie-shaped wedges. Serve warm or at room temperature with a petite salad of mixed greens.

The Berghoff on closing night, February 28, 2006.

CARLYN'S KIDS' PANCAKES

Makes about 20 pancakes | *Making breakfast for dinner is a Berghoff solution for how to put in a ten-hour day and still sit down to a hot dinner together. Pancakes with eggs or bacon became a family favorite dinner. Pancake mixes are convenient, but you can't get big fluffy pancakes like these out of any box. Beating the egg whites separately and folding them into the batter—Carlyn uses a rubber spatula to fold—makes for a light, cloudlike pancake. Shapes are not just for kids. When you look at all the cookie cutters available—stars, moons, hearts, animals, trees, leaves, seasonal, and holiday cutters—you'll find something to amuse and delight adults as well as children. It's also fun to make one or two big pancakes to share, depending on the size of your skillet or griddle.*

2 cups all-purpose flour

3 tablespoons granulated sugar

1 tablespoon baking powder

¹/₄ teaspoon salt

2 cups buttermilk

3 large eggs, separated

1 teaspoon vanilla extract

3–4 tablespoons unsalted butter

Real maple syrup, as needed

Combine the flour, 2 tablespoons of the sugar, the baking powder, and the salt in a large bowl. Add the buttermilk, egg yolks, and vanilla, and whisk until smooth. Using an electric mixer, beat the whites in a separate medium-size bowl to soft peak stage. Add the remaining 1 tablespoon of sugar and beat until stiff but not dry. Gently fold into the batter.

On a large griddle or in a heavy skillet, melt enough butter to coat the griddle over medium-low heat. In batches, pour batter by one-quarter cupful onto the hot griddle. Cook until the pancakes are golden brown, about 3 minutes per side. Transfer to plates. Using cookie cutters, cut out fun shapes and sizes. Serve with warm maple syrup.

FRENCH TOAST STICKS

Serves 8 | *Okay, when Carlyn says, "Sprinkle French Toast Sticks with powdered sugar and serve with warm maple syrup," that doesn't mean you have to eat them with a fork. Sometimes she likes to dip them in the maple syrup (individual containers, please) and eat them with her fingers. Warm the maple syrup in a glass or microwave-safe container in the microwave for a few seconds.*

1 (1-pound) loaf brioche or kosher egg bread (challah) (about 24 pieces)

8 large eggs

2 cups milk

2 tablespoons vanilla extract

2 tablespoons Grand Marnier (or other orange-flavored liqueur)

1 tablespoon granulated sugar

1/2 teaspoon ground cinnamon

1/2 cup melted unsalted butter

2-3 tablespoons confectioners' sugar (in shaker)

Real maple syrup as needed, warmed

Preheat the oven to 250°F.

Cut the bread into 1-inch-thick slices, cutting each slice into thirds to make it into sticks.

In a large bowl, whisk together the eggs, milk, vanilla extract, Grand Marnier, granulated sugar, and cinnamon. Soak half the bread sticks in the egg mixture for about 5 minutes. Turn over the sticks and soak for 5 minutes more. Remove and place the soaked bread sticks in a 9 by 13-inch baking dish. Repeat with the remaining bread sticks.

In a heavy 12-inch nonstick skillet, heat 2 tablespoons of the melted butter over moderate heat. Cook the bread sticks (as many as will fit in one layer) for 2 to 3 minutes on each side, or until puffed and golden brown. Transfer to a baking sheet and keep warm in the oven. Cook the remaining sticks in the remaining butter, following the same method.

Serve with confectioners' sugar and warm maple syrup.

THE
FAMILY PARTY

Yours and Ours

WHEN ENTERTAINING AT HOME the Berghoff family flies solo. Neither Jan nor Carlyn has the benefit of the restaurant's and catering company's chefs and staffs. For that reason, they serve sit-down dinners only for up to eight guests. After that, they favor the buffet.

The Buffet

As soon as Carlyn realized that she liked catering and opened Artistic Events, she developed a sense of style "and a love for buffets," she says, "even though they require careful planning." For example, if the buffet is too small in its quantity and variety of dishes, then the portions look skimpy—as if you are going to run out of food.

The best aspect of a buffet is its variety—the opportunity it gives your guests to choose among dishes. Jan's weekly Sunday brunch (see page 265) is an excellent example.

When Carlyn designs a buffet, she goes back to the basics. First, decide your center of the plate, your protein, then design the rest of the menu from there. For example, if you choose halibut and chicken breasts, then roast the chicken for color, and grill the fish for the same reason. After you've settled on the center of the plate, pick the vegetables that are in season and will bring the most color to your table. Three vegetables are a good choice, such as Roasted Vegetables (page 186), Szechuan Green Beans (page 182), and Eggplant Ratatouille (page 179).

When it comes to salad and bread on a buffet, your guests will eat both, but not as much as they would at a sit-down dinner. The same applies to butter. And, even if you provide salad and bread plates, they will tend to put everything on one plate.

The starch is your next consideration. It can be hot or cold, depending on the time of year. The Berghoffs like to do room-temperature buffets, always keeping food safety in mind. For starches, potatoes are the obvious choice: white or sweet, mashed, gratinéed, fried, chips, roasted, even grilled. But don't forget grains and pastas: wheat berries, couscous, tabbouleh, wild rice, rice pilafs, pasta salads. One potato dish and one grain dish make for variety.

Now the buffet is almost complete and you can move on to hors d'oeuvres. Pick some that can sit on a counter or a table for guests to help themselves, such as Chef Matt's Spinach Dip (page 30); a German Cheese, Meat, and Fruit Board (page 34); or Sweet Potato Chips with Green Onion Dip (page 38). Also pick one or two that you can pass around hot, either directly from the kitchen or made ahead and reheated, such as Beer-Battered Vegetables (page 32) or Mushroom Strudel (page 36). Try to serve one vegetarian option, such as Creamed Spinach-Stuffed Mushrooms (page 42) or Hazelnut Quesadilla with Chihuahua Cheese and Red Pepper Sauce (page 44).

Dessert for a buffet can be extra special and can be set out after the dinner has been removed, or placed on a separate dessert table. Small bites, whole cakes and pies, bowls of fun candy, plates of cheese, fresh fruits on skewers, dried fruits, ice cream, and brandy snifters filled with berries and zabaglione sauce are just a few options. The sky's the limit.

Sit-down in Style

If you are going to cook and serve a sit-down dinner for eight by yourself, then the obvious choice is to do it family style, with an emphasis on the style. For example, Carlyn and Jan usually serve a cold first course, such as an appetizer salad or a room-temperature quiche wedge, nicely garnished. This is served in a small plate placed on the dinner plate that has been lined with a pretty folded paper napkin, before the guests sit down. When that course is cleared, the napkin is removed, leaving a pristine dinner plate. The rest of the meal is served family style on platters and casseroles of your choosing, and this is where you have the opportunity to be creative. Showcase your favorite casseroles and serving pieces. These can be contemporary, old-fashioned hand-me-downs from family members, your best china, vintage finds from flea markets, or interesting ethnic pieces from other countries. It's okay to mix or match as long as you stay within a theme.

When it's time for dessert, there are two ways to serve it: Clear the center of the table and place the dessert or desserts down the center, as Carlyn often does. Or, set up a dessert buffet on a separate side table.

In any event, set the dinner table the day before the dinner, placing glassware and plates upside down so they remain dust free.

When to Hire—or Ask for—Help

Carlyn and Jan are often asked that question and their answer always is, "How much time do you want to be a guest at your own party?"

Up until Carlyn's second child was a year old, she says, "I did everything myself when I entertained. I thought it was just expected. Then I realized I had no time to be a guest. And at the end of the party, I really needed help getting the dishes washed and put away and the house back in order. That's when I started exploring options for help."

One option is to cohost a party with a friend. That way you share the expense, the work, the fun, and the glory.

A second option is to hire a neighborhood teen. But make sure you make your expectations clear and write them down on a list. Also be careful about keeping a teenager away from contact with liquor.

A third choice is to work through a staffing agency in your area.

When to Rent Dishes

How many plates you have is one answer to that question. Carlyn and Jan believe that any number over thirty guests calls for rentals and help of some kind. You can find rental companies by looking in the Yellow Pages or searching on the Internet. They advise, when you rent, getting the cleanup option, so all you need do at the end of the party is rinse the dishes and put them in the crate for the rental company to pick up and wash.

Party Checklist

Here's a simple ten-step checklist for a party.

1. **Timing**—Pick the time of day (which will determine your menu), and the date for your party. Check to make sure it doesn't conflict with holidays or other party plans.

Send out invitations that cover the who, what, when, where, and why of the party, and ask for an RSVP or regrets-only by a certain date—and don't forget your phone number.

2. **Logistics**—Plan some logistics. Plan for seating, so every guest can sit somewhere, even in other rooms. You can borrow or rent folding chairs and even arrange them in groups around small tables. If you have pets, where will they be kept during the party? Do you need a babysitter, or are your kids old enough to help? Plan for the trash, and how to move it out of sight. If you are going to hire help, rent dishes, and so on, reserve those services early. If it's an outside party, have a rain plan. If it's summer, plan a strategy for bugs. Plan for parking. Lastly, inside or outside, summer or winter, think about where you will put coats, boots, umbrellas, etc., from the minute the guests step in the front door.

3. **Tableware**—Decide if you will use china and glassware, or paper plates and disposable cups and glasses.

- The ratio for disposables for a cocktail party is: 4 plates (7-inch), 2.5 forks, 1.5 knives, 10 cocktail napkins, and 6 glasses per person.

- For a cocktail party with china: 2.5 plates (7-inch), 1.5 forks, 1 knife, 10 cocktail napkins, and 4 glasses per person.

- For a dinner buffet using disposables, add 3 dinner-size plates, 3 dessert plates (4-inch), 2 large napkins, and 2 heatproof cups per person.

- For a dinner buffet using china, add 2 dinner-size plates, 1.5 dessert plates (4-inch), 2 large linen napkins, and 1 cup and saucer per person.

4. **Shopping**—Plan your menu, making two shopping lists: one for products that are not perishable, such as disposables, wine, liquor, unchilled beverages, etc. And one for the actual food you will need for the party. Shop for the nonperishable items days ahead, and store them.

5. **Layout**—If you are planning a buffet, sketch it out on paper, deciding where the food, plates, and glassware will go. Plan where the bar and dessert station will be. Select all your serving bowls, plates, and serving utensils and identify them with sticky notes. Select your linens or disposables: tablecloths and napkins. Walk through the probable paths of the guests and make sure there is enough room so they don't create a traffic jam. Also, clear enough surface areas away from the buffet so guests have a place to leave dishes, glasses, and cups.

6. **Decor**—Plan your enhancements. Will you have flowers in small vases or bowls in several places—low, so people can see across them—or one large flower arrangement in a central spot? Candles can be placed in candlesticks or a candelabra on the dining table or tables, or small votive candles can be placed strategically on mantelpieces, tables, and on the buffet. Background music should complement the party theme and the season, but it should always be in the background—loud enough to be heard but not so loud that it drowns out conversation. Put the music on before guests arrive. If it's a children's party, you will want to plan and fill goodie bags in advance. And some grown-up parties are enhanced by nicely wrapped party favors.

7. **Cleaning**—Two days before the party, clean the house and/or yard. Plan what you will need for the inevitable spills, and have the supplies handy.

8. **Shopping and Last-Minute Preparations**—Go shopping for food (write your shopping list based on actual recipes, so you don't forget anything). Prepare and cook as much as possible in advance. The day of the party, make last-minute food preparation; buy ice and chill drinks three hours before the party begins. If your space is limited in the kitchen or bar area, chill your drinks in ice in the bathtub. Check to make sure you have extra toilet tissue and hand towels.

9. **Finishing Touches**—Set the table or the buffet. You can also do this a day in advance. Take a shower. Take a picture of the buffet. Be a guest at your own party and have fun.

10. **Be Your Own Next Party Planner**—If your dinner or buffet was successful, write out the menu, date it, and put it in a loose-leaf binder

along with the recipes for it. If some of the recipes need improvement, make notes. If some didn't work out, delete them. After a year you will have a unique party planner complete with menus and recipes for all seasons. After several years you will have a family treasure for future generations.

Below, we offer some garnishing tips and suggested menus for the kinds of parties we like to give, parties that range from Oktoberfest to backyard barbecues, cocktail parties, brunches, and soup, sandwich, and salad suppers.

Garnishes for Dishes and Trays

There are many easy yet eye-catching ways to garnish plates and platters. One of the quickest and most dramatic is to completely line or cover serving plates with edible, inexpensive food items. For example, a tray covered with baby spinach leaves makes an attractive presentation for miniature appetizer quiches or crab cakes. A tray lined with packed brown sugar is a perfect way to present miniature pastries in paper or foil cups.

Fresh and Dried Savory Platter Linings

Use these to cover plates completely or to place in rows between food:

- Carrot and cucumber ribbons: Slice large carrots and seedless cucumbers into wide, thin slices with a vegetable peeler. Lay them side by side to cover the plate bottom, or weave the strips in a basket pattern.

- Citrus slices and wedges: Use lemon, lime, or orange slices to cover the plate bottom, or line up wedges in side-by-side rows.

- Kumquats, grapes, or cherry tomatoes: Halve these and place, cut side down, to cover the plate or platter.

- Sliced starfuit and pineapple chunks: Arrange in side-by-side rows on platters.

- Baby carrots, stemmed cherries, fresh cranberries, dried apricot halves, frozen defrosted green peas, or canned corn kermels: Completely cover plates and platters with these.

- Fresh dill, fennel, tarragon, sage, rosemary, baby spinach, arugula leaves, or bean sprouts: Cover plates and platters completely. Also, lay in strips between rows of food.

- Chives and wheatgrass: Cut to fit and line plates and platters.

- Walnuts, pecans, cashews, sliced or slivered almonds, pumpkin seeds, sunflower seeds, black and white sesame seeds, or cinnamon sticks: Pour onto platters and tilt to cover evenly. Arrange cinnamon sticks in rows.

Linings for Dessert and Sweet Platters

Use these to line trays. Be sure the garnish enhances the food and the recipe, in case some of the small garnishes stick a little to the foods.

- Any of the fruits and nuts in the previous list

- Brown sugar, packed

- Chocolate chips

Four ideas for garnishing trays. *Clockwise from top left:* Carrots, chives, M&M's, and starfruit.

- Coconut flakes, plain or toasted

- Toffee chips, butterscotch chips

- Chocolate shavings

- Peppermint candies

- Candy canes

- M&M's

- Candied nuts

- Cinnamon "red hot" candies

- Chocolate sprinkles, rainbow sprinkles

- Cocoa powder

- Banana chips, raisins and other dried fruits

- Colored gelatins, made from dried gelatin mixes: Pour on bottoms of trays and plates and chill. Also cut out shapes with cookie cutters and place on top of the gelatin sheet.

Party Menus

A Cocktail Party Menu

This menu has a balance of items that can be made in advance, allowing you to be a guest at your own party.

The Menu:

- Chef Matt's Spinach Dip (page 30) with assorted crudités
- Miniature Grilled Kabobs, four bites per skewer, two or three varieties
- Chicken Saltimbocca Skewers (page 39)
- Pesto Cheesecake (page 46)
- Sweet Potato Chips (page 38)
- Dilled Shrimp on Cucumber Cup (page 43)
- Bruschetta (page 45)
- Mixed nuts or Candied Pecans (page 80)
- Grapes Rolled in Cream Cheese (page 48)

A Summer and Fall Beer Menu

This menu is perfect for a neighborhood event.

The Menu:

- Beer-Battered Vegetables (page 32)
- Brie Chicken Skewers (page 40)
- Mixed Nuts or Candied Pecans (page 80)
- Creamed Spinach-Stuffed Mushrooms (page 42)
- German Cheese Platter (page 34)
- Grilled Portobello Mushrooms (page 31)
- Mushroom Strudel (page 36)
- Sweet Potato Chips (page 38)
- Bratwurst (page 102)
- Root Beer Floats (page 213)
- Seasonal Beers

A Soup, Salad, and Sandwich Menu

Simple, simple, simple and tailor made for everyone's eating habits. Great for lunch or supper. You can let your kids pick the soup and sandwich flavors.

The Menu:

- Beef Barley Soup (page 64)
- Baby Spinach Salad (page 86)
- Reuben (page 100), or Black Forest Ham and Brie Panini (page 106)
- Sacher Torte Cakes (page 232)

A Sandwich Buffet Menu

This is a great way to throw a party after a sports event with your family and friends. You can even ask guests to bring a prepared dish or ingredients.

For a party of eight, choose two sandwiches, one side dish, the chips, the vegetable relishes, and the beverages.

For a party of sixteen to twenty, prepare the entire menu.

The Menu:

- Tuna Salad Sandwich on Berghoff Home Rye (pages 122 and 110)
- Berghoff Roasted Turkey Breast on Olive Bread with Basil Aïoli (pages 105, 112, 125)

- Bratwurst on buns with Berghoff Brown Mustard (page 102)
- Grilled Vegetable Wrap (page 120)
- Salad Caprese (page 90)
- German Potato Salad (page 81)
- Crudités (select from celery, radishes, scallions, seedless cucumber coins, sliced jícama, cauliflower and broccoli florets, cherry tomatoes, baby carrots, and sugar snap peas)
- Chips, an interesting assortment
- Wine, beer, soft drinks
- Lemonade with or without vodka

Alternate Suggestion:

In place of the Bratwurst on buns, set up a panini station (you can even appoint someone to man the panini grill) and grill either of the following recipes. Serve them hot as they come off the grill.

- Black Forest Ham and Brie Panini (page 106), or
- Brie and Raspberry Grilled Cheese Sandwich (page 117)
- For the sweet tooth, something simple, such as Sacher Torte Cakes (page 232), Pistachio Cheesecake Squares (page 230), Pecan Diamonds (page 229), or purchased cookies

Set-Up:

- Centerpieces for the buffet can be flowering seasonal potted plants in uniform pots set on the same size and color plates or saucers.

- Use sturdy color-coordinated disposable plates, napkins, cutlery, cups, and glasses, but use your own serving utensils, bowls, pitchers, and platters.
- Place all the breads, presliced, in napkin-lined baskets. Remember that you can buy wonderful bakery breads as well as bake your own. Slice breads right before serving time.
- Make the tuna salad a day in advance and refrigerate, covered, so the flavors can fully develop and meld. Before serving, stir well, taste for seasoning (does it need salt? A little pepper?) and pile it into a serving bowl. You can garnish it with celery sticks for guests who would like to avoid bread (yes, even at a sandwich buffet). If you have a large enough platter to hold the bowl and leave room for garnishes, we suggest the following:

Two different colors of tomatoes—red and yellow, or red and orange—sliced, makes a dramatic impact; two different kinds of pickles—sweet coins and dill spears; a pretty green pile of lettuce leaves (romaine, Bibb, red leaf lettuce, even iceberg), carefully washed and dried (nothing throws a wet blanket on a good sandwich like soggy lettuce); sliced red, green, orange, or yellow sweet bell pepper rings. If your platter is not large enough to hold the bowl of tuna salad and garnishes, then make a separate platter of garnishes.

- To avoid the last-minute rush, cut up all vegetables, preslice the tomatoes, and wash and dry lettuce, but store them all in the fridge in their own separate zippered plastic bags. Inside each bag, place a paper towel to absorb the extra moisture. This not only keeps vegetables fresh and crisp but avoids flavor transfer—who wants to bite into a tomato that tastes like a green pepper, or a radish that reeks of green onion?

- For the turkey breast, slice the meat thinly, shingle it in the center of a platter, and garnish the platter with fresh basil leaves that guests may tuck into their sandwiches.

- Bread becomes soggy when condiments are spread on too far in advance. So put the condiments in bowls on the side, and let guests choose and spread their own.

- For a party with a minimum of last-minute preparation, consider preparing and serving wraps. Wraps will hold longer than bread without becoming soggy.

- Stock up on beverages and restock the ice cooler as the supplies run low.

- Serve all beverages in bottles and cans packed in an ice cooler, except for the lemonade. This can be served from two large pitchers, one without vodka, one with.

A Picnic Menu

When you're thinking about a picnic menu, think about bringing along the grill and serving hot sandwiches using sausages. Once grilled, bratwurst, knockwurst, and Thuringer need only a bun and a slather of mustard. Also, pack

Grandmother's Relish Tray

One of our fondest and most enduring memories is going to Grandmother's house for Sunday dinner. Carlyn Berghoff, third-generation Herman's mother, and fourth-generation Carlyn's grandmother and namesake, was known for her roasts and her gravy. When Jan married Herman, his mother, Carlyn, taught her to make good gravy. Grandmother's Sunday dinners were served in style on good china set upon a hand-crocheted lace tablecloth. And every meal began with soup. But no matter what the meal—pork roast, or prime rib with mashed potatoes and sautéed carrots—winter, spring, summer, or fall, the one constant on the dining table was the relish tray. It was oblong in shape, about nine inches long, and made of cut glass. And it held, in groups, the crispest radish roses, carrot and celery sticks, and pimiento-stuffed green olives. That relish tray was the perfect accompaniment to any and every meal. And every so often, Grandmother would add a cut-glass dish of cottage cheese sprinkled with paprika and garnished with curly parsley. (Back then, we had not yet been introduced to flat-leaf [Italian] parsley.)

wraps, which hold up longer than sandwiches without becoming soggy. We think picnics are a great way to empty out your refrigerator of relishes, dips, and cheeses. Think of a picnic as finger-food delights.

The Menu:

- Smoked Salmon Wrap with Capers and Dilled Cream Cheese (page 121)
- Grilled Knockwurst on buns (page 102)
- Smothered Onions (page 102)
- Chicken Waldorf Salad, bread optional (page 78)
- Chef Matt's Spinach Dip (page 30) with crudités, or low-fat Boursin cheese with celery and carrot sticks for dipping
- Assortment of cheese cut in wedges, chunks and slices
- Ready-to-eat fruit: melon wedges (watermelon, cantaloupe, and honeydew), strawberries, small bunches of grapes, garnished with mint.
- Your favorite condiments: jars of olives, marinated artichokes, pepperoncini, pickled okra
- Bottles and cans of iced beverages packed in a cooler
- For the sweet tooth: jumbo chocolate chip or oatmeal cookies, or Pecan Diamonds (page 229)

Set-Up:

- If you aren't going any farther than the backyard, all you need are a couple of trays to transport the food and utensils.

- If you have a destination farther afield, the packing becomes very important. Let's assume you are going to a park or a concert. You need a blanket, perhaps some foldable beach chairs, and a cooler on wheels, which will make it easy to transport from the car to the picnic site. Ice or freezer packets will keep it cold.
- Place all perishables in the cooler in zippered plastic bags or covered plastic containers, along with beverages of choice.
- In a separate container (maybe a grocery cart on wheels), pack disposable plates, cutlery, cups, napkins, and serving utensils.
- You can either grill on site (in which case bring a grill, charcoal, and grilling supplies), or grill the sausages and onions at home and serve them at room temperature.
- Don't forget bug spray, a citronella candle, hand wipes, sun block, a trash bag, good weather, and a sunny disposition.

A Fall and Winter Buffet

Jan and Carlyn believe that as soon as it gets cold, people's taste buds crave a different style of food. This buffet is geared for crisp or chilly weather.

The Menu:

- Baby Spinach Salad (page 86)
- Pot Roast or Sauerbraten (pages 144 and 143)
- Mashed Potatoes (page 178)
- Roasted Vegetables (page 186)
- Apple Strudel (page 210)

A Spring and Summer Buffet

Carlyn says, "As soon as there is one day over seventy degrees, my eyes eat differently. Brown food, so welcome during cold weather, is gone for now, and I'm ready for color, color, color."

The Menu:

- Chilled Grape Gazpacho (page 68)
- Crab Cakes (page 163)
- Wheat Berry and Wild Rice Salad (page 189)
- Eggplant Ratatouille (page 179)
- Almond Pear Tartlets (page 226)

Oktoberfest Menu

The Menu:

- Sauerkraut (page 181)
- Bratwurst in beer (page 102, finish on the grill)
- Barbecued chicken thighs (see Note)
- Your choice of buns
- Corn on the cob in husks
- Beer, wine, and root beer
- Huge pretzels, and Düsseldorf mustard for dipping
- Apple strudel (page 210)

Note: Marinate chicken thighs in Balsamic Vinaigrette Marinade (page 92) or the marinade of your choice, in a zippered plastic bag for 2 hours; then grill till done.

How-To:

For fifteen to twenty guests, you will need:

- 36 brats and 36 buns
- 3 pounds Sauerkraut (page 181)
- Beer, wine, and soft drinks
- 20 chicken thighs
- 20 corn on the cobs, soaked in water for 2 to 3 hours
- 20 large, soft pretzels
- 3 recipes Apple Strudel (page 210)

Kabob Bar Menu

The Menu:

- Zesty Garlic Shrimp, grilled on skewers (page 197), or Sesame Seed Tuna (page 198)
- Chicken Saltimbocca Skewers (page 39)
- Bratwurst, Knockwurst, and Smoked Thuringer, cut and skewered, finished on the grill (page 102)
- Lamb or beef kabobs (marinate $1^1/_2$-inch lamb or beef cubes in Balsamic Vinaigrette [page 92], and grill until done)
- Grilled vegetables (page 203)
- S'mores on the Grill (page 205), or
- Seasonal Berry Shortcake (page 224)

How-To:

For fifteen to twenty guests, you will need:

- 3 proteins (one seafood, one poultry, one meat, about 9 pounds total)
- One assortment of 3 or 4 vegetables (about 4 pounds), plus 4 pounds of small new potatoes

- Use one recipe marinade for both seafood and vegetables, a second recipe for meat and poultry.

- Marinate the seafood; cover and refrigerate for 20 minutes.

- Cut the vegetables into chunks and marinate, covered, in the refrigerator, for 1 hour.

- Cut the poultry, beef, lamb, or pork into 2-inch cubes and marinate, covered, in the refrigerator, 2 hours.

- Season whole new potatoes with herbs, spices, and olive oil, and roast in the oven. Bring out on skewers on a platter.

- Drain all marinated protein and vegetable items, and present separately on platters.

- Discard all marinades unless they can be boiled for 10 minutes prior to basting. If this is not possible, prepare batches of new marinades to baste and serve as sauce.

- Presoak wooden or bamboo skewers in hot water for 30 minutes.

- For small 6-inch skewers, plan on six items (meat, poultry, seafood, vegetables) per skewer; 12 items for long 12-inch skewers

- Let guests assemble their own skewers from the variety of ingredients.

- Appoint a grillmeister who will grill the skewers.

A Mashed Potato Bar

Provide glass or disposable plastic martini or rocks glasses, a chafing dish full of hot mashed potatoes, and a series of toppings as follows:

Menu I:
- Mashed Potatoes (page 178)
  Toppings:
  Bacon bits
  Sour cream
  Chopped chives
  Basil oil
  Blue cheese crumbles
  Chili con carne
  Pesto

Menu II:
- Mashed Potatoes (page 178)
  Toppings:
  Pureed sweet potatoes
  Cooked chopped shrimp
  Cooked chopped lobster
  Lump crabmeat
  Salmon roe
  Crème fraîche
  Dill Beurre Blanc Sauce (page 157)
  Sweet Potato Chips (page 38)

Menu III:
- Mashed Potatoes (page 178)
  Toppings:
  Chicken à la king
  Beef stew
  Gravy
  Chopped roasted vegetables
  Creamed Spinach (page 170)
  Sautéed diced mushrooms
  Corn relish

How-To:

- Set out martini or rocks glasses, along with napkins, spoons, and forks on the left side of the buffet.

- Keep potatoes warm in a crockpot or chafing dish in the center.

- Arrange toppings around and to the right of the potatoes, in dishes with serving spoons.

A Dessert Party

This is fun for the holidays and a great way to house-jump by courses.

The Menu:

- Sacher Torte Cakes or Flourless Chocolate Cake, thinly sliced (pages 232 and 209)

- Pecan Diamonds (page 229)

- Pistachio Cheesecake Squares (page 230)

- Apple Strudel (page 210)

- White Chocolate Mousse with Raspberry Sauce (page 220)

- Seasonal berries

- Coffee bar

- Champagne

How-To:

- Serve the Sacher Torte Cakes on a large platter with a bowl of Raspberry Sauce on the side, or slice the Flourless Cake very thinly, twelve slices per cake.

- Serve the White Chocolate Mousse in a glass bowl topped with chocolate shavings. Serve raspberry sauce in a pitcher on the side.

- Serve mixed berries in a large glass bowl, with a small bowl of whipped cream on the side.

Jan's Brunch Buffet

This is another great way to entertain differently. A brunch buffet is welcome and wonderful around the holidays.

The Menu:

- Fresh boiled shrimp served cold with cocktail sauce

- Rolled smoked salmon with dill sauce and wedges of pumpernickel

- Green salad (romaine and a mesclun mix) with Lemon-Dijon Vinaigrette (page 93)

- Freshly cut seasonal fruit

- Oven-baked asparagus spears topped with shaved Parmesan (or seasonal vegetables of choice)

- Thick, crisp applewood-smoked bacon

- Tomato, Basil, and Fresh Mozzarella Quiche (page 238)

- Black Forest Cake or Flourless Chocolate Cake or Sacher Torte Cakes, (pages 214, 209, and 232)

- Apple Strudel or Almond-Pear Tartlets (pages 210 and 226)

- Champagne, Mimosas, Chambord-champagne cocktails

- Freshly squeezed orange juice

- Coffee and tea

First row, left to right: Lindsey, Sarah, and Todd McClure. *Second row, left to right:* Timothy Berghoff, Jan Berghoff, Herman Berghoff, Julie Berghoff, and Peter Berghoff. *Back row, left to right:* Jim McClure and Carlyn Berghoff.

In closing, we—Jan and Carlyn—both hope that you
and yours have as much fun cooking and entertaining
as our family has for the past hundred years.

Berghoff chefs. *Clockwise from top left:* Matthew Reichel (Berghoff), Paul J. Larson (CBC), Enrique Sta Maria (Berghoff pastry), and Encarnacion Reynozo (Chon) (CBC pastry).

SPEAKER J. DENNIS HASTERT

Whenever I talk to friends and family about going out to dinner in Chicago, someone inevitably suggests heading back to the Berghoff. That is because the Berghoff Restaurant is a Chicago tradition - the place that visitors must see, the place that locals want to return to time and again.

It is my honor to congratulate this historic establishment on its 107th Anniversary.

The Berghoff is a model in excellence because it is true to its tradition. The restaurant's visitors immediately notice its high ceilings, hand-crafted murals and bold woodwork. They are further impressed by the Berghoff's seasoned and professional staff, and a family feel that lets customers know they are more than just another diner on a busy day.

But the true secret to the success of the Berghoff is clear: the food. The Berghoff offers a menu that changes with the seasons - but the quality is consistently second to none. While many of us enjoy the German house specialties, the menu offers everything from American cuisine to seafood and salads. There is a lot to choose from, but regulars take heart in the fact that you really can't go wrong.

I am pleased to congratulate the Berghoff family on this anniversary, and applaud the decision to let the rest of us in on some of the recipes that make the restaurant great. Given the tradition of excellence, there is no reason to doubt that even after 107 years, the Berghoff's best days are still ahead.

Sincerely,

J. Dennis Hastert
Speaker of the House

P.O. Box 625 • Batavia, IL 60510 • (630) 879-1988

STATE OF ILLINOIS
NINETY-FOURTH GENERAL ASSEMBLY
HOUSE OF REPRESENTATIVES

House Resolution No. 1045

Offered by Representatives Harry Osterman-Barbara Flynn Currie

WHEREAS, A Chicago landmark recently closed its doors after 107 years of service to the citizens and visitors of our great State; and

WHEREAS, The Berghoff Restaurant, opened in 1898 by Herman Joseph Berghoff as Berghoff Cafe, closed for the final time on Tuesday, February 28, 2006; and

WHEREAS, The restaurant has been owned and operated by three generations of Berghoffs, most recently by Jan and Herman Berghoff and their family; it was initially opened to showcase Herman Berghoff's celebrated Dortmunder-style beer; originally located at the corner of State and Adams streets, one door down from its present location, the bar sold beer for a nickel and offered sandwiches for free; and

WHEREAS, The restaurant itself was a connection to years gone-by; the large dining rooms were paneled in wood and covered with pictures of Chicago's past; a display case held "liquor license Number One", granted to Herman Berghoff because he was the first person waiting in the line on the day Prohibition was repealed; and

WHEREAS, While the menu would change regularly, the restaurant was famous for its delicious German food, including sauerbraten, wienerschnitzel, creamed spinach, and freshly baked apple strudel, as well as its beer; several generations of Illinoisans have enjoyed the tradition of Berghoffs; therefore, be it

RESOLVED, BY THE HOUSE OF REPRESENTATIVES OF THE NINETY-FOURTH GENERAL ASSEMBLY OF THE STATE OF ILLINOIS, that we recognize the many years of contributions made by the Berghoff Restaurant in Chicago; and be it further

RESOLVED, That a suitable copy of this resolution be presented to the Jan and Herman Berghoff family as an expression of our esteem.

Adopted by the House of Representatives on March 23, 2006.

Michael J. Madigan

Michael J. Madigan, Speaker of the House

Mark Mahoney

Mark Mahoney, Clerk of the House

A resolution

Presented by ___Alderman Edward M. Burke___ on ___January 11, 2006___

Whereas, Chicago is a place of great culture and diversity thanks to its many immigrants who have brought with them the traditions and heritage of their home countries; and

WHEREAS, Chicago is known as a "City of Neighborhoods" where the wealth of these customs greatly enhance the quality of life for all people of Chicago; and

WHEREAS, Herman Joseph Berghoff is one such immigrant who has made a name for himself and his family by sharing a taste of his German homeland with all of Chicago; and

WHEREAS, The Berghoff has been family-owned and operated for more than one hundred years, making an indelible mark on the community at large; and

WHEREAS, The Berghoff has been a place of great historical significance in the City of Chicago; and

WHEREAS, Herman Joseph Berghoff opened the Berghoff to serve his Dortmunder-style beer and sandwiches, and it grew into a full-service restaurant that has served Chicagoans for 107 years; and

WHEREAS, The Berghoff made history in the city by being the first establishment to get a liquor license after Prohibition ended, in 1933; and

WHEREAS, The Berghoff was the background for a pivotal point in the fight for the equality of women, when seven members the National Organization for Women sat at the bar and insisted on service in what was a men-only establishment; and

WHEREAS, The Berghoff has seen ten Chicago Mayors and thirteen Illinois Governors, since it regained its liquor license in Chicago in 1933; and

WHEREAS, The Berghoff has served as a backdrop to thousands of Chicago family memories, during which generations of Chicago families joined in celebration together; and

WHEREAS, members of the Berghoff family will continue to entertain and serve Chicago after the Berghoff closes its doors, as Carlyn Berghoff will maintain the spirit of her great-grandfather by keeping the bar that serves his famous beer and using the restaurant to create a new home for her company, Artistic Events by Carlyn Berghoff Catering, Inc; and

WHEREAS, through their tireless service and generous hospitality, the Berghoff family has contributed much to the people of the City of Chicago; now, therefore

BE IT RESOLVED, that we, the Mayor and the members of the Chicago City Council, assembled here this 11th day of January 2006, do hereby congratulate and thank the Berghoff family for their service and dedication to the City of Chicago; and

BE IT FURTHER RESOLVED, that a suitable copy of this resolution be presented to Herman and Jan Berghoff and Carlyn Berghoff as a token of our esteem.

Mayor

City Clerk

Index

advertisements, 7, 8, 26, 195, 213
Ahi Tuna, Sesame-Crusted, 156
aïoli, 125, 203
Almond-Pear Tartlets, 226–27
Almonds, Candied, 172
Ancho Chile Dressing, 160–61
appetizers, 30–51, 254
Apple Cake, Old-World, 212
Apple Chutney, 40–41
Apple Pancakes, Bavarian, 240
Apple Strudel, 210–11, 220
Artistic Events by Carlyn Berghoff Catering,
    12–13, 45, 48, 70, 86, 150, 226
Asian Pear and Chicken Salad, 80
Asian-Style Vegetables, 154–55

bacon, 243, 246
Balsamic Dressing, Cherry, 82
Balsamic Vinaigrette, 31, 92
Banana-Coconut Chicken, 200
bar, setting up, 25–26, 239, 263–65
Barbecued Pesto Turkey Breast, 195
barbecues. See grilling
Barley Soup, Beef, 64
basil. See also Pesto
    Creamy Tomato Basil Soup, 61, 69
    Quiche, Tomato and Fresh Mozzarella,
        238–39
    relish, 152
Bavarian Apple Pancakes, 240
beans
    Crimson Red Lentil and Fava Bean Relish,
        188
    White Bean and Cabbage Soup, 58
beef. See also Corned Beef
    Barley Soup, 64
    Berghoff Beer-Braised Brisket, 104
    Bourbon Short Ribs, Berghoff, 196
    Pot Roast, 144

Sauerbraten, 143
sausages, 102, 103
Tenderloin, Marinated, 201
Tenderloin, Stuffed, with Fontina and Dried
    Tomatoes, 148–49
beer. See also specific types of beer
    free lunch and, 96, 97
    parties, 24–25, 27–28
    Prohibition, ix, 7, 8–10, 25, 26, 244
Beer (Brewer's) Bread, Berghoff, 114–15
Beer-Battered Vegetables with Teriyaki Sauce,
    32–33
Beer-Braised Brisket, Berghoff, 104
Beet and Goat Cheese Tower, Mixed Greens
    with, 91
Beets with Oranges and Candied Almonds,
    172–73
Benedict, Berghoff Eggs, 242–43
Benedict, Harry, 242
Benedict, Mrs. LeGrand, 242
Bergeron, Victor, 200
Berghoff, Alfred Charles, 3, 5, 8
Berghoff, Carlyn. See also Artistic Events by
    Carlyn Berghoff Catering
    entertaining notes of, 254–55
    grilling notes of, 192–205
    life of, viii, 12–13, 15, 18, 96–97
    recipes noted by, 38, 44, 58, 118, 164, 185,
        196, 232
Berghoff, Carlyn (first generation), 58, 86, 261
Berghoff, Clement, viii, x, 5–6, 8, 9, 10–11
Berghoff, Franz Anton, 1
Berghoff, Gustav, 3–4
Berghoff, Hannah, 5, 8
Berghoff, Henry, 2–5
Berghoff, Herman (third generation)
    favorites, 238
    life of, viii, 11–12, 17, 18–19
    recipes noted by, 112, 114, 146, 175

Berghoff, Herman Joseph, viii, x, 2, 24, 54, 56,
    236
    life of, x, 1–10
Berghoff, Hubert, 3
Berghoff, Jan
    Brunch Buffet, 265
    entertaining notes of, 254–55
    life of, viii, 12, 17, 18–19
    recipes noted by, 65, 74, 112, 140, 180, 198,
        213
Berghoff, Leo Henry, 3, 5, 8
Berghoff, Lewis Windthorst, viii, x, 5, 8, 9,
    10–11
Berghoff, Lizette Boelhauve, 1
Berghoff, Mary Elizabeth, 8
Berghoff, Peter, viii, 12, 13, 18
Berghoff, Robert Sixtus, 5, 8
Berghoff, Timothy, viii, 12, 13–15, 18
Berghoff, Todd, 97
Berghoff brothers, viii, x. See also specific names
    of Berghoff brothers
Berghoff Café, viii, 6–8, 13, 24, 55. See also
    Berghoff Restaurant
    lower-level (2003), 17, 106
    O'Hare International Airport (1998), viii, 13,
        18, 246
Berghoff Restaurant
    chefs, 15–17, 155
    closing down, 17–18, 249, 268–71
    customers, 13–15, 17–18
    government recognition of, 268–71
    100th Anniversary of, 15
    management, x, 10–13
    memories of, 13–15
    Oktoberfest, 192, 193
    waiters, 13, 41, 75
Bergo soda pop, 7, 9, 213
Berry Shortcake with Lemon-Chantilly Cream,
    Seasonal, 224–25

beverage station, coffee and, 239
Bistro-Style Lamb Shank, 140–41
Blackened Swordfish Sandwich, 108–9
Black Forest Cake, 214–16, 220
Black Forest Ham and Brie Panini, 106–7
Black Olive Tapenade with Walnuts, 124
Bloody Marys, 239
Blueberry Mini-Muffins, 247
Blueberry Pie, 218–19
Blue Cheese Croutons, 84–85
Blue Cheese Dressing, Berghoff, 84
Blue Cheese Terrine, 88
Bouillabaisse, 158–59
bourbon, Berghoff, 7, 28–29
Bourbon Short Ribs, Berghoff, 196
Bratwurst, 102, 103, 145
bread
    buffet, 253, 260
    crumbs, 157, 211
Bread, Berghoff Beer (Brewer's), 114–15
Bread, Olive, 112–13
breakfast
    for dinner, 250
    menu, 236–37
Breakfast Gratin with Leeks and Swiss Cheese,
    Carlyn's, 248
Breakfast Sandwich, Berghoff, 246
Breuer, William, 5
Brewer's Bread, 114–15
Brie and Raspberry Grilled Cheese Sandwich,
    117
Brie Chicken Skewers with Candied Pecans and
    Apple Chutney, 40–41
Brie Panini, Black Forest Ham and, 106–7
Brisket, Berghoff Beer-Braised, 104
broth, 55, 66, 67, 164–65
brunches, 236–37, 239, 265
Bruschetta with Pears, Gorgonzola, and
    Walnuts, 45
B. Trentman & Son, 3, 4
Buffalo Bill, 2
Buffalo mozzarella, 90, 238–39, 249
buffets
    brunch, 236–37, 239, 265
    dessert, 208
    food temperature and, 161
    layout, 256
    planning, 253–54
    salad bar, 75
    sandwich, 96–97, 259–60
    seasonal, 262, 263
    side dishes, 168
    tableware for, 256
Butternut Squash Soup, 69, 70

Cabbage, Corned Beef and, 142
Cabbage, Red, 180
Cabbage Soup, White Bean and, 58
Cajun Salmon Salad, 79
Cajun Sauce, 108
cake(s)
    Apple, Old-World, 212
    Black Forest, 214–16, 220
    chocolate, 214–15
    crumbs, 211, 216

Flourless Chocolate, 209
    Sacher Torte, 232–33
    yellow, 214–15
    Yule Log, 222–23
Cannon, James, 16
Capers, Smoked Salmon Wrap with, 119, 121
Caprese, 90, 116
caramel sauce, 212
Carlyn's Breakfast Gratin with Leeks and Swiss
    Cheese, 248
Carlyn's Kids' Pancakes, 250
Carlyn's vinaigrettes, 93
Catfish, Stir-Fried, 154–55
Cauliflower Fritters, 187
Centliver beer, 5
Century Room, 18
cheese(s). See also specific types of cheese
    about, 34–35, 90
    Beet and Goat Cheese Tower, 91
    Blue Cheese Terrine, 88
    Brie and Raspberry Grilled Cheese Sandwich,
        117
    Carlyn's Breakfast Gratin with Leeks and
        Swiss Cheese, 248
    German Cheese, Meat, and Fruit Board,
        34–35
    Panko-Crusted Goat Cheese Salad, 82–83
    pesto, 46–47
    sauce, 242–43
Cheesecake Squares, Pistachio, 230–31
chefs, 15–17, 155
cherry
    filling for Black Forest Cake, 214–16
    reduction for Chicken Waldorf Salad, 78
Cherry Balsamic Dressing, 82
Chicago, 6–7, 8–10
Chicago City Council, 270–71
chicken
    about, 66, 150
    Banana-Coconut, 200
    Broth, 66
    Crêpe Bites, Curried, with Peanut Sauce, 49
    Salad, Asian Pear and, 80
    Saltimbocca Skewers with Pesto Cream Dip,
        39
    Schnitzel, 132–33
    Skewers, Brie, with Candied Pecans and
        Apple Chutney, 40–41
    Soup, 65
    Valenciano, 150–51
    Waldorf Salad, 78
Chihuahua Cheese, 44
children's foods, 65, 75, 205, 247, 250
Chips
    Berghoff, 175
    Sweet Potato, with Green Onion Dip, 38
chocolate
    cake, 214–15
    Cake, Flourless, 209
    Death by, 232
    Mousse, White, 220–21
Christmas food, 18, 230–31
Chutney, Apple, 40–41
Clam Chowder, New England, 62–63
Clapp, Janice Edith, 12. See also Berghoff, Jan

cleaning, 256
Cobb Salad, 84–85
cocktail parties, 24–25, 255, 259
Coconut Chicken, Banana-, 200
coffee and beverage station, 239
condiments, 34, 103, 113, 261
Cordon Bleu, Veal, 137
Corned Beef
    and Cabbage, 142
    Hash, 244–45
    Sandwich, 99
Coronato, Linda, 202
Crab Cakes, 163
Cranberry Aïoli, 125
Cream, Lemon-Chantilly, 224–25
Cream Cheese, Dilled, 121
Creamed Spinach, 168, 170–71
    Dip, Chef Matt's, 30
    Stuffed Mushrooms, 42
Creamy Ranch Dressing, Berghoff's, 92
Creamy Tomato Basil Soup, 61, 69
Crème Brûlée, 228
Crêpe Bites, Curried Chicken, with Peanut
    Sauce, 49
Croutons, Blue Cheese, 84–85
crust, 218, 230–31, 238–39
Cucumber Cup, Dilled Shrimp, with Boursin
    Cheese, 43
Curried Chicken Crêpe Bites with Peanut
    Sauce, 49
customers, 13–15, 17–18

Dark Beer, Berghoff Genuine, 28
Death by Chocolate, 232
decor, 256, 260
Delmonico's, 242
desserts
    about, 208, 210
    buffet v. sit-down dinner, 254
    garnishing platters of, 257–58
    menu, 208, 219, 265
Diezinger, Augustine, 16
Dill Beurre Blanc, 157
Dilled Cream Cheese, 121
Dilled Shrimp Cucumber Cup with Boursin
    Cheese, 43
Dip
    Green Onion, 38
    Pesto Cream, 39
    Spinach, Chef Matt's, 30
dishes. See tableware
Dortmund, Westphalia, Germany, 1, 4
Dortmunder beer, 5, 7, 24
Dressing, Ancho Chile, 160–61
dressing, salad, 88, 92–93. See also vinaigrette

East End Bottling Works, 4, 5
egg wash, 218–19
Eggplant Ratatouille, 179
Eggs Benedict, Berghoff, 242–43
18th Amendment, 8
entertaining, 24–29, 253–65. See also party
    planning
Espresso Crème Brûlée, 228

family crest, 117
family style serving, 254
Fava Bean Relish, Crimson Red Lentil and, 188
filling
    Black Forest Cake, 214–16
    Blueberry Pie, 218–19
    Pecan Diamonds, 229
    Pistachio Cheesecake, 230
    quiche, 238–39
    sandwich, 97
    Seasonal Berry Shortcake, 224
fish. *See also* salmon; tuna
    Bouillabaisse, 158–59
    Halibut Livornese with Sautéed Spinach, 153
    marinating, 193
    Pan-Seared Tilapia with Tabasco Broth, 164–65
    Stir-Fried Catfish with Asian-Style Vegetables, 154–55
    Swordfish Sandwich, Blackened, 108–9
    Whitefish with Basil Relish and Sautéed Spinach, 152
Fish Broth, 67
Float, Root Beer, 213
Flourless Chocolate Cake, 209
Fontina and Dried Tomatoes Stuffing, 148–49
food safety, 194
Frangipane, 226
free lunch, 96, 97
French Toast Sticks, 251
Frey, Emil, 35
Frittata with Proscuitto and Fresh Mozzarella, 249
frozen foods
    ahead of time, 38, 40, 55, 66, 67, 176, 216, 229, 247
    buying, 37, 170, 227, 239
Fruit Board, German Cheese, Meat, and, 34–35
fruits, 34, 217, 237, 247

ganache, 222–23, 232
garlic, dried, 171
Garlic Shrimp, Zesty, 197
garnishes, 257–58
Gazpacho, Chilled Grape, 68, 69
German Cheese, Meat, and Fruit Board, 34–35
German Fries, 174
German Potato Salad, 81
Goat Cheese
    Grapes Rolled in, 48
    Salad, Panko-Crusted, 82–83
    Towers, Beet and, 91
government recognition, 268–71
Grape Gazpacho, Chilled, 68, 69
Grapes Rolled in Goat Cheese, 48
Green Beans, Szechuan, 182–83
Green Olive Tapenade with Hazelnuts, 124
Green Onion Dip, 38
Grilled Cheese Sandwich, Brie and Raspberry, 117
grilling
    about, 192–94
    Beef Tenderloin, Marinated, 201
    Carlyn's notes on, 192–205
    Chicken, Banana-Coconut, 200

picnic menus and, 262
Portobello Mushrooms, 31
Sausage, Italian, 202
Short Ribs, Berghoff Bourbon, 196
Shrimp, Zesty Garlic, 197
S'mores, 205
Tuna, Sesame Seed, 198–99
Turkey Breast, Barbecued Pesto, 195
Vegetable Wrap, 119, 120
Vegetables with Red Pepper Aïoli, 203

Halibut Livornese, 153
Ham, Black Forest, and Brie Panini, 106–7
ham hocks, 56, 58
hash browns, 248
Hastert, J. Dennis, 268
Hazelnut Quesadillas, 44
Hazelnuts, Green Olive Tapenade with, 124
Hefe Weizen Beer, Berghoff, 28
Herbed Bread Crumbs, Salmon with, 157
Herb Vinaigrette, Carlyn's Fresh, 93
Herman Berghoff Brewing Co., 4–5
Hertenstein, Karl, 15–16, 170
holiday food, 208, 222, 230–31, 265
Home Rye, Berghoff, 110–11
Honey Salmon, 162
hors d'oeuvres, 30–51, 254
horseradish, 113
Hussein, Mohammed, 15, 16, 74

Illinois House of Representatives, 268, 269
Indiana (Fort Wayne), 2, 5
invitations, 255
Italian food, 45, 136
Italian Sausage, 202

Jäger Schnitzel, Pork, 146
Jansen, Henry, 6
Jansen, Mary, 6
J. E. Capps & Co., 2
Johnny Wagner's German band, 17
Joseph Huber Brewery, 12

kabobs. *See* skewers
Kay, Reuben, 100
kids. *See* children's foods
kitchenware, 38, 228
Knockwurst, 102, 103, 145

Lach, Alma, 212, 220
Lager, Berghoff Original, 28
Lamb Shank, Bistro-Style, 140–41
Larson, Paul, 48, 50, 267
Leeks and Swiss Cheese, Carlyn's Breakfast Gratin with, 248
leftovers, reinventing, 96, 244, 249
lemon(s)
    for garnish, 129
    zest, 225
Lemon Aïoli, 125
Lemon-Chantilly Cream, 224–25
Lemon-Dijon Vinaigrette, 93
Lemon-Pepper Mayonnaise, 187
Lentil Soup, 56–57

Lentils, Crimson Red, and Fava Bean Relish, 188
lettuce, about, 85, 260
liquor licenses, 7, 8, 9–10, 25

Mai Tai, 200
main dishes, about, 128–29
mandoline, 38
MAO (monoamine oxidase) inhibitors, 188
marinade(s)
    about, 193–94
    Balsamic Vinaigrette, 31
    Banana-Coconut Chicken, 200
    Beef Tenderloin, 201
    Italian Sausage, 202
    Pork Tenderloin, 147
    Sauerbraten, 143
    Steak Salad, Berghoff, 76
    Zesty Garlic Shrimp, 197
Marsala, Veal, 139
Mashed Potatoes, 50, 169, 178, 264–65
Mayer, Johanna, 3, 5
Mayer, Julia, 4
Mayer, Lorenz, 3
Mayer, Mary Sophia, 4, 6
Mayer, Theresa, 2–3
Mayer, Walburga, 3, 6
mayonnaise
    lemon-pepper, 187
    wasabi, 106
McClure, Jim, 192
Meat, and Fruit Board, German Cheese, 34–35
meats, 34, 135, 194
menu, Berghoff
    "1914," 116, 136
    "1932," 71, 105
    breakfast, 236–37, 244
    changes, viii, 9, 80, 106, 128, 244
    cheese, 35
    desserts, 208, 219
    Mai Tai, 200
    memorial, 18
    planning, 256
    prices, 10, 11, 32, 35, 55, 136, 237
    salad, 75
    sandwich, 97, 105
    soup, 54–55
menus, example party
    beer, 259
    beer tasting, 27
    bourbon tasting, 28–29
    brunch, 265
    cocktail, 259
    dessert, 265
    kabob bar, 263–64
    Oktoberfest, 263
    picnic, 261–62
    sandwich, 259–60
    seasonal, 259, 262, 263
mimosas, 239
Mint, Peas with, 185
Mousse, White Chocolate, 220–21
mozzarella, 90, 238–39, 249
Muffins, Blueberry Mini-, 247
Munich, Germany, 193, 210

Mushroom(s)
Creamed Spinach Stuffed, 42
Grilled Portobello, 31
Ragout, Veal and, 138
Soup, 59
Strudel, 36–37
mustard, 93, 103

National Organization for Women (NOW),
28, 270
near beer, 9, 26
New England Clam Chowder, 62–63

O'Hare International Airport, viii, 13, 18, 246
Oktoberfest, 15, 192, 193, 210, 263
old-world foods, 212, 240–41
Olive Bread, 112–13
olive tapenade, 124
100th Anniversary, 15
onion rings. See Beer-Battered Vegetables with
Teriyaki Sauce
Onions, Smothered, 102
Oranges and Candied Almonds, Beets with,
172–73
Osso Buco, 136

Pancakes
Bavarian Apple, 240
Carlyn's Kids', 250
Potato, 176–77
Pancetta, Baby Spinach Salad with, 86–87
Panini, Black Forest Ham and Brie, 106–7
Panko-Crusted Goat Cheese Salad, 82–83
Pan-Seared Tilapia with Tabasco Broth, 164–65
party planning, 24–25. See also buffets
bar setup, 25–26, 239, 263–65
beer tasting, 27–28
beverage station, 239
books, making your own, 256–57
bourbon tasting, 28–29
checklist, 255–57
cocktail, 25–26, 255, 259
German Cheese, Meat, and Fruit Board for,
34–35
grill, 192–94
help for, hiring, 254–55
menus, 27–29, 259–65
salads, 75, 88
sit-down dinner, 254
Pasta Salad, Roasted Vegetable, 89
pastry, 37, 210, 227
Pea Soup, Split, 60
Peanut Sauce, Curried Chicken Crêpe Bites
with, 49
Pear, Asian, and Chicken Salad, 80
Pears, Gorgonzola, and Walnuts, Bruschetta
with, 45
Pear Tartlets, Almond-, 226–27
Peas with Mint, 185
Pecan Diamonds, 229
Pecans, Candied, 40, 80
pesto, 123, 125
Pesto Cheesecake, 46–47
Pesto Cream Dip, 39
Pesto Turkey Breast, Barbecued, 195

Pesto Turkey Salad Sandwich, 123
Phelan, Tim, 14
phyllo dough, 37
picnics, 26, 89, 97, 118, 261–62
Pie, Blueberry, 218–19
Pistachio Cheesecake Squares, 230–31
planning. See party planning
platter linings, 257–58
pork
Brat, 102, 103
Jäger Schnitzel, 146
Rahm Schnitzel, 134–35
Schlacht Platte, 145
Tenderloin, 147
Pot Roast, 144
potato(es), 169, 264–65
Berghoff Chips, 175
Chips, Sweet, with Green Onion Dip, 38
Gallette, 184
German Fries, 174
hash browns, 248
Mashed, 50, 169, 178, 264–65
Pancakes, 176–77
Red Potatoes Vinaigrette, 204
Salad, German, 81
presentation, 128–29. See also serving dishes
prices, menu, 10, 11, 32, 35, 55, 136, 237
Prohibition, ix, 7, 8–10, 25, 26, 244
Proscuitto and Fresh Mozzarella, Frittata with,
249
Prudhomme, Paul, 79
Prussia, 1, 2
Pudding, Rice, 217

Quesadillas, Hazelnut, 44
Quiche, Tomato, Basil, and Fresh Mozzarella,
237, 238–39

Ragout, Veal and Mushroom, 138
Rahm Schnitzel, 134–35
Ranch Dressing, Berghoff's Creamy, 92
Raspberry Grilled Cheese Sandwich, Brie and,
117
raspberry sauce, 232
Ratatouille, Eggplant, 179
rationing, 11
Red Cabbage, 180
red peppers
aïoli, 125, 203
roasted, 109
sauce, 44
Red Potatoes Vinaigrette, 204
reductions, 78, 82
Reichel, Matt, 267
about, 17
creations, 30, 100, 175, 176, 246
favorites of, 61, 172, 179
Spinach Dip, 30
Relish
Basil, 152
Crimson Red Lentil and Fava Bean, 188
Tray, Grandmother's, 261
Reuben, Arthur, 100
Reuben on Rye, 100–101
Reynolds, Bill, 68

Reynozo, Chon, 226, 232, 267
Ribs, Berghoff Bourbon Short, 196
Rice Pudding, 217
Root Beer, Berghoff, 9
Float, 213
roulade, Yule Log, 222–23
roux, 59, 144, 153
Rye
Berghoff Home, 110–11
Reuben on, 100–101

Sacher, Franz, 232
Sacher Torte Cakes, 232–33
Salad, 74–75, 85, 88, 253
Asian Pear and Chicken, 80
Cajun Salmon, 79
Caprese, 90
Chicken Waldorf, 76
Cobb, 84–85
Crimson Red Lentil, 188
German Potato, 81
Mixed Greens with Beet and Goat Cheese
Tower, 91
Panko-Crusted Goat Cheese, 82–83
Roasted Vegetable Pasta, 89
Spinach, 86–87
Steak, Berghoff, 74, 76–77
Tuna Sandwich, 122, 260
Wheat Berry and Wild Rice, 189
salad dressing, 88, 92–93. See also Vinaigrette;
specific salad recipes
Salmon
Cakes, 160–61
with Herbed Bread Crumbs, 157
Honey, 162
Salad, Cajun, 79
Wrap, Smoked, 119, 121
salsa, 150–51
Saltimbocca Skewers with Pesto Cream Dip, 39
Salvator beer, 5
sandwich(es). See also spreads
about, 96–97
Beer-Braised Brisket, Berghoff, 104
Black Forest Ham and Brie Panini, 106–7
Blackened Swordfish, 108–9
Bratwurst, 102, 103
Breakfast, Berghoff, 246
Brie and Raspberry Grilled Cheese, 117
buffets, 96–97, 259–60
Caprese, 116
Corned Beef, 99
Knockwurst, 102, 103
menu, 259–60
New York, 112
Pesto Turkey Salad, 123
Reuben on Rye, 100–101
Roasted Turkey Breast Sandwich, Berghoff,
105
Thuringer, Smoked, 102, 103
Tuna Salad, 122, 260
wraps, 118–21
sauce, 161
Cajun, 108
caramel, 212
cheese, 242–43

Chicken Schnitzel, 132
Dill Beurre Blanc, 157
Halibut Livornese, 153
Honey Salmon, 162
Lemon-Pepper Mayonnaise, 187
Marsala, 139
Peanut, 49
Pork Tenderloin, 147
Rahm Schnitzel, 134–35
raspberry, 232
red, 132
Red Pepper, 44
Sauerbraten, 143
sour cream, 134–35
stir-fry, 154–55
Stuffed Beef Tenderloin, 148–49
Teriyaki, 32–33
White Chocolate Mousse as, 220
white wine, 50
Sauerbraten, 143
Sauerkraut, 100–101, 145, 181
sausages, 103, 202
Schlacht Platte, 145
Schnitzel, 130–35, 146
"Scratch House," x, 13, 128
seafood. See also fish; Shrimp
    Bouillabaisse, 158–59
    Crab Cakes, 163
Seasonal Berry Shortcake with Lemon-
    Chantilly Cream, 224–25
seasonal menus, 259, 262, 263
seating, 255
secrets, 55, 81, 99, 113, 130, 176, 180, 211,
    225, 227
Seelos, Annette, 100
serving dishes, 35, 247, 254
    buffet, 161, 253, 254
    linings for, 257–58
    renting, 255
    unique, 48, 70, 223
serving meals, 161, 254–55
Sesame-Crusted Ahi Tuna, 156
Sesame Seed Tuna, 198–99
17 West, 18
Shallot Vinaigrette, Roasted, 86
Sherry Vinaigrette, 91
shopping, 256
Shortcake with Lemon-Chantilly Cream,
    Seasonal Berry, 224–25
Shrimp
    Dilled, Cucumber Cup with Boursin Cheese,
        43
    Martini, 50–51
    Zesty Garlic, 197
side dishes, 168–69
sit-down dinner party, 254
skewers, 192, 263–64
    Brie Chicken, with Candied Pecans and
        Apple Chutney, 40–41
    Saltimbocca, with Pesto Cream Dip, 39
    Sesame Seed Tuna, 198–99
Smoked Salmon Wrap with Capers and Dilled
    Cream Cheese, 119, 121
Smoked Turkey Wrap, 118–19
S'mores on the Grill, 205

Smothered Onions, 102
soda pop, Bergo, 7, 9, 213
soup(s), 54–55, 67, 161. See also stew
    Butternut Squash Soup, 69, 70
    Chicken, 65
    Chilled Grape Gazpacho, 68, 69
    Creamy Tomato Basil, 61, 69
    Lentil, 56–57
    Mushroom, 59
    New England Clam Chowder, 62–63
    shots, 68, 69
    Split Pea, 60
    substitutions in, 70
    White Bean and Cabbage, 58
sour cream sauce, 134–35
spinach. See also Creamed Spinach
    Eggs Benedict, Berghoff, 242–43
    Salad with Pancetta, 86–87
    sautéed, 152
Split Pea Soup, 60
spreads, 113
    aïoli, 125
    Blue Cheese Terrine, 88
    Cajun Sauce, 108
    Dilled Cream Cheese, 121
    olive tapenade, 124
    Reuben on Rye dressing, 100
    Smothered Onions, 102
    wasabi mayonnaise, 106
Squash Soup, Butternut, 69, 70
Sta Maria, Enrique "Bong," 16, 267
Steak Salad, Berghoff, 74, 76–77
Steinem, Gloria, 28
stew, 161
    Bouillabaisse, 158–59
    Ragout, Veal and Mushroom, 138
Stir-Fried Catfish with Asian-Style Vegetables,
    154–55
Streicher, Adriana, 140
Strudel
    Apple, 210–11, 220
    Mushroom, 36–37
Summer Solstice Wit Beer, Berghoff, 28
Sunday brunch, 236–37, 239, 265
Sunday dinner, 261
Sweet Potato Chips with Green Onion Dip, 38
Swiss Cheese, Carlyn's Breakfast Gratin with
    Leeks and, 248
Swordfish Sandwich, Blackened, 108–9
Szechuan Green Beans, 182–83

tableware, 254, 255–56, 260. See also serving
    dishes
tapenade, 124
Tartlets, Almond-Pear, 226–27
tasting, beer and bourbon, 27–29
temperature, food, 161, 194
tenderloin, 147–49, 201
Teriyaki Sauce, Beer-Battered Vegetables with,
    32–33
Thanksgiving, 105, 222–23
Thompson, William "Big Bill" Hale, 9
Thuringer, Smoked, 102, 103
Tilapia, Pan-Seared, with Tabasco Broth,
    164–65

tips, 55, 81, 99, 113, 130, 176, 180, 211, 225,
    227
tomato(es)
    Basil, and Fresh Mozzarella Quiche, 238–39
    Basil Soup, Creamy, 61, 69
    paste, 55
    for sandwich buffets, 260
Tosi's Restaurant, 12, 15, 137
Trentman Company. See B. Trentman & Son
Tschirky, Oscar, 78
Tuna
    Salad Sandwich, 122, 260
    Sesame-Crusted Ahi, 156
    Sesame Seed, 198–99
Turkey
    Breast, Barbecued Pesto, 195
    Breast Sandwich, Berghoff Roasted, 105
    Salad Sandwich, Pesto, 123
    Wrap, Smoked, 118–19

veal
    Bratwurst, 102, 103
    Cordon Bleu, 137
    Marsala, 139
    Mushroom Ragout, 138
    Osso Buco, 136
    Wiener Schnitzel, 130–31
vegetable(s)
    Asian-Style, 154–55
    Beer-Battered, 32–33
    cutting, 38, 260–61
    decorative, 35
    Grilled, 119, 120, 203
    marinating, 193–94
    Pasta Salad, Roasted, 89
    Roasted, 186
    Wrap, Grilled, 119, 120
Vinaigrette, 91–93
    Balsamic, 31, 92
    Red Potatoes, 204
    Roasted Shallot, 86

waiters, 13, 41, 75
Waldorf-Astoria, 78, 242
walnuts, 45, 91
wasabi mayonnaise spread, 106
weddings, 40, 43, 150, 184
Wheat Berry and Wild Rice Salad, 189
whipped cream, 214–15, 224–25, 227
whiskey. See bourbon
White Bean and Cabbage Soup, 58
White Chocolate Mousse, 220–21
White Wine Sauce, 50
Whitefish with Basil Relish and Sautéed
    Spinach, 152
Wiener Schnitzel, 130–31
Wild Rice Salad, Wheat Berry and, 189
World Colombian Exposition, 6, 7
wraps, 118–21

Yule Log, 222–23

17/west at the Berghoff